Behavioral Interventions in Schools

Behavioral Interventions in Schools

A Response-to-Intervention Guidebook

David Hulac ▪ Joy Terrell
Odell Vining ▪ Joshua Bernstein

Routledge
Taylor & Francis Group
New York   London

Routledge
Taylor & Francis Group
711 Third Avenue
New York, NY 10017

Routledge
Taylor & Francis Group
2 Park Square
Milton Park
Abingdon, Oxon OX14 4RN

© 2011 by Taylor and Francis Group, LLC
Routledge is an imprint of Taylor & Francis Group, an Informa business

Printed in the United States of America on acid-free paper
10 9 8 7 6 5 4 3 2

International Standard Book Number: 978-0-415-87584-4 (Hardback) 978-0-415-87585-1 (Paperback)

Library of Congress Cataloging-in-Publication Data

Behavioral interventions in schools : a response to intervention guidebook /
    David M. Hulac ... [et al.].
        p. cm.
    Includes bibliographical references and index.
    ISBN 978-0-415-87584-4 (hardback : alk. paper) -- ISBN 978-0-415-87585-1
    (pbk. : alk. paper)
    1. School discipline. 2. Classroom management. 3. Problem
children--Behavior modification. I. Hulac, David M. II. Title.

LB3012.B43 2011
370.15'28--dc22   2010009244

Visit the Taylor & Francis Web site at
http://www.taylorandfrancis.com

and the Routledge Web site at
http://www.Routledge.com

Contents

Series Editors' Foreword

The *School-Based Practice in Action* series grew out of the coming together of our passion and commitment to the field of education and the needs of children and schools in today's world. We entered the process of developing and editing this series at two different points of our careers, though both in phases of transition – one (RWC) moving from the opening act to the main scene and the other (RBM) from the main scene to the final act. Despite the fact that one of us was entering the peak of action and the other was leaving it, we both continue to face the same challenges in and visions for education and serving children and families.

Significant transformations to the educational system, through legislation such as the *No Child Left Behind Act* and the reauthorization of *Individuals with Disabilities Education Act* (IDEA 2004), have led to broad, sweeping changes for the practitioners in the educational setting, and these changes will likely continue. It is imperative that as school-based practitioners we maintain a strong knowledge base and adjust our service delivery. To accomplish this, there is a need to understand theory and research, though it is critical that we have resources to move our empirical knowledge into the process of practice implementation. For this reason, it is our goal that the books included in the *School-Based Practice in Action* series truly offer resources for readers to put directly "into action."

To accomplish this, each book in the series will offer information in a practice-friendly manner and will have a companion CD with reproducible and usable materials. Within the text, readers will find a specific icon that will cue them to documents available on the accompanying CD. These resources are designed to have a direct impact on transitioning research and knowledge into the day-to-day functions of school-based practitioners. We recognize that the implementation of programs and the changing of roles come with challenges and barriers and, as such, these may take various forms depending on the context of the situation and the voice of the practitioner. To that end, the books of the *School-Based Practice in Action* series may be used in their entirety and present form for a number of practitioners; however, for others, these books will help them find new ways to move toward effective action and new possibilities. No matter which style fits your practice, we hope that these books will influence your work and professional growth.

We had the privilege of starting the *School-Based Practice in Action* series with one of the "hot topics" in the field of education and school psychology—Response to Intervention (RTI). Dr. Matthew Burns and Dr. Kimberly Gibbons provided our series an outstanding reference with *Implementing Response to Intervention in Elementary and Secondary Schools: Procedures to Ensure Scientific-Based Practices,* which offered a practice-friendly guide to assist schools in putting the RTI process into practice to improve academic outcomes for children. However, despite this excellent resource, there remained a need in the literature for a book that focused on using the same scientific-based principles of RTI and applied them to enhance social and behavioral outcomes for children.

As we continued to explore this need to bridge the gap in literature between positive behavioral support and RTI, we were pleased to receive the manuscript for this book. David Hulac, Joy Terrell, Odell Vining, and Joshua Bernstein provided a well-written guidebook that exceeded our original thoughts. In this book, *Behavioral Interventions in Schools: A Response to Intervention Guidebook,* Hulac and colleagues fill this need for a resource that ties together these important concepts within the field. They offer a concise and user-friendly review of positive behavioral supports that can be easily implemented within every classroom. We believe their well-defined procedures for the execution of intervention and their ready-to-use forms will be an invaluable resource for school-based practitioners, teachers, and administrators. The opportunity to work with these authors has been both enjoyable and rewarding. We must thank them for their efficiency, which allowed us to produce this book in a timely fashion.

The continued growth and expansion of the *School-Based Practice in Action* series would not be possible without our relationship with Mr. Dana Bliss and Routledge Publishing, who from the start have supported our vision and have trusted our judgment on topics and manuscripts to be included in this series. We are grateful for their belief in our idea of having a book series focusing on "action" resources dedicated to enriching practice and service delivery within school settings. Their dedication and belief in meeting the needs of school-based practitioners made the *School-Based Practice in Action* series a reality and a resource we are truly proud to be a part of the series. We hope that you enjoy reading and implementing the materials in this book and the rest of the series as much as we have enjoyed working with the authors on developing these resources.

Rosemary B. Mennuti, EdD, NCSP
Ray W. Christner, PsyD, NCSP

Series Editors, School-Based Practice in Action Series

Introduction

Imagine a school—whether it be a large urban elementary or a small rural country school. The faculty and staff are hardworking, putting in a tremendous amount of time and effort to guarantee the safety and educational growth of the students. Like most schools, some of the students are eager to learn, whereas some seem as though they would prefer to be elsewhere. Though unmotivated and poorly supported students are familiar to most professional educators, many teachers and administrators are frustrated by students who present as defiant and have difficulty meeting behavioral expectations. Susan's story provides a glimpse into a school discipline system that inadvertently increases behavior problems.

SUSAN'S STORY

At the elementary school last month, a fourth grader named Susan came to the attention of the discipline office. Susan had not been in much trouble in the past; in fact, she was described by her teachers as a quiet and unassuming girl. Breaking from her historic nondisruptive behavioral pattern, Susan had been in three fights in the last 2 weeks and sent to the principal's office 10 times in the last month, all related to aggressive acting-out behavior. The teachers wondered at the sudden and dramatic change in Susan's behavior. When the school counselor interviewed Susan and her parents, there was no indication of significant concerns outside of school. However, the counselor did uncover some pertinent information.

Susan has often been teased by classmates about her body weight, physical conditioning, and coordination. When the class engaged in competitive team sports, Susan was often the last student picked. One month ago, while playing basketball during physical education (P.E.) class, Susan inadvertently hit her classmate Nancy's mouth in a collision during gym. The injury caused Nancy to begin bleeding. Nancy called Susan several names that drew the attention of all in attendance. Embarrassed and belittled before her peers, Susan pushed Nancy to the floor. When the gym teacher reentered the room, he saw Nancy lying on the court with a bleeding lip. Mistakenly assuming the minor injury was due to the physical altercation rather than an accidental collision, the teacher sent Susan to the office.

During the course of the next 2 weeks, Susan frequently engaged in aggressive behavior during P.E. and was sent to the office for each infraction. The counselor's report, based upon his interview with Susan, indicated that Susan has been acting out to avoid participation in P.E. Her aggression resulted in spillover altercations occurring outside of P.E. The administration was aware that at least three of these disagreements ended in physical altercations. Susan was suspended for 3 days and told she would face a 10-day suspension if another similar action occurred. Following the 3-day suspension, Susan's behavior only got worse. Not only did the incidence of fighting increase, but also Susan's teacher noticed that the quality of her schoolwork deteriorated. When she took the federally mandated assessment, she failed the test and was in danger of failing the fourth grade.

THE SCHOOL'S PLAYGROUND

Meanwhile, Nancy's behavior was indicative of an increase in violent behaviors of students in the school. The administration considered a proposal to remove recess from the school's schedule following several years of parent complaints regarding schoolyard bullying and several dramatic fights, some of which resulted in serious injury. Those advocating removing the recess period felt that the student body in general did not deserve the privilege of having recess. By removing recess, they argued that a clear message would be sent to all students that poor behavior would not be tolerated.

The school removed recess, but once the period was removed, the school found that the number of fights in the hallway increased. Teachers reported that students seemed restless in class and were not paying as close attention as they had in the past. Soon, other parents complained that their children, who were not receiving recess, were missing out on valuable exercise and socialization time.

A small group of teachers recommended that the school implement a system of positive behavior supports. Many of the other teachers thought such a system would take away valuable instructional time. However,

- Ms. White had to stop her lecture 9 times in 10 minutes to ask Billy and Suzy to stop talking.
- Mr. Red was unable to provide small-group assistance to a group of struggling students because other students were throwing pencils from across the room.
- Every day, Ms. Black needed 10 minutes to get her class calmed down after lunch before she could start her lesson.
- Mr. Green received a subpoena to appear in court to testify about a fight that he broke up outside of his classroom.
- Ms. Purple met with Jason's mother three times, and had to call home during her planning period several times during the past week alone.
- Ms. Yellow needed 10 minutes to fill out each onerous office referral form for sending Annette to the office.
- Many teachers were spending half of their classroom time managing behavior problems rather than providing instruction.

THE REACTION OF THE SCHOOL STAFF

As a professional working in a school, you probably recognize that the reactions of the school staff to many of these incidents were counterproductive. Traditional punishment-based disciplinary measures are frequently ineffective and may often exacerbate existing behavior problems. Understanding the context through which schools make disciplinary decisions is important. Schools are required to provide safe learning environments for their students. A common solution to problems that disrupt a learning environment is to administer harsh punishments. Those school personnel who administer these punishments hope that the offending child will be reluctant to misbehave again. They also hope that other students in the school will vicariously learn that disruptive behavior will result in a harsh punishment, making other students reluctant to misbehave. Unfortunately, the administration of punishments is typically ineffective at improving school climate and reducing behavior problems.

PUNISHMENT DOES NOT WORK!

SCHOOL SAFETY AND FEDERAL LAW

Federal law has provided schools with a portion of parental authority, meaning that schools have a responsibility for the protection of students under their care (Alexander & Alexander, 1998). These laws include Title IX and the Americans with Disabilities Act, which provide the legal mandates that schools must protect students from harassment that may prevent them from receiving an education, which is thought to be a property right guaranteed by the 14th Amendment of the U.S. Constitution. School safety received more attention in light of the school shootings of the late 1990s. The No Child Left Behind Act of 2001 (aka NCLB 2001) mandated school reporting of incidents of violence or drug crimes occurring within the school setting. NCLB (2001) also required schools to implement evidence-based prevention programs to reduce the incidence of violence within the school settings. These laws coincided with the nationwide movement of American schools toward zero-tolerance policies.

ZERO-TOLERANCE POLICIES

Following the increased attention given to urban gangs in the late 1980s, many school systems began incorporating policies whereby students bringing weapons, drugs, or other gang paraphernalia into the schools or committing violent acts were immediately suspended or expelled from the educational setting. Those who practiced zero-tolerance policies made several assumptions (Skiba, 2008):

- Strong, mandated punishments for offenses would result in a consistent and fair disciplinary message. Considering the context of the behavior could only weaken this disciplinary message.
- Punishments as deterrents served as the most effective means of maintaining discipline in a school.
- Removing students who misbehave would improve the school climate and the learning environment for the remaining students.

These zero-tolerance guidelines grew in their acceptance and became more popular throughout the country. While the initial scope of the policies was meant to address dangerous and violent behaviors, schools began to apply zero-tolerance principles to disruptive and irritating behaviors that did not necessarily represent a threat to the safety of the school. This shift reflected a national trend in schools favoring punitive models of behavioral intervention (Evenson, Justinger, Pelischek, & Schulz, 2009).

LIMITATIONS TO PUNISHMENT-BASED DISCIPLINARY SYSTEMS

There remains a diminishing body of supporters for more traditional, punitive behavioral management techniques in school systems. It is common to hear a teacher say, "I have no behavior problems in my class. When students act out, they are removed from my class." Similarly, principals may acknowledge few behavior problems because they suspend and eventually expel those students violating the school's ethical code. These attitudes, unfortunately, ignore many of the flaws inherent in discipline systems that emphasize punishments to instill and enforce disciplinary expectations.

Problems with Punishment-Based Systems

A task force of the American Psychological Association made several key findings when investigating the current application of zero-tolerance, punishment-based policies across schools in the United States (Skiba, 2008; Skiba et al., 2006). The first was that suspension and expulsion rates across schools with zero-tolerance policies differed widely. Moreover, students from minority backgrounds were expelled at a higher rate than their Caucasian peers. Ironically, a policy that was intended to be more consistent was not implemented consistently.

The second finding was that zero-tolerance practices were not developmentally appropriate for many students under the age of 15, who frequently had not fully developed the skills necessary to resist peer pressure, foresee the effects of their behaviors, and manage their impulses. Although school personnel viewed these behaviors as deliberate and thought out, misbehaviors caused by poor judgment were managed in ways that threatened the ability of students to learn those skills in an appropriate educational setting. Perhaps most ironically, schools that suspended and expelled students at higher rates performed more poorly on measures of schoolwide academic achievement than did schools with similar demographics and socioeconomic levels. Finally, although the entire focus of zero-tolerance policies was designed to improve school

culture, schools with high suspension and expulsion rates
have more negative school cultures than do other schools
(Skiba et al., 2006).

To better understand why many of these punitive policies
continue to fail, it is important to investigate some of the
practical drawbacks of harsh punishments. Schools utilizing punishment as their primary method of behavior management may fail to meet their students' needs for a variety
of reasons.

Failure to Promote Desirable Behavior

Punishment, although it may reduce problem behaviors in
the short run, does not promote desirable behaviors (Bear,
2008). Students may learn not to yell out in class, but they do
not learn how to get the teacher's attention appropriately. For
example, Susan is experiencing a real-life dilemma, which is
how to manage difficult friendships and take part in activities
in which she has little success. When she returns to school following a suspension, she will continue to exhibit deficits in her
social skills. Likewise, playground fights represent poor conflict management skills on the parts of the students. Removal
of recess does not improve student conflict resolution skills.

Suppression of Behavior Does Not Generalize to Other Settings

Punishment may inadvertently teach a student to only avoid
performing a behavior when an adult is watching (Skinner,
1974). For example, students may become aggressive only when
they know an adult is not in the area. The suspensions may
even teach Susan that a behavior is acceptable if she does not get
caught. A punishment model may reduce problematic behaviors
only when adults with the authority to punish are watching.

Punishments May Encourage Students to Be Aggressive

Perhaps most seriously, punishments may increase student
aggression against those with less power (Bear, 2008). Because
students may see authoritarian school systems inflicting painful consequences upon them, they may learn to use aggression
against those weaker than themselves. By using his power to
suspend Susan, the school administrator has modeled the use
of power for aggression. Thus, Susan and others may learn that
she must increase her power for aggression to more effectively
control others.

Punishments May Cease to Be Punishing

Many schools utilize a hierarchy of punishments for their discipline management. Through this hierarchy, a less restrictive punishment, such as after-school detention, is followed by parent phone calls, brief suspensions, longer suspensions, and then expulsions. Such practices often encourage a student to habituate or become accustomed to a punishment. Thus, if a school continues to remove recess as a response cost, the students may soon become used to living without recess, and the loss of the privilege will lose its salience to change behavior.

Suspensions May Reward Some Students and Damage Communities

An additional and unintended consequence of suspensions and expulsions is that some students find the time away from school rewarding (Atkins et al., 2002). By the time Susan is in the seventh grade, her parents may decide to leave her unattended at home during suspensions so that they do not miss work. Being away from school may provide some of the students who are most likely to act out with opportunities to be unsupervised in the community. At this point, a suspension has lost its ability to reduce problem behavior, and is likely to serve as a vehicle that increases problem behaviors both in and out of school.

It should be noted that we, the authors, do not advocate the extreme position of removing all punishments from school systems. There may be students who require suspension and expulsion. However, our position is that these occurrences should be rare, and should only occur when a school has exhausted its behavioral repertoire of positive, preventative measures designed to encourage desirable behaviors, or a student's behavior presents an immediate danger to the safety of others in the school. Similarly, it is unlikely that teachers will refrain from issuing reprimands, or sending students to the principal's office. In fact, effective techniques for reprimands are recommended in this book. Similarly, the book describes procedures for sending students to the discipline office. However, those providing educational and mental health services to schools must be aware of the resources and years of research at their disposal. Fortunately, most of this research points toward positive methods that teachers, administrators, and related school personnel can use to elicit desirable behaviors.

FEDERAL PUSH TOWARD POSITIVE BEHAVIORAL SUPPORTS

Recently, the federal government has encouraged schools to develop positive behavior supports (PBS) for students in schools (Sugai & Horner, 2002b). The No Child Left Behind Act of 2001 encouraged schools to take a preventative approach to school discipline using strategies proven effective by scientific research. In order to receive funding, schools needed to have plans that included "appropriate and effective discipline policies" and "prevention activities" (NCLB, 2001).

The Individuals With Disabilities Education Act of 2004 (aka IDEA 2004) also encouraged schools to alter the way they responded to student misbehavior—particularly for students with disabilities. For instance, when developing an individual education plan (IEP) for a student whose behavior impeded his or her learning or that of others, the IEP team had to consider the use of positive, nonpunitive behavioral interventions and supports to address the behavior (IDEA, 2004). The goal was to teach or elicit appropriate replacement behaviors rather than merely stopping misbehavior. To do so required school personnel to examine and alter the student's school environment.

To encourage this change, the creators of IDEA 2004 sought to provide funding for increased behavior supports and research-based, systemic interventions in schools; staff training in positive behavioral interventions and supports, behavioral intervention planning, and classroom and student management techniques; and the development and/or implementation of specific curricula, programs, or interventions aimed at addressing behavioral problems (IDEA, 2004). In light of these findings, the current recommended approach to discipline is the use of schoolwide systems that include a continuum of support for all students. These systems consist of proactive strategies for teaching and supporting appropriate student behavior to create positive school climates (IDEA, 2004). Consequently, schools have begun to look at strategies that impact the school community as a whole rather than singling out misbehaving students.

WHAT ARE POSITIVE BEHAVIORAL SUPPORTS?

While the faculty, parent groups, and administration at Susan's school may agree that suspension and the removal of recess are undesirable choices, they probably feel as though they have no other choice. What else can be done? Frequently, experts in behavior management are asked questions by teach- ers such as "What should I do if a student hits another student? Shouldn't that child be sent to the office?" The question is fair, but not the best question to ask. A better question is "How can I reduce the likelihood that a child will hit another student?" This new heuristic is at the core of PBS. Rather than asking how to react, the questions should instead be "How can I pre- vent behavior problems?" or "How can I create environments that elicit behaviors that are desirable?"

Positive behavior supports have been described by scholars and practitioners using a spectrum of definitions and termi- nology ranging from the elaborate to the elementary. For our purposes, we take the middle ground, discussing PBS at a level above that used in everyday, casual conversation but not so technical that semantics become the primary focus. For this reason we chose a definition from Turnbull, Turnbull, Shank, Smith, and Leal (2002) describing PBS as "systemic and indi- vidualized strategies for achieving important social and learn- ing outcomes while preventing problem behavior" (p. 337).

Positive behavior supports can improve the overall morale of both students and teachers. As a consequence, PBS schools find the following:

- More teaching time (Scott, 2001)
- Higher test scores (Lassen, Steele, & Sailor, 2006)
- Happier teachers (Nelson, 1996)
- Better instruction (Colvin & Fernandez, 2000)
- Fewer trips to the school office (Nelson, 1996)

HOW DOES RESPONSE TO INTERVENTION FIT?

Positive behavior supports provide multiple tiers of preven- tion-based interventions. However, a PBS system will fail if it does not include a team willing to systematically review data on student behavior. Many of us have worked in schools where a positive intervention had been put into place, but was quickly written off. Some school staff members may say things like "We tried that years ago, and it just doesn't work." Although an intervention might be effective according to some research base, it may not be working effectively in your school. Does that mean there is a problem with the intervention? Or does it mean the intervention is not being implemented correctly? Does it mean the intervention needs to be changed slightly?

Response to intervention (RTI) is a problem-solving model that evaluates interventions to determine whether they are serving their stated purpose. Interventions that are not effective should be changed or removed. Interventions that are effective should be supported. As described by Figure 1.1, problem identification lends itself to intervention. If that intervention is not evaluated, new problem-solving processes cannot begin, and interventions are unlikely to be successful.

WHAT TO EXPECT FROM THIS BOOK

Positive school settings are good for teachers and students! Most educators agree with this sentiment, but few understand how to create and achieve positive results. Although harmonious relationships between adults and children seem to be easy, the truth is that schools are too often stressful places for both students and adults. Developing a positive school climate requires significant effort from school employees who are frequently facing meaningful challenges with the current expectations. Who has time to go through the research to understand how to develop and implement a PBS system? If you work in a school with behavior problems, this manual is designed for you. Whether a small group of students causes many problems, certain classes of students appear unwieldy, or a whole student body seems to be out of control, educational and mental health

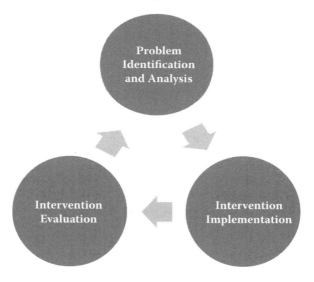

Figure 1.1   Schoolwide problem-solving model.

professionals responsible for providing consultation or direct services to schools will find this manual to be valuable.

Rather than describing details about theories of classroom and school behavior management, this guide specifies best practices to help teachers and administrators create positive supports in their schools. The applied procedures are clearly spelled out and forms are included. It is our expectation that school educational and mental health providers will already have many of the tools necessary for putting PBS systems into place.

THREE-TIER SERVICE DELIVERY

The premise of PBS is based on the assumption that application of behavior principles in a school setting will increase prosocial behaviors and contribute to the establishment of a more positive learning environment. The emphasis on these two goals bears restating and additional attention. The presence of an increased frequency of appropriate behaviors translates into a decrease in the number of socially unacceptable behaviors (aka discipline problems). A reduction in discipline referrals generally means that students are complying with school and class rules and causing less disruption to the learning environment. More time on academic tasks translates into an increase in performance feedback to help students master material. A more positive learning environment is the desire of parents and teachers regardless of political, religious, or social beliefs. Society as a whole benefits when our children learn in a setting where they feel safe, accepted, and encouraged.

A three-tiered triangle visually conveys the concept of a primary, secondary, and tertiary service delivery model. The base of the triangle is the largest, the middle third is smaller, and the top of the triangle is the smallest. Tier I, the bottom third, represents the 80–85% of students benefiting from primary service delivery (e.g., teaching expectations and reinforcement for positive behavior). It is on this level that a majority of data for school, grade, and class is aggregated (Tidwell, Flannery, & Lewis-Palmer, 2003). Although percentages may vary, a PBS model with an ineffective Tier I is easily identified by the high percentage of students requiring Tier II and III services. Educational systems are not designed and cannot adequately allocate intensive services to large numbers of students. Thus, Tier I interventions and behavior management strategies must be effective at encouraging all students to demonstrate positive school behavior. Depending on the student population, the intensity of Tier I interventions will vary. If not, day-to-day activities will entail "putting out fires" (e.g., dealing with problem behaviors) as much as enhancing learning opportunities. Similarly, poor classroom and schoolwide management practices may trigger maladaptive and problematic behaviors in students who require Tier III interventions. Effective Tier I interventions not only reduce the number of students requiring intensive Tier III interventions but also support them.

In essence, designing a discipline model with effective Tier III interventions but poor Tier I interventions is like trying to stand an elephant on a wedding cake. Those providing individualized functional behavioral assessment and creating behavior plans are overwhelmed and do not have the time to adequately address each student's unique behavioral needs. Teachers are required to implement multiple behavior plans in a classroom, taking away their attention from instruction delivery and classwide management. The school office is overwhelmed by the number of students sent for behavioral referrals. The school lacks the necessary foundation and crumbles when attempting to withstand the weight from above. When behavior management systems rely on reactive disciplinary measures in which they assume that students should already know how to behave, an inverted triangle forms that is incapable of supporting itself. (See Figure 1.2.)

Tier II often involves the implementation of predetermined interventions for the 10–15% of students identified as behaviorally at risk (Crone & Horner, 2003). The majority of students receiving Tier II services should demonstrate improved behavior as a result of a robust, research-based intervention. This is not to say that every student will respond positively to a given intervention. Instead, we suggest that *most students* should respond in a positive manner when empirically validated interventions are administered consistently and with fidelity. Failure to do so would suggest that the selected intervention, treatment integrity, or data analysis should be reexamined. Tier III represents the use of functional behavior assessment to understand the causes and reasons behind problematic behaviors.

The application of RTI principles to behavior is not a new idea. The multitiered system, high-quality school and classroom management for all students, targeted interventions for those at risk of severe behavior problems, and individual problem solving using functional behavior assessment techniques closely mirror the structure of RTI systems designed to prevent

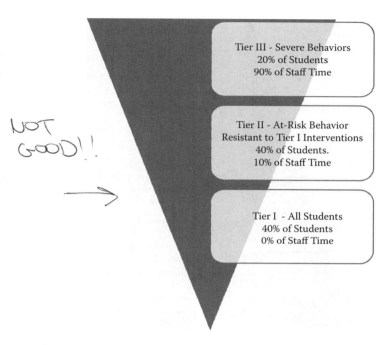

NOT
GOOD!!

→

Figure 1.2   A pyramid headed for collapse.

and remediate reading or other academic problems. Concepts such as intervention integrity, school-based problem-solving teams, data-based decision making, and reliability and validity of data are all integrated into this model.

This manual will serve as a guide for school personnel to work with a school-based problem-solving team responsible for early intervention and schoolwide problem solving. This team will oversee the implementation of a comprehensive, data-based plan for their school to effectively manage student behavior. To be most effective, school-based teams should implement each chapter's objectives sequentially.

The chapters are organized in an adequately based pyramid order as demonstrated by Figure 1.3. As the teams work through the chapters, the number of students served will decrease, but the severity of the behavior problems will increase. Chapters 3 through 9 discuss the stages involved in implementing a positive behavioral climate in the whole school. These practices will influence all students throughout the school. Chapters 10 and 11 provide a procedure for problem-solving teams to identify and resolve schoolwide and classwide behavior problems that persist or develop after

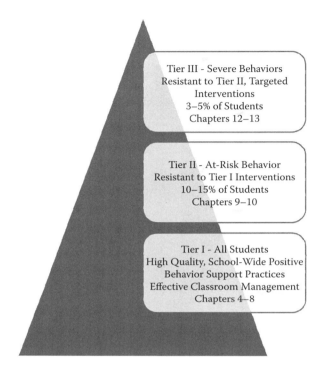

Tier III - Severe Behaviors
Resistant to Tier II, Targeted
Interventions
3–5% of Students
Chapters 12–13

Tier II - At-Risk Behavior
Resistant to Tier I Interventions
10–15% of Students
Chapters 9–10

Tier I - All Students
High Quality, School-Wide Positive
Behavior Support Practices
Effective Classroom Management
Chapters 4–8

Figure 1.3   Organization of chapters.

the faithful implementation of initial prevention procedures. Chapters 12 and 13 will articulate ways to identify students who may need even more intense and individualized intervention than is provided at Tier II.

This book primarily describes an application of a positive behavior support system that is effective for most students and most behavior problems. By following the procedures in this book, a problem-solving team will provide teachers with tools that are effective with most children. Schools who apply this system will find a reduction in many problem behaviors throughout the school. However, we do not provide detailed interventions for students who have serious mental health and behavioral challenges and who may require psychiatric treatment. Although many of these interventions have helped improve the behavior of such students, providing behavior supports to the most challenging students requires extensive training in functional behavioral techniques, psychotherapy, or psychiatric or pharmacological consultation. Such training is outside the scope of this volume.

Most chapters will follow the standardized format below:

- Introduction.
- Concepts to be introduced.
- Links to previous discussions.
- Description of forms. Perhaps one of the most difficult tasks for new teams is to take information from a model and convert it to meaningful forms that allow for comprehensive data collection and tracking. These forms are provided.
- Necessary resources. To successfully complete the tasks outlined in a particular chapter, a school-based problem-solving team may need some resources, including knowing what people are essential for the decisions to be made, what information will need to be collected, and what materials will be helpful to the team.
- Procedures: At this point in the chapter, the reader will learn what steps a problem-solving team should take to effectively implement this portion of the manual.
- Initial procedures.
- Secondary procedures.
- Follow-up procedures.
- Monitoring and integrity checks: The best interventions fail if they are not executed properly. When learning to implement a new system, it is important that school personnel receive feedback on how effectively an intervention is being put into place.
- Conclusion.

WHAT DID SUSAN'S SCHOOL DO?

Fortunately, Susan's school, with support from parent groups, began to implement positive behavior supports. For Susan, the school recognized that her behavior problems began to stem from her participation in the gym class. The teacher, recognizing that bullying was central to the difficulty, chose different ways to pick teams, included more individual sports rather than team sports, and began to initiate procedures whereby students quietly lined up at the beginning and end of gym class. The gym teacher also began teaching students about sportsmanship and provided more supervision for the more contentious team sports in gym class. Susan began keeping track of her own aggressive behaviors, as did the other students. By simply tracking their behaviors, the number of aggressive acts decreased.

The problem-solving team began to review the office discipline referrals (ODRs) from recess to determine exactly where fights were most often breaking out. They found that the swing sets and the ball field were the areas where the most fights took place. The fights on the ball field occurred when there were too few balls, resulting in a majority of students not touching the football. In the playground during recess, teachers began to more closely monitor areas where fights were frequent. They interacted with students more frequently and increased the number of positive teacher–student interactions. They also made more balls available on the ball field to allow more students an opportunity to play. These interventions reduced the incidents of fighting from one per day to two per month.

SUMMARY

School personnel must serve as advocates for kids. At times, we may feel as though we are in direct conflict with the role of others who wish to maintain order and safety for all children in the school setting. Fortunately, this conflict is manageable. Behavioral RTI programs meet and evaluate many of the security needs that administrators and parents value while supplying the additional benefit of providing nurturing and safe learning environments for each student.

Of course, the process requires commitment, and schools are sometimes resistant to change. This manual facilitates the process that schools go through to focus on the positive aspects of education. Frequently, we lose sight of the joy involved in those "aha" moments of helping children learn to read, conduct a difficult science lab, or balance an algebraic equation for the first time. We want to bring joy back into the classroom—for teachers and for students. That joy is at the core of a positive behavior support system. Good luck!

Building the School-Based Problem-Solving Team

INTRODUCTION

The scope of providing behavioral interventions in a response to intervention (RTI) framework requires a great deal of people power. This chapter focuses on the question of "Who?" Who is responsible for implementing this process? Who does the work and the training? Typically, a school building-level committee takes on the responsibility for putting positive behavior supports (PBS) into place. Throughout this book, we refer to this group of people as the *problem-solving team*.

School-based problem-solving teams have many different names, including *child study team*, *school building-level committee*, and *teacher assistance team*. Initially, the primary function for these teams was to collectively determine whether special education referrals were warranted (Chalifant, Pysh, & Moultrie, 1979). Part of that responsibility was to determine if a child needed a simple intervention to continue to receive educational benefit from a general education classroom. However, there were some who worried that prereferral teams were actually preventing students from getting the services that they needed. Thus, many school teams began to focus on moving student referrals quickly to special education referrals and became rubber stamps for those wishing to get the student evaluated (Schwanz & Barbour, 2005). Although many students were being evaluated for special education, these prereferral teams failed to provide effective interventions for their students. Interventions either were not research based or were not implemented with a sufficient degree of integrity to successfully remediate the mild education deficits that students were experiencing (Carter & Sugai, 1989).

However, many schools have seen the benefit of having groups of educators work together to solve problems within the school. For individual students, many teams are implementing effective interventions. Although these teams may recommend special education evaluations, their primary goal is to help children find success in regular education classes (Iverson, 2002). The purview of these groups has expanded. Today, effective problem-solving teams have taken on additional responsibilities to include screening, identification, and management of behavioral problems (Eber, Lewis-Palmer, & Pacchiano, 2002; Nelson, Benner, Reid, Epstein, & Currin, 2002; Tyre, 2003; Walker, Zeller, Close, Webber, & Gresham, 1999). Instead of merely reacting to individuals, these teams solve schoolwide problems, and even provide effective prevention services. School-based problem-solving teams, as described by this manual, play an active role in preventing, identifying, and resolving behavior problems.

One individual is unable to effectively support a child's behavior across community, home, and school settings. Instead, a network approach in which stakeholders across settings work together for the purpose of improving student behavior is more effective at providing consistent and comprehensive interventions (Dunlap, Newton, Fox, Benito, & Vaughn, 2001). A team, then, must collaborate in constructing, implementing, and setting the criteria to evaluate the effectiveness for PBS plans (Carr et al., 2002). The successes of PBS programs are due, in large part, to the ability of PBS teams to first collaborate and work together to achieve goals (Bambara, Gomez, Koger, Lohrmann-O'Rourke, & Xin, 2001). Conflicts within the group lead to dissension amongst team members and the potential undermining of its success (Jolivette, Barton-Atwood, & Scott, 2000). When stakeholders buy into the cause, work well with one another, and take ownership, they can better meet their stated goals (Tyre, 2003).

CONCEPTS TO BE INTRODUCED

- The problem-solving team

LINKS TO PREVIOUS DISCUSSIONS

The problem-solving team is the "who" described in this manual. It is the problem-solving team that makes most of the decisions, provides the training, and reviews and evaluates how well a school system, classroom, or individual student is responding to behavioral interventions.

PEOPLE NEEDED

Problem-solving teams vary in size, but generally consist of five to eight team members whose responsibility it is to lead in the prevention, identification, and remediation of socially inappropriate behaviors (Scott & Hunter, 2001). The problem-solving team should be composed of individuals with the following roles (one person may function in multiple roles).

> *Building-level administrator*: Most frequently the principal, this person brings true authority to the committee and controls financial and human resources. The administrator also represents the school to the broader community.   *Principal*
>
> *Teachers*: Selection here is critical as the teachers should have a thorough understanding of not only the school curriculum but also the school culture. Both regular education and special education teachers will provide crucial expertise.
>
> *Intervention expert*: This person must have a thorough knowledge of research-based interventions that are effective for managing a variety of children. Whereas the school psychologist may be itinerant, the intervention specialist is often housed at one school. This may be a school counselor, a special education teacher, or a teacher with training in managing problematic behaviors.
>
> *Data expert*: Understanding data collection, entry, and interpretation are traits of a data expert. He or she is responsible for ensuring the accuracy of the school's data.
>
> *Other individuals*: The problem-solving team should also consult with paraprofessionals, hallway and playground monitors, lunchroom personnel, bus drivers, custodians, secretarial staff, and/or, most importantly, *parents*.

What Are the Roles of the Members of a Problem-Solving Team?

The problem-solving teams have a broad range of responsibilities within the school that include developing positive behavioral support and schoolwide academic screening systems, and selecting academic and behavioral interventions for high-risk students (Lane, Gresham, & O'Shaughnessy, 2002) who for the most part are having difficulty adjusting to the school environment (Lane, Barton-Arwood, Nelson, & Wehby, 2008). If a child's academic skills prevent him or her from being successful in the classroom, behavioral interventions will invariably fail at improving problematic behavior (Witt, Gilbertson, & VanDerHeyden, 2007). Thus, problem-solving teams may need to address a child's academic and behavioral needs (Sugai & Horner, 2002a). However, due to the magnitude of this responsibility, and given the academic resources currently available, this manual seeks to address the more difficult task of behavior management.

It is also important to note that students who require intensive functionally based interventions may best be supported by an IEP team focused solely on the needs of that individual child. In this particular manual, we do not make recommendations about when a child should be evaluated for or placed into special education. Instead, it is our hope that special education services are used when a child's behavior precludes him or her from meeting the behavioral expectations of a school with high-quality Tier I and Tier II service provisions in place.

It is noted here that most interventions outlined in this text are effective when used with elementary and middle school students. The same practices may or may not be effective in high schools, as school size and the quantity of various adult interactions increase the complexity of planning. Secondly, the cognitive and emotional development of high school students may demand an intervention model more relational than behavioral in its approach.

What Are the Expectations of the Problem-Solving Team?

Ultimately, leadership in schoolwide behavioral management falls to the building's administration. Within each individual classroom, the teacher is responsible for behavioral management. However, schools overcome challenging behaviors with students when every adult takes responsibility for supporting every child. The tasks of the problem-solving team, then, are consultative and supportive in nature. The problem-solving team is the best prepared entity for schoolwide behavior management, which involves communicating best practices in classroom management and training teachers how to implement the various interventions. For the implementation of classroom management practices, the school problem-solving team can only serve as support systems for willing teachers. The following list of tasks is not comprehensive, but instead outlines the nature of this ambitious undertaking.

Tasks of the Problem-Solving Team

- Design schoolwide positive behavior support system.
- Implement schoolwide token economy.
- Review classwide and schoolwide management procedures.
- Review the implementation integrity of the schoolwide positive behavior support system.
- Review office discipline referral data to identify areas of the school that need intervention.
- Review classroom data to identify means of improving classrooms whose students frequently manifest many behavioral problems.
- Support teachers in identifying students who need additional supports.
- Support teachers in monitoring the integrity of Tier II behavioral supports.
- Enter progress-monitoring data on intervention effectiveness.
- Support teachers in the identification of students requiring intensive behavior supports.
- Develop and implement Tier III behavioral supports.
- Review the progress of students receiving individualized behavior supports.

FINAL THOUGHTS

Some administrators feel obligated to create problem-solving teams to "make sure we meet federal and state educational guidelines." Many may disagree with these individuals' perspective or rationale, but their motives should not be disregarded and ignored. School personnel from around the country have shared similar thoughts. With a troubled economy and job security in question, self-preservation manifests itself through compliance with district and state practices, often regardless of whether they meaningfully contribute to improving student outcomes. However, such an approach runs the risk of bogging down a team with paperwork, and removing much of the creative spark that is essential for students to be successful. A problem-solving team that implements positive interventions will both prevent many problems that can come to the attention of legal authorities, and be able to provide data necessary to show the effectiveness of different research-based interventions. Following best practice is not only effective but also highly defensible in court.

This chapter has documented some of the history of problem-solving teams. We have also recommended who should be on the team. However, the exact models of supporting our students and teachers are determined by individual schools. Team members should be willing to work with others. Response to intervention is not only a concept for working with individual students, but also can be applied to whole schools and to teams. Thus, the real mettle of the team will be measured not when they have had their first success, but by their response to a failure. If the team is able to use the failure as a learning opportunity, it has the potential to benefit students and staff for many years.

CHAPTER 2 TASKS

Goal: Create a problem-solving team responsible for implementing a positive behavior support system in the school.

Task 1. Secure permission, and support from the school's principal. The committee will need the following:
- Teachers and school staff with time to meet
- A meeting location
- Access to discipline data and other information about student behavior
- A commitment for the principal to serve on the committee

Task 2. Identify and secure commitments from individual staff members.
- The members of the staff should have a variety of experiences, and should include the following:
  - Data expertise
  - Administrator
  - Intervention specialist
  - General and special education teachers
  - Others who the team feels are appropriate
- Each member should be committed to positive behavior management.
- Each member should be able to meet at an agreed upon time.

Task 3. Begin training the team on the tasks at hand, and prepare a course of action.
- See subsequent chapters.

3

Understanding Positive Behavior Support

T his chapter offers an overview of the thinking and ideas that taken together constitute the roots of positive behavior support (PBS) systems. PBS relies upon an integration of behavioral and educational principles that have a demonstrated utility in allowing educators, parents, and helping professionals to understand individual behavior. These behavioral and educational principles, when selectively and systematically integrated into an applied public health model, become a PBS system. Key concepts related to these behavioral and educational principles are also explored. This chapter will offer more than a review of existing PBS practice; we describe a crucial third pillar to PBS systems, systematic program evaluation. Through the use of systematic program evaluation assessment tools, a PBS system becomes more than simply a best practice behavioral intervention plan. A PBS system becomes a behavioral response to intervention (RTI) practice whereby schools can measure how well students are responding to the strategies designed to elicit desirable behaviors.

As noted above, the PBS model described in this writing integrates practices from multiple methodologies. This blending of behavioral science technology with the most recent advances in educational and cognitive science facilitates practitioners' abilities to (a) provide effective intervention to student populations, (b) monitor the effectiveness of the individual and group interventions, and (c) provide ongoing schoolwide assessment of the effectiveness of PBS systems. An overview of the salient theories underlying these methods is briefly outlined here and further elaborated in subsequent chapters. Finally, this chapter discussion ends with an overview of the historic and current research supporting these methodologies.

BEST PRACTICES IN PBS

The best PBS programs integrate multisystems in seeking to reduce problem behaviors (Barrett, Bradshaw, & Lewis-Palmer, 2008; Walker et al., 1996). While such comprehensive prevention efforts draw upon the contributions of a diversity of social science theories and research, positive behavior support relies upon three veins of social science research and technology. First and foremost, PBS relies upon the application of methods derived from behavioral and humanistic psychology. These behavioral and humanistic psychology practices are focused on eliciting and reinforcing desirable student behaviors (Sugai et al., 2000). The origins of PBS stem from the assumptions that all students deserve to be treated with dignity and respect, and benefit from being provided with opportunities to act as stakeholders in their education (Carr et al., 2002). Second, PBS depends upon the use of educational techniques and principles designed to teach students the skills necessary to enjoy effective and satisfying social interactions. These skills help students to meet established conduct expectations and improve the likelihood of students achieving sufficient developmental and academic progress in school and beyond. To perfect these social skills and achieve the target academic and interpersonal outcomes, school staff members must routinely provide differentiated social and behavioral skill instruction. This sort of supportive instruction is delivered at various levels: schoolwide, classwide, and to identified groups and individuals. These social and behavioral skill development sessions are organized to be supportive, fun, and interactive, and to foster student engagement. The PBS system is structured so that these opportunities for social skills learning are available until all students can be safe and effective in all settings (e.g., class, hall, and restroom). The final ingredient of a successful PBS system is derived from the science of program evaluation and response to intervention (RTI) progress-monitoring practices.

One of the most critical uses of schoolwide data evaluation is the discovery of conditions that provoke student misbehavior. These antecedent circumstances become targets for review and alteration. Using data to identify and remediate situations that contribute to students' social, behavioral, or academic difficulty is at the heart of PBS. Individual student performance can also be the target of analysis. Ongoing systematic review of students' response to high-quality intervention, both individually and collectively (e.g., schoolwide, gradewide, or classwide), is another central application of the program evaluation component of the PBS system described. Program evaluation facilitates ongoing program alteration and reform. In this way, the educational environment is continuously being directed toward improved facilitation of students' desirable behavior and a maximization of learning opportunities. In essence, a behavioral response to intervention model is data-driven positive behavioral support practice.

The key to PBS is the integration of the aforementioned underlying components into a public health model of service provision whereby multitier prevention strategies are employed. These three elements of PBS (behavioral and humanistic psychology, educational technology, and program evaluation) work in a complementary and interdependent fashion to create a safe and welcoming setting for children and staff alike. A public health perspective by definition is prevention focused, emphasizes academic achievement, promotes positive behavior, and strengthens the school community (Strein, Hoagwood, & Cohn, 2003). A schoolwide, public health–oriented, three-tiered prevention model is effective in guaranteeing an efficient and successful response to a full spectrum of behavioral health and academic concerns (Friedman, 2003; Hunter 2003; Strein et al., 2003). This approach includes universal (primary prevention), targeted (secondary prevention), and intensive (tertiary prevention) intervention efforts. The majority of the student population (70–85%) will most likely not have serious academic, emotional, social, or behavioral difficulties (OSEP Technical Assistance Center, n.d.). These relatively untroubled students benefit from universal prevention efforts such as a schoolwide positive behavioral support system and the appropriate implementation of an evidence-based curriculum (OSEP Technical Assistance Center). Smaller percentages (up to 30%) of students are actively at risk for developing academic or behavioral disorders. Fewer than 5% of students will manifest intense problem behaviors (OSEP Technical Assistance Center). This distribution of student needs should serve as a guide to inform the allocation of human and fiscal resources to address academic and behavioral health concerns.

Under the auspices of a schoolwide, public health-oriented, three-tiered prevention model, early academic intervention and positive behavioral support are provided without incurring the delays inherent in an evaluation-focused system

(Friedman, 2003; Strein et al., 2003). In this way, all students receive universal interventions. These positive discipline strategies (e.g., simple and concise school rules, frequent rewards and incentives for appropriate behavior at the classroom and schoolwide levels, and a curricular emphasis on social skills and problem solving), along with evidenced-based curricula, help prevent students from developing or creating behavioral problems (Strein et al.).

PSYCHOLOGICAL PRINCIPLES UNDERLYING PBS

Edward Thorndike (1913) described the Law of Effect, which had two important components:

1. Subjects' responses that are followed by pleasant or satisfying stimuli will be strengthened and occur more often in the future.
2. Those responses accompanied or closely followed by aversive stimuli will be less likely to occur again.

Thorndike's First Law of Effect in particular laid the groundwork for the development of the principles of positive reinforcement. This notion of positive reinforcement was expanded by B. F. Skinner's development of free operant conditioning procedures. Skinner (1938) posited that subjects could be trained to perform certain skills through the differential application of reinforcement and punishment. Specifically, by providing reinforcement to behavior that approximated the target behavior, Skinner found that he could shape behavior. Skinner's "shaping" technique involves reinforcing (i.e., rewarding) a series of successive approximations of a target behavior. By reinforcing small steps toward a target behavior, a rat or a mouse could be encouraged to perform tasks such as running through a maze or pressing a lever a certain number of times. The term *operant* in Skinner's operant conditioning refers to the subject's action or operation on the environment as a means of gaining reinforcement (e.g., giving a child a desired pencil if, and only if, he or she says, "Please"). Skinner described three different parts of a behavior: the operant behavior; the operant antecedent, or the stimulus that elicited a particular behavior; and the operant function, or the consequence of the function. A more thorough description of the ABCs of behavior is delineated in Chapter 12, "Understanding the Function of Behavior."

As behavior principles began to be applied to human subjects in the 1950s and 1960s, it became more apparent that these principles could be utilized to provide more effective interventions to people in need. Applied behavior analysis (ABA) allowed practitioners for the first time to effectively provide behavioral intervention. Early (and continuing) applications of ABA targeted people who suffer from chronic conditions such as mental retardation and autism. In particular, Carr's (1977) seminal work on the functions of self-injurious behavior encouraged the use of functional behavioral assessments whereby an investigator would examine the subject's environment to determine eliciting antecedents and functions of a problematic behavior. During the 1980s, these practices were generalized to individuals with less chronically debilitating conditions, including emotional disturbance and learning disorders. Today, positive behavior support reflects the application of functional behavioral assessments to studying antecedents and consequences with entire groups of students in schoolwide and classroom settings (Carr et al., 2002).

Reinforcement

Offering incentives (i.e., reinforcement) is one of the pillars of positive behavior support. PBS is in large part based upon the science of operant conditioning. Perhaps the greatest challenge to the success of a positive behavior support system is finding a set of rewards that are consistently effective in fostering student motivation. Students must value the rewards the school staff offers. If the rewards are not providing a behavioral incentive, they are not acting as behavioral reinforcement. To help establish a set of effective incentives, this PBS system recommends an incentive program reliant upon several overlapping reinforcement strategies. At the core of the system is a token economy. A *token economy* is a powerful first-level intervention that includes the distribution of tokens (e.g., tickets) that are redeemable for prizes at a "store." There are two important components of effective *token economy systems*: (a) The value of the offered rewards must be great enough to provoke student interest, and (b) students must expect to be able to perform the specified tasks successfully if they apply themselves. To achieve these, school staff members must select rewards carefully.

Table 3.1 Definition of Behavioral Terms

Reinforcers	Events that follow behavior and increase the future probability of that behavior
Punishers	Events that follow behavior and decrease the future probability of behavior
Extinction	Behavior stopping when no longer reinforced
Primary reinforcer	An environmental event that satisfies a student's biological needs (food, water, warmth, sex. etc.)
Secondary reinforcer (conditioned reinforcer)	Any event that acquires reinforcing effects for a student because it has been associated with a primary reinforcer
Generalized secondary reinforcers	Environmental events associated with several reinforcers
Operant antecedents	The context in which the response occurs; events that precede a response; also called the *discriminative stimulus*
Operant behavior	The response itself
Operant consequence	The reinforcer of the behavioral response
Positive reinforcement	Any stimulus that a student finds pleasurable and that, when present, increases the likelihood of response
Negative reinforcement	Any stimulus a student finds aversive that, when removed, increases the likelihood of a response
Token economy system	A systematic reward system whereby students earn points or other tokens that may be exchanged for objects or for access to activities the child enjoys

To better understand a *token economy system*, take the example of currency. The physical attributes that collectively constitute our coins and bills are not innately reinforcing. By itself, a dollar bill cannot do anything. However, the ability to exchange coins and bills for other tangible items and services makes them valuable. These tangible items and services are *primary reinforcers*. Put simply, money is a *secondary reinforcer* used to acquire primary reinforcers. Paying students for good behavior with tickets that are exchanged for valued prizes creates an *incentive-based economy*. Table 3.1 provides definitions of many of the behavioral terms that will be utilized throughout this text.

What Rewards Can Be Considered?

Weekly and monthly rewards for a consistent pattern of appropriate behavior may include a pizza party lunch, a dress-down (i.e., nonuniform) day, a Friday recess, movie passes, or any other group reward. Positive behavior armbands signify which children can receive these tangible rewards (e.g., popcorn, snowballs, and prizes) or attend fun activities (e.g., parties, school outings, and fun days). However, determining what rewards should be offered may require the administration of schoolwide *preference assessments*. A school that conducts an effective preference assessment with its student body will know what activities and items students find most rewarding as well as the categories of reinforcement (Schanding, Tingstrom, & Sterling-Turner, 2009). Although a complete list of possible rewards and activities is impossible to determine, Appendix D includes some ideas that school faculty can use as incentives in helping students.

Do Rewards Undermine Intrinsic Motivation?

There are some who contend that providing students with incentives for working is tantamount to bribery and encourages students to become reliant upon adults for approval (Kohn, 1993). Others have argued that extrinsic methods of motivation may work to discourage a child from becoming internally motivated to perform an action (e.g., Deci, Koestner, & Ryan, 2001). However, it is important that school staff members understand that *bribery* describes an incentive for performing an illegal, unethical, or immoral act. In many ways, giving students tokens serves a similar purpose as giving an employee a bonus for meeting performance criteria. Several reviews have demonstrated that the prudent use of extrinsic motivators does not have damaging effects on students' motivation or achievement (Akin-Little, Eckert, Lovett, & Little, 2004). In fact, these researchers argue that the use of rewards *awesome* and praise may actually increase a student's intrinsic motivation to perform tasks (Akin-Little et al., 2004).

Methods for Rewarding Students

However, to be effective, reward systems, including systems of praise, must be contingent upon completing a task or sufficiently meeting some criteria. Merely giving rewards to students who fail to meet a prearranged outcome will not change behavior. Rewards must be provided when promised, and *not* to students who have failed to meet particular criteria. Similarly, rewards must be made available on multiple occasions. Finally, once the behaviors have generalized, reward systems must be given on an intermittent reinforcement schedule or, in the case of individual behavior plans, gradually withdrawn (Akin-Little et al., 2004) Teachers and administrators quickly undermine their own reinforcement systems when they provide rewards to students who are not demonstrating desired behaviors.

There are several sets of criteria frequently used to determine whether a student or group of students should be rewarded. Students earn rewards for actively performing some action or deed deemed worthy of targeting for reinforcement. For example, they may help other students, help teachers, or serve as classroom mediators. Students may also receive rewards for avoiding problematic behaviors. Students may receive tokens for demonstrating a consistent pattern of no office referrals, not being late to class, or not being sent to the principal's office. Another method rewards a student for taking active steps to avoid negative behavior. Additionally, students will be reinforced for demonstrating an appropriate replacement behavior. For example, imagine a student who has historically responded to being teased by her second grade peers with disruptive and sometime aggressive acting out. This young girl has participated in a social-skills program, and today you witness her responding to being teased by walking away (an appropriate replacement behavior).

EDUCATIONAL PRINCIPLES UNDERLYING PBS

Most children recognize what constitutes socially acceptable interpersonal interactions and general codes of conduct. Yet, no child is born with this knowledge. Some children have the benefit of concerned and involved caretakers. These fortunate children have learned from their caregivers' patient demonstrations, modeling, guided instruction, corrective feedback, and praise how to exhibit socially appropriate behavior. However, many children are not as fortunate, and they often enter the school system without the benefit of understanding socially acceptable interpersonal interactions and general codes of conduct. These children are not necessarily impaired in any way other than that they have not been taught the expectations of their new environment. They simply never had someone take the time to teach them how to behave properly. All children need to receive instruction on how to behave. This sort of instruction is a prerequisite to academic instruction. These all-too-often overlooked principles represent a central tenet of PBS and applied behavioral analysis.

An important notion of behavioral analysis is that a student is more likely to display a desirable behavior if that behavior is a fluent part of his or her repertoire (Carr et al., 2002). A basic assumption of the PBS model (as described above) is that students will be less likely to display conduct problems if they know, have been taught, and have practiced the behaviors that meet conduct expectations. Best practices in delivering targeted instruction include five necessary components: targeting skills at a student's level, teaching explicitly, including an appropriate level of challenge, giving frequent opportunities to practice, and providing immediate feedback (Burns, VanDerHeyden, & Boice, 2008). Skills will be most likely demonstrated when they are taught to fluency. The same is true for student behavioral expectations. Good behavioral management involves direct instruction of behavioral expectations that allows students to practice good behavior, receive feedback on their performance, and demonstrate fluency.

[handwritten margin note: Best practices in delivering targeted instruction]

[handwritten margin note: practiced FB are important!!]

These simple but essential rules to developing children's social skills can be applied at the schoolwide level, in classrooms, or individually to students. Schoolwide application involves students receiving explicit instruction on behavioral expectations in common areas such as playgrounds, lunchrooms, libraries, school offices, and hallways. Opportunities must be made available for schoolwide training days where students have the chance to practice desired behaviors until those behaviors become fluent. This is a common practice among schools that implement PBS.

Best practices in classroom management encourage teachers to instruct students on behavioral expectations for transitions such as entering and leaving the classroom or moving from one subject to another, and instructional periods such as independent work time, group work, or teacher-led instruction. Students who receive individualized behavioral interventions may receive social-skills training or other types of instructionally based interventions whereby they learn the behaviors necessary to best access classroom instruction.

PRINCIPLES OF PROGRAM EVALUATION UNDERLYING PBS

Program evaluation involves the application of statistical methods and other empirical tools to determine how effectively an organization is meeting a series of goals and objectives. Best practices in program evaluation involve several necessary steps:

1. Identifying value-based goals that describe the aims of a particular program
2. Describing these goals as meaningful, observable and measurable outcome-based objectives
3. Collecting meaningful data that relate to the objectives
4. Analyzing the data to provide support for these objectives
5. Making recommendations based on the data (Fitzpatrick, Sanders, & Worthen, 2004)

A behavioral response to intervention system involves a program evaluation of the school's discipline program. In doing this thorough and systematic analysis, a school will go through several program evaluation steps:

1. The creation or development of social and behavioral goals for students
2. Turning the identified goals into behavioral objectives that are observable and measurable
3. Systematically measuring target behaviors and establishing a method of data analysis
4. Regular schoolwide screenings to identify students, classrooms, areas of the school, and times of the school day when behavioral interventions are needed
5. Systematic progress monitoring to determine if an individual or a group of individuals is responding to a high-quality intervention
6. Reviews of intervention implementation to determine whether interventions are put in place appropriately and with fidelity

The last two components of the PBS program evaluation describe the utilization of RTI technology in analyzing behavior problems (Gresham, 2004). When a school implements RTI to address academic problems, universal screenings typically involve the schoolwide administration of curriculum-based measures to provide objective data to identify students who may have difficulty in reading, mathematics, or written expression (Burns & Gibbons, 2008). In behavioral measurements, instruments tend to have less evidence of reliability and validity. Thus, a combination of quantifiable data that schools already collect such as grade point average, office discipline referrals, or suspensions and expulsions is analyzed in conjunction with qualitative analyses such as teacher report and staff observation to identify students who may be struggling to meet the school's behavioral expectations.

Similarly, RTI for behavior involves systematic progress monitoring to determine if a child is responding to a high-quality, research-based intervention (Lewis & Sugai, 1999). Typically, progress monitoring involves the weekly administration of curriculum-based measures that are analyzed to determine whether a student is making adequate progress toward a goal. Behaviorally, quantifiable measures such as office discipline referrals may also be analyzed to determine whether a child is responding to behavioral supports. However, other pieces of information such as systematic direct observations of behavior are also included in progress monitoring as well as other target behaviors that serve as quantitative variables.

CONCLUSION

Program evaluation, high-quality instruction, and the implementation of high-quality psychological principles underlying student motivation are all critical pillars of any positive behavioral support system. High-quality reinforcement systems are most effective when used in conjunction with program evaluation systems. Similarly, it is impossible to simply teach students effective behaviors without also reinforcing those behaviors. Although some PBS systems may involve only teaching and reinforcement, a high-quality system must also evaluate effectiveness through a response to intervention lens (Gresham, 2004). The program evaluation component allows school leaders to understand how well or even if individual students, classes of students, or larger groups of students are responding to interventions.

No behavioral system should be constant. The ongoing program evaluation allows for the process to change as needed so that it remains effective. Consequently, the students receive meaningful reinforcement and targeted instruction. Figure 3.1 describes how these effective data management, behavioral instruction, and reinforcement principles come together in an antecedent–behavior–consequence model.

By better understanding the theory underlying positive behavior support, school problem-solving teams will be able to

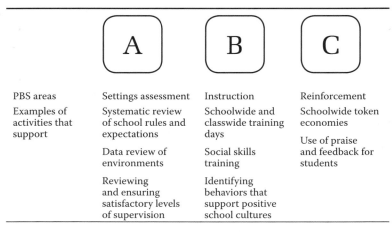

A	B	C
PBS areas	Settings assessment	Instruction	Reinforcement
Examples of activities that support	Systematic review of school rules and expectations	Schoolwide and classwide training days	Schoolwide token economies
	Data review of environments	Social skills training	Use of praise and feedback for students
	Reviewing and ensuring satisfactory levels of supervision	Identifying behaviors that support positive school cultures	

Figure 3.1   Activities that support operant antecedents, behaviors, and consequences.

design and tailor the information provided to their individual school. Most importantly, however, we will stress the importance of finding positive ways to manage and shape student behavior rather than punitive methods. In building all three pillars, teachers and students will create a school setting that is fun and meaningful for all.

4

Preventing Schoolwide Misbehaviors

INTRODUCTION

Hallways, lunchrooms, playgrounds, and other common areas are often difficult to manage due to a reduction in structure, less specific rules, and interaction with an environment that offers more opportunities to engage in problem behaviors. This chapter focuses on schoolwide behavioral safety strategies that address the development of structured environments, teaching of school expectations, and removal of many opportunities to act out. Although these approaches may look different from interventions with individual students, conceptually they are very similar. The two important components of positive behavior support—creation or alteration of environments that limit stimuli that may cause problem behaviors, and building students' skills to demonstrate appropriate behaviors (Carr et al., 2002)—are applied to physical locations with the highest rate of behavior problems.

CONCEPTS TO BE INTRODUCED

- Strategies for schoolwide management of common areas
- Schoolwide procedure training days (aka rotation stations)
- Precorrection or precuing
- Overcorrection or overpracticing
- Active supervision

LINKS TO PREVIOUS DISCUSSIONS

This chapter in conjunction with Chapter 5 describes steps that increase the likelihood of all students succeeding in a safe environment. Adhering to these recommendations helps school problem-solving teams eliminate or reduce many precursors of problem behaviors. This chapter primarily deals with the prevention of schoolwide problems and does not focus on explicit problem-solving or identification procedures for periods of the school where frequent problems may occur. These interventions are described more thoroughly in Chapter 8.

FORM TO BE INTRODUCED

Form 4.1: Schoolwide Integrity Check Form

PEOPLE NEEDED

- Facilitator to guide schoolwide behavioral expectations.
- Team to plan schoolwide training days.
- The entire school faculty is involved in schoolwide training days.

INFORMATION NEEDED

Many authors have documented heightened levels of violence occurring in school common areas. In a review of one elementary school's process to create a positive behavior support (PBS) system, Marchant et al. (2009) demonstrated that more than 55% of office discipline referrals (ODRs) generated by the school occurred in areas outside of the general classroom. Over 60% of the ODRs occurred during or immediately after morning recess or lunch. Observations suggest that bullying rates increase 4.5 times on the playground compared to the classroom (Craig, Pepler, & Atlas, 2000). In an analysis of peer aggression across multiple schools and ages, over 15,000 students were asked to indicate the locations where they were bullied (Bradshaw, Sawyer, & O'Brennan, 2007). Another evaluation of a school's discipline program found that 70% of all aggressive student interactions occurred outside of the classroom setting. The hallway (highlighted by 15.4% of elementary school students and 29.2% of middle school students), the cafeteria (20.3% and 23.4%, respectively), and P.E. (10.2% and 19.5%, respectively) were highlighted by more than 10% of students. In elementary school, 30% of elementary school students indicated that they had been bullied on the playground. Other schools have found hallway behavior to be an area

most violence/ aggression happens outside the classroom

requiring intervention (Clonan, McDougal, Clark, & Davison, 2007). Although prevalence rates of school behavior problems by location will vary among schools, there is little doubt that increased opportunity for social interaction and fewer staff members monitoring common areas increase the probability of behavior problems—many of which can threaten the physical health of students and school staff members.

Ironically, many schools focus disciplinary efforts on remediating individual student behavior while ignoring many behavior problems routinely occurring in common areas (Oswald, Safran, & Johanson, 2005). In essence, they are treating the symptoms while ignoring the source of the problem. Imagine the futility of spending each day attending to visitors who have fallen into a sinkhole in your backyard while failing to address the problem of the actual sinkhole. Such is the case when we spend a disproportionate amount of our mental and physical resources dealing with "problem kids" while minimizing the environmental sinkhole they may be encountering.

Although PBS systems have been shown to dramatically improve students' compliance in nonclassroom settings (Leedy, Bates, & Safran, 2004; Oswald et al., 2005), some may be hesitant to allocate teacher time for improvement of common area discipline. However, Marchant et al. (2009) identified behavior problems initiated during recess, during lunch, or in the hallway that carried over into the classroom and required teacher intervention. Thus, it is little surprise that Luiselli, Putnam, Handler, and Feinberg (2005) were able to increase the amount of time that teachers spent on instruction and that students spent on task and in instruction, by focusing behavior management efforts on nonclassroom settings.

INTERVENTION PRINCIPLES IN MANAGING COMMON AREAS

Earlier, in Chapter 3, we described three critical principles of managing any behavior: prevention, instruction of desirable behavior, and reinforcement of desirable behavior while removing reinforcement for undesirable behavior. However, implementing these principles on a large scale requires the school staff to work together. A facilitator is responsible for ensuring fluid transitions within the problem-solving process rather than belaboring points through less productive staff venting sessions. The primary goal eliciting desirable behaviors from students must remain at the forefront of these discussions. To bring about ideal behaviors, schools should ask and answer four important questions:

- How do we want students to behave?
- What means will we use to teach students expected behaviors?
- What are the behavioral management expectations for faculty or staff?
- How do we create environments that minimize triggers for problem behavior?

Defining Rules and Expectations

Although school rules remain constant, behavioral expectations often vary among the playground, hallways, lunchroom, and school office. It is important to not only know what a student is prohibited from doing but also operationally define the behaviors a student is expected to demonstrate at school. Behavioral expectations of students in common areas may be unclear. Thus, the school staff must determine what behaviors are expected of students in different school locations.

Rules and expectations must be positively stated. Educators have frequently been prone to establish sets of negatively stated rules—what students ought not to do. When focusing on what students are not allowed to do, students do not learn what they are expected to, can, and should do. Telling students they are not allowed to run may be translated into the understanding that they should stand still, jog, walk quickly, walk slowly, or sit down. Any of these options could be interpreted as viable alternatives to "not running." Ambiguity begets rule violations and ODRs, which drain valuable and finite school resources such as teacher and administrator time. When thinking about this, ask how quickly students should move, where they should stand, what they should do while waiting, where they should not go, how loudly they are able to talk, and what they should do with their hands and materials.

Appropriate expectations and procedures should be established for times of transition when students move from one area to another. These times may include the beginning and ending of the school day, changing classes, entering and exiting the cafeteria, visiting restrooms, or moving to and from the auditorium for assemblies. They should also be created for periods when students remain in one area. These include the lunchroom, playground, assembly halls, school bus, or school office.

Procedures

When creating common area procedures, staff members should recall that following desired procedures should make simultaneous engagement in opposing, undesirable behavior almost impossible. In other words, the staff should promote alternative behaviors that are incompatible with many problem behaviors. For example, a student who is walking with her hands folded in front of her will be unable to hit other students. Similarly, if students are staying to the right side of the hallway, they will not run into students passing in the opposite direction.

Procedures should be stated in a simple and straightforward manner. If a procedure is too complicated, students will not remember how to follow it. Procedures should:

- Describe expected behaviors, not prohibited behaviors.
- Help schools run smoother by allowing students to spend less time in transition, and be more fully prepared to engage in activities that promote academic, social, or physical development.
- Be practiced (this is discussed in depth later in the chapter).

Procedure Examples

Although the following list of hallway procedures is not exhaustive, it serves as a starting point for school problem-solving teams as they facilitate a "procedures" discussion.

Hallway Procedures:

- Students walk in the hallway. One foot must be on the ground at all times.
- Students walk down the right side of the hallway.
- When walking down the hallway, students keep their hands together in front of them.
- Groups of three or more students will travel the hall in a single-file line.
- When talking in the hallway, students will use a voice that allows only the people next to them to hear them speak.

Examples of playground procedures are as follows:

- Students will check out and return balls only from the monitor on duty.
- Students waiting to play basketball will stand against the wall.

Examples of lunchroom procedures include the following:

- Students remain seated at their tables until instructed to line up.
- Students sit only with their class during lunch.
- When the lights are turned off, students hold up two fingers to signify silence.
- Students pour leftover liquids down the drain, place leftover food into another container, and throw their paper plates in the trash.

Teaching Appropriate Student Behaviors

In a recent community theater musical, we observed 40 children aged 5–11 walking onto a stage quietly and quickly, singing a piece of a musical chorus, and walking back off stage to the delight of the crowd. This all occurred in 120 seconds. We also happened to know that many of these students had displayed challenging behaviors in classrooms, in church Sunday schools, and even during the play rehearsals. What was the key to this social-engineering marvel? It was practice, practice, and more practice. The children did not walk onto stage without several patient adults lining them up, having them practice walking onto and off the stage. When the children made mistakes, they practiced again. As Shakespeare wrote, "All the world's a stage, and all the men and women merely players: They have their exits and their entrances...." In theater, entrances and exits are practiced—and the same can be true for school.

Schoolwide Training and Overcorrection

Some procedures require students to perform a series of tasks. Just as teachers provide instruction to remediate academic problems and help students meet academic goals, many students need explicit instruction in behaving appropriately. Effective curricula and lesson plans are necessary to help students learn, practice, and master the appropriate behaviors.

Procedures and expectations are taught through direct instruction to move students from "knowing" desired behavior to "doing" desired behavior. First, students must be able to recognize the expectations. For example, students learn how they are expected to walk in the hallway. This acquisition stage is essential, but students who have only acquired knowledge are not yet proficient at converting that knowledge to practice. Many of us have worked with students who, when asked, successfully recite classroom expectations. For example, when asked, "What is the rule about how fast we walk in the hallway?" a student may be able to say, "Students must walk at all times in the hallway." When cued in a calm setting, this student can recite the rules. However, when faced with peer pressure and without adequate practice, the student may, to the exacerbation of her teacher, still run in the hallway. We rely on our habitual behaviors during stressful situations. When teaching procedures and expectations, teachers make the behaviors so fluent that they become habits. Lining up, walking down the hallway, taking napkins off the tray, and throwing out trash should all be practiced so frequently that students perform the actions as second nature.

PBS practitioners encourage schoolwide behavioral training days whereby faculty and staff teach behavioral expectations for various school areas. The premise is that acceptable behaviors should be systematically taught, relying on the same techniques used to teach academic skills. There is no assumption that students "should already know how to behave." Burns, VanDerHeyden, and Boice (2008) outlined practices for providing effective instruction. These include the use of explicit instruction whereby the teacher directly explains, models, and guides students in the development of behavior skills. These lessons should be correctly targeted such that students are able to understand the directions. Once students have learned the skills, they need frequent opportunities to respond to and practice the behavior. In fact, these practice sessions should occur frequently at first such that students eventually perform the tasks automatically. If a student does make a mistake, immediate teacher feedback should direct the student to perform the desired behavior. Finally, if several students have difficulty learning a particular portion of a procedure, an overcorrection technique can be used to help the students acquire the skills more effectively. It is not enough to implement procedures on a single day. Intermittent practice with feedback assures skill generalization to a variety of settings.

Training days involve explicit instructions as described above. In fact, best practices involve using easily followed, scripted lesson plans. These lesson plans should be included in school resources such as faculty and staff handbooks and student handbooks (Sugai et al., 2000). Once appropriate behaviors are taught, students then need effective reminders and sufficient supervision to enhance and reinforce desirable behaviors.

Adult Interaction with Students

If students performed all behaviors fluently and habitually, there would be no need for adult monitoring. Of course, some students will always need adult supervision. As educators, our actions are under constant surveillance by those students with whom we interact. Thus, our interactions with students serve two purposes: to remind students of school expectations (precorrection), and to redirect students wavering from the designated behavioral path (active supervision). Strategic placement of educators throughout a school allows successful implementation of these tasks.

Precorrection

Precorrection has also been an important component for effective interventions on playgrounds (Fraznen & Kamps, 2005; Lewis, Colvin, & Sugai, 2000) and middle school hallways (Oswald et al., 2005). Establishing common area rules and procedures allows effective use of precorrection strategies. These antecedent intervention strategies remind students to demonstrate appropriate behaviors that follow the expectations of the school faculty (Lewis et al., 2000). Colvin, Sugai, Good, and Lee (1997) provided a precorrection strategy for an elementary school that identified problem areas such as entering the building, transitioning to and from lunch, and exiting the building upon dismissal. Through this primary intervention, teachers reminded students of three rules: walking, keeping hands and feet to self, and using quiet voices. This strategy, along with active supervision, resulted in a substantial decrease in problem behaviors (Colvin et al., 1997).

Active Supervision

Researchers have demonstrated that active supervision is effective at reducing minor behavioral difficulties in elementary school (Haydon & Scott, 2008; Lewis et al., 2000), middle school (De Pry & Sugai, 2002), and high school (Johnson-Gros, Lyons, & Griffin, 2008) settings. Active supervision assumes that students are less likely to engage in inappropriate behaviors if they are aware of adult supervision. Simply stated, when adults are visible in an area and actively engage with students, students' behaviors improve.

Many teachers and staff report hall and supervisory duties as stressful at best or boring at worst. Those responsible for common area monitoring may be observed visiting with other staff, grading papers, or choosing not to actively engage students (Lewis et al., 2000). Active supervision is quite different. During active supervision, school faculty and staff move constantly among the students, scan the area to ensure that all students are safe, interact by greeting and praising students, redirect problem behaviors, and provide corrective feedback. Those providing active supervision do not engage in personal or extensive work-related conversations with other adults or with students (Lewis et al.). In many ways, active supervision is enriching for teachers as they find new and creative ways to recognize and interact with students.

ACTIVE

supervision

Johnson-Gros et al. (2008) outlined six important features of active supervision:

- Those who are supervising a common area arrive on time.
- Those who supervise stay on duty the entire period.
- When students come together in groups, the monitor walks to within 2 feet of that group of students. A teacher uses an irregular movement pattern so that students who wish to misbehave cannot predict when a teacher will look in their direction.
- Escorting students through the common area encourages a monitor to help some students move quicker. This is especially appropriate for a crowded hallway or thoroughfare where students move from one area to the next.
- Scanning involves teachers constantly moving their heads and eyes to observe the behaviors that are occurring in the common area. Thus, students have the ability to see where the adult is looking, and they know that the adult's attention will soon focus in their direction.
- Teachers interact with students on a regular basis using smiles, touching shoulders, saying hello, or offering some form of interaction. Monitors may consider praising those students who are following the expectations, and providing reminders to rule violators (Lewis et al., 2000).

Of course, one monitor can realistically monitor only a given perimeter depending on population density. Thus, problem-solving teams may recommend staffing-level adjustments to areas with many students or potential blind spots such as hidden corners or spaces behind cabinets or doors.

Identifying Other Sources of Problem Behavior

Occasionally, structural obstacles or scheduling irregularities increase the difficulty in supervising and managing particular student behaviors. Using data collected within the PBS model should guide decision makers in determining when, where, and what infractions can be most readily improved with the least amount of disruption or change (e.g., the flow of traffic, changes of bell schedules, and the location of teachers during nonstructured time).

Some problems require more than modifications in school policy. Changing when bells ring, moving furniture, and adjusting the directions of traffic flow are effective ways of eliminating problem behaviors. For example, one school (see Figure 4.1) was laid out in a square entirely on one level. Initially, students went both ways in the halls, leading to numerous collisions and physical outbursts. The school administration decided to have all students move in one direction, which subsequently reduced the number of physical altercations in the crowded hallways as well as the number of students late to class. Another school found that one intersection of the school had a bathroom, a water fountain, and lockers in one area. Students retrieving materials from their lockers inadvertently disrupted

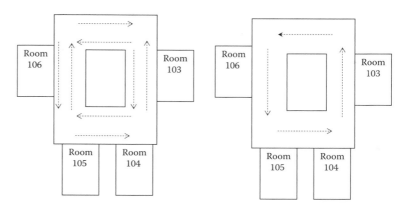

Figure 4.1   Hallway traffic problems.

traffic flow in one direction. Thus, the school administration relocated the lockers, and traffic flowed more freely.

A second challenge may entail the timing of the school bell. For example, one middle school reported congested hallways when students transitioned between classes while others were released for lunch. Resolving the issue meant the creation of two passing periods: The first bell set signified when students were to leave the lunchroom and move to their classroom. The second set of bells marked the period when other students would leave their class and go to lunch.

Another school found that students running in hallways after lunch were disrupting classes and requiring excessive time to calm down before receiving their lessons. The schools had teachers escort students from the playground and walk them in lines from the lunchroom to their classes. In a different instance, a school reported routine playground altercations involving swings. The next year, conflicts were minimized when the school increased the number of swings available. All of these intervention examples describe steps that staff members took to intervene and prevent further problem behavior at a systems level rather than only targeting individual students.

Additional Ideas

These are suggestions that, from our experience, have proven to work well in preventing behavior problems and creating safe common areas. School should be a safe, fun place that students look forward to attending. The following recommendations are not intended to create a boot camp-type system where students must walk lockstep on the second square to the right, with hands firmly clasped together and eyes directly, perfectly forward. Establish as many rules, regulations, and expectations as are necessary, but allow as much freedom as possible. Prevention-oriented systems, like any tool, can be abused or used in ways not intended if school personnel fail to remember that positive behavior supports are meant to improve the school climate rather than provide a method to punish students.

Hallways

- Prior to passing periods, encourage teachers to remind students about the expectations.
- Encourage teachers to dismiss students from class rather than allow students to leave as soon as the bell rings. Frequently, teachers ask students to sit quietly, and then release small groups of students at a time.

- Teach students to walk on the right side of the hall.
- Teach students to walk with their hands folded in front of them.
- If possible, consider slightly altering the bell schedules to prevent large groups of students from being in the hallway at the same time. For example, a middle school may decide to allow only seventh graders to move during some passing periods, and eighth graders to move after the seventh-grade passing period has ended.
- Ensure that all staff members on hall duty follow the steps of active supervision as delineated by Johnson-Gros et al. (2008).

Recess

- Make sure that students have fun things to do to avoid boredom by securing enough playground equipment such as balls, jump ropes, and tether balls (Doll, Zucker, & Brehm, 2004).
- When there is a shortage of playground equipment, create procedures whereby students wait in lines until equipment becomes available or engage in play activities that do not require equipment. These are also situations where students can be encouraged to create their own system for preventing disagreements.
- Observe the layout of the playground and find areas that are frequently hidden from adult sight. Either restrict students from entering those areas, or ensure that adults can see those areas.
- During recess, active supervision by a highly visible and evenly distributed adult presence provides a safe place for all students.
- Consider adjusting where adults stand for hall duty so they do not stand in the same place. Students who misbehave may be foiled if teachers are standing in unexpected places!

Cafeteria

- The expectations of active supervision for teachers on duty continue to be in place.
- Create a signal whereby a teacher can get students' attention quickly. This signal should include verbal and visual components so students can both see and hear that an adult needs attention (Sprick, Knight, Reinke, &

McKale, 2006). Both teachers and students will need to practice this signal in the cafeteria setting.

- Once a student finishes eating, ensure that procedures are set up for throwing away trash, leftover food and liquids, and dishes. Train students on places or stations where they should move. Ensure that activities are available for students when they have finished eating.
- Frequently, the noise level of cafeterias is a major concern for school teachers and administration. Consider teaching students how to talk quietly, and allow them to practice the appropriate noise level.

Lesson Plan for Schoolwide Training Day

- Washington Elementary School held a schoolwide training day on the second day of school. Faculty set up individual stations to teach students the procedures of different areas. Mr. Red, Ms. White, Ms. Yellow, and Ms. Black ran four stations within the cafeteria.
- Mr. Red led teaching stations instructing students about the procedures for lining up and getting food.
  - He instructed each group of students to practice lining up against the wall.
  - He then called the students and taught them to walk to the lunch-serving counter.
  - Each student took one tray, one napkin, and one piece of silverware.
  - The students then got their food, said please and thank you, paid for their lunch, and walked to the tables.
- Ms. White led a teaching station about students walking from the cafeteria to the tables.
  - Students practiced walking along the yellow tape to their assigned lunch table.
  - Students practiced holding their trays with two hands.
  - Students practiced sitting at their tables, putting down their trays, and remaining seated.
- Ms. Black led a teaching station about student behavior at the lunch table.
  - Students practiced talking in a quiet voice.
  - Students learned that when a teacher turned off the lights, they needed to be silent and listen to directions.

- Ms. Black taught the students to raise their hands prior to getting up to throw away their trash.
- Ms. Yellow led a teaching station instructing students on appropriate procedures for disposing of their trays.
  - Students learned to throw their leftover food in one receptacle, their liquids in another barrel, and their garbage in the trash container.
  - The teachers showed the students where to put their silverware, plates, and trays, and how to set down the materials slowly and carefully.
- Students then practiced walking through the exit door on the way to recess.

After Mr. White demonstrated the appropriate behavior, each student walked through the procedure, receiving frequent praise from Mr. White. When a student performed one of the procedures incorrectly, that student received a polite reminder of the appropriate way to do it, and was allowed to practice again. When a student performed a task correctly, he or she received a positive behavior token. Once each student had performed the tasks, the entire class walked through the procedures. When the entire class successfully followed each procedure, they all received an additional positive behavior token.

Schoolwide Training Day Example
Playground (Mr. White and Ms. Black)

Kindergarten	8:00–8:30 a.m.
First grade	8:30–9:00
Second grade	9:00–9:30
Third grade	9:30–10:00
Fourth grade	10:00–10:30
Fifth grade	10:30–11:00

Cafeteria (Mr. Red and Ms. Orange)

First grade	8:00–8:30 a.m.
Second grade	8:30–9:00
Third grade	9:00–9:30
Fourth grade	9:30–10:00
Fifth grade	10:00–10:30
Kindergarten	10:30–11:00

Hallway (Ms. Green and Ms. Yellow)

Second grade	8:00–8:30 a.m.
Third grade	8:30–9:00
Fourth grade	9:00–9:30
Fifth grade	9:30–10:00
Kindergarten	10:00–10:30
First grade	10:30–11:00

Bathrooms Next to Gymnasium (Custodians and One Male and Female Teacher)

Third grade	8:00–8:30 a.m.
Fourth grade	8:30–9:00
Fifth grade	9:00–9:30
Kindergarten	9:30–10:00
First grade	10:00–10:30
Second grade	10:30–11:00

School Bus, Front of School (School Bus Driver and Principal)

Fourth grade	8:00–8:30 a.m.
Fifth grade	8:30–9:00
Kindergarten	9:00–9:30
First grade	9:30–10:00
Second grade	10:00–10:30
Third grade	10:30–11:00

Procedures for Start of the School Day, Main Office (Assistant Principal and Head Secretary)

First grade	8:00–8:30 a.m.
Second grade	8:30–9:00
Third grade	9:00–9:30
Fourth grade	9:30–10:00
Fifth grade	10:00–10:30
Kindergarten	10:30–11:00

CONCLUSION

When we release large groups of students into one area, behavior problems may increase. In these types of settings, it is difficult to exert adult control. In schoolwide settings, it is crucial that teams think proactively and ask themselves, "How can behavior problems be avoided?" When we ask this question, we recognize that we have control over much more than we previously thought. We control the schedule, where we as adults station ourselves, what we as adults do, and how many kids are allowed in one area at one time. We are also able to instruct and are experts in providing good instruction.

By following the outline provided and implementing the recommended interventions, problem-solving teams can maintain safe and effective schools by providing positive but clear directives. Of course, school problem-solving teams may need to teach procedures throughout the year due to changes in student and staff population. In the next chapter we outline means for establishing orderly classrooms, and later in Chapter 8 the problem-solving team learns to identify and intervene in schoolwide problems.

CHAPTER 4 TASKS

- Members of the problem-solving team guide the school staff through a discussion of schoolwide procedures that include the creation of rules and expectations for hallways, common areas, recess, the gym, the cafeteria, and bathrooms. Expectations should allow for smooth movements through areas and should be designed to be incompatible with problem behaviors. (See examples of expectations and procedures in this chapter.)
- All school staff members learn the expectations for observation duties, including the principles of precorrection and active supervision. (See the "Coach Card for Active Supervision of Common Areas" in Appendix B.)
- The problem-solving team develops lesson plans for teaching students how to follow the expectations in different areas of the school. These lesson plans include the principles of explicit instruction that is correctly targeted to student abilities, frequent opportunities for students to practice, regular feedback from the instructor, and overcorrection procedures for areas in which students are not demonstrating the desired behaviors (Burns et al., 2008). (See the "Lesson Plan for Schoolwide Training Day.")
- The school staff will conduct a schoolwide procedure teaching day to give students hands-on opportunities

to learn and practice effective behaviors. Students or classes who continue to experience difficulty after the training day may benefit from additional practice (see the "Schoolwide Training Day Example").

- Members of the problem-solving team complete the "Schoolwide Integrity Checklist Form" (Form 4.1, Appendix A) and determine whether procedures are being taught effectively. The integrity checks occur once per 9-week period (e.g., after the first month and in early November, late January, and early April).

- Schedule schoolwide procedure training sessions as needed throughout the school year. Factors to consider include team-recommended expectation changes, the number of new students entering school, or the problem behaviors that students are demonstrating.

- Continue to observe common areas to identify frequent problems that may be fixed through rearranging furniture, changing traffic patterns, moving supervisors, or changing schedules.

- Experiment wisely, but be willing to make mistakes! Working with large groups of people is difficult, and no implementation is done perfectly.

5

Preventing Classroom Misbehaviors

INTRODUCTION

Classroom management is the hallmark of all good teaching. More instructional time and fewer discipline problems are products of effective management strategies (Dwyer, Osher, & Hoffman, 2000; Safran & Oswald, 2003; Scott & Barrett, 2004; Walker, Ramsey, & Gresham, 2005). As described earlier, schoolwide behavior management involves the application of antecedent, behavior, and consequence models to large groups of students (Carr et al., 2002). Certainly each child has a unique set of triggers and consequences for the array of different behaviors he or she may display. However, many of the triggers for misbehavior can be eliminated through classroom management practices. Teachers can take steps to remove the opportunity for problem behaviors to occur. Similarly, a teacher can build triggers whereby ideal behaviors may be elicited. Thus, the focus of this chapter is on describing methods that teachers may implement to reduce the need and frequency of problem behaviors.

CONCEPTS TO BE INTRODUCED

- Time in
- Developing and teaching rules
- Teaching procedures and routines
- Consistent and regular praise

LINKS TO OTHER CHAPTERS

Previous chapters addressed the concept of PBS and strategies for incorporating PBS into the school environment. This chapter builds upon previous concepts and practices by incorporating the principles of ABA and good instruction into the classroom environment. Later chapters will engage in discussion regarding the development of (a) the token economy system and (b) keys to preventing and identifying potential problems in the classroom.

FORM TO BE INTRODUCED

Form 5.1: Classroom Self-Monitoring Form

PRINCIPLES OF EFFECTIVE CLASSROOM MANAGEMENT

Every teacher plans to teach something when he or she comes to school. Whether the explicit curriculum involves teaching first graders how to read, students with special needs how to perform well in a job interview, or twelfth-grade honor students how to integrate differential equations, teachers expect students to learn new facts or skills, or develop new attitudes toward different subjects. Classroom management comes almost naturally for some educators, but most of the rest of us need additional time, support, and training to hone these skills. Some teachers have the opportunity to work with populations of students who demonstrate almost no behavioral disruptions. The students believe that learning the school's curriculum will help them in the future. The parents support the work of the teacher and the school, and the students value the teacher's expertise. Many of those reading this text may have displayed those characteristics when they were in school. Unfortunately, these desirable characteristics are not embedded within every child who comes to school. Many children lack an appreciation for learning and teacher expertise. These children need to learn how to behave in the classroom as well as how to read, write, and understand mathematics in the world. Our responsibilities as educators are vast: We must educate all children, regardless of their backgrounds or their desire to learn.

Fortunately, as educators, we are the most powerful force in the environments in which students learn. Some environments elicit learning behaviors better than others. Think of settings where we may occasionally demonstrate ineffective learning behaviors. Imagine yourself at a conference presentation where an "expert" standing before 500 teachers begins and continues speaking in a monotone voice. The sound system works sporadically, and the presentation addresses only abstract and theoretical concepts. We are trapped in a setting absent of clearly defined expectations while forced to engage in an undesirable task led by an individual seemingly uninterested in arousing our attention. Many may be thinking, "I bet this person never works with children!" Looking around the room, we notice one teacher checking her e-mail on her cell phone while another has pulled out his Blackberry and is looking at basketball scores from the previous night. Some are conversing amongst themselves, and others have simply left the room for an early lunch. How do the behaviors change when a dynamic presenter uses creative ways to share information, addresses a topic that we find relevant, and involves participants in choral responding? Suddenly, the number of people checking their e-mails decreases, and the number of side conversations diminishes. People are probably laughing or thinking to themselves, "I can't wait to get back to my classroom so I can try this!" What has changed? The participants are the same, but the environment is different. Our behaviors change. Fortunately, we can establish educational settings more conducive to eliciting desired social behaviors.

Research on classroom management teaches that manipulating the environment significantly impacts behavior. Although many note that internal factors influence learning potential, educational researchers from 40 years ago began to find that teacher variables related highly to student behaviors (e.g., Kounin, 1970). A body of recent literature reveals that expert teachers rely more on preventative classroom management strategies and less on appealing to student efforts to control their own behaviors when creating effective learning environments (Bondy, Ross, Gallingane, & Hambacher, 2007; Little & Akins-Little, 2008; Şetürk, 2006). Teachers with classes demonstrating higher levels of on-task behaviors, more instructional time, and the greatest degree of academic student gains spent more time on organization, had clearer rules, and set higher expectations than did teachers with more disruptive behaviors (Stronge, Ward, Tucker, & Hindman, 2007). In other words, students demonstrated different behaviors for different teachers, making it clear that educators had more influence or power than was previously believed in managing student behaviors.

But what are some of the things that teachers do to improve student classroom behavior? The following section outlines many of the basic classwide interventions that teachers can implement to improve the behaviors of all students. Many of these interventions that are recommended for the classrooms were originally designed to elicit appropriate behaviors from those individuals demonstrating the most serious behavior problems. When applied to a large group, they may actually improve the behaviors of those one or two students in the class who are most frequently disruptive. After all, students with behavior problems are most disruptive in classrooms that do not have clear classroom management plans. Although the interventions are not proverbial silver bullets in that they eliminate all misbehavior, they can reduce behavior problems for all students.

CRITICAL INFORMATION

Think about what you find effective when *you* are being instructed:

- First, you need to know the expectations and how to get answers to your questions.
- Second, the task expectation should be attainable. Challenging goals are desirable, whereas unrealistic expectations invoke resentment. In addition, you would likely appreciate acknowledgment of your achievements.
- Third, highly engaging activities are optimal. Quietly sitting atop a hard wooden or plastic chair or desk seat while passively taking notes that could have been conveyed on a handout brings out little joy, even in the most dedicated. Yet, actively learning and applying new information and skills create a positive and enjoyable experience.

Rule Development and Expectations

Madsen, Becker, and Thomas (1968), in a seminal study, investigated the effect of rules on children's behavior. They found that clearly explaining classroom expectations resulted in a 50% reduction in problem behaviors. This suggested that teachers can prevent a number of problematic behaviors by explicitly and clearly explaining and having students recite school and class rules. Numerous studies have examined the impact that posting rules has made on student behaviors. A comprehensive literature review by Simonsen, Fairbanks, Briesch, Myers, and Sugai (2008) found that those teachers who posted rules increased student engagement in academic work, and decreased disruptive behaviors.

What Are Good Rules?

A teacher must carefully devise the rules and expectations for students. In general, *expectations* refer to ways that students should behave in class, and *rules* tell the students how to do so. The best rules meet several important criteria:

- They promote safety in the classroom.
- They allow each student the opportunities to receive the maximum benefit from instruction.
- They minimize disruption.
- They create and protect instructional time.

Rules define general expectations for student behavior. Clear rules should be

- Positively phrased
- Simple and clear
- Descriptive of observable behaviors
- Enforceable (Miltenberger, 2001)

The following are examples of ineffective rules:

- Don't talk over one another (negatively stated).
- Be respectful (too ambiguous).
- Spend 2 hours every night on homework (not enforceable).

Once rules and expectations are created, a teacher must effectively convey the rules to students. As described earlier, one method for increasing rule visibility and compliance is by printing the rules in a large, clear font and posting them in the classroom. Similarly, having the students rehearse and regularly recite the rules helps to ensure recollection and overlearning of the rules. A teacher should also consider using examples for class expectations. While addressing the rules, a teacher should give examples of appropriate conduct as well as behaviors that violate the rule or the expectation.

Example of Rule Instruction

Ms. White had five rules for her class:

1. All students will quietly direct their eyes toward the teacher when she addresses the class.
2. Students will comply with teacher directives.
3. A quiet voice will be used when talking to another student in the classroom.
4. All students will keep their hands by their sides or on their desks and will not place them on others.
5. Only the materials necessary for the completion of classwork are to be on a student's desk.

At the beginning of the school year, Ms. White reviewed these rules and had each student recite them. Her next step was providing examples of each rule. For rule number 1, when she began speaking to the whole class, she instructed her students to direct their attention to her and to stop their individual discussions. The class practiced the rule 1 activity until a pattern of successes was established. For rule number 3, she demonstrated speaking in both a quiet and loud voice. Her students then practiced and received feedback on speaking at the designated volume. Early in the semester, she recognized students using a quiet voice and redirected students using louder voices.

Developing Classroom Procedures and Routines

Think about the number of steps that teachers use to prepare students for academic lessons at the start of each day. The teacher retrieves students from the playground and transports them to the classroom. She instructs them to hang up their jackets and backpacks, remove their boots, and locate and sit at their desks. Then, she takes attendance, collects homework, determines which students are having a hot lunch, relays daily announcements, passes out reading materials, instructs students to get out necessary materials, and prepares any audio and visual equipment. These steps often take less than 10 minutes to complete. The expectations are extensive. Each step provides opportunities for students to misbehave, refuse to follow a directive, or disrupt the classroom flow. It is the organized teacher who has clear expectations and procedures for what students must do.

Procedures are methods for accomplishing daily routines. They refer to a variety of steps students follow to participate in instruction, to transition from or into instruction, or to transition from the classroom to other parts of the building.

For example, procedures may include the following:

- Students line up outside of Ms. Green's door and wait quietly outside of the classroom prior to the start of the day.
- When entering the classroom, students walk to their desks.
- When at their desks, students remove their homework folders from their backpacks and place the folders on their desks.
- At the end of the social studies lesson, a designated student collects and places all books on the shelf.
- When the bell rings, students stay in their seats until dismissed by the teacher.

By creating routines for specific, frequently occurring activities, students have clear expectations and are better able to engage in learning. By establishing and rehearsing classroom procedures, teachers maximize students' comfort level by providing a consistent and structured routine. This benefits students by allowing them to meet clearly defined expectations (Metzler, Biglan, Rusby, & Sprague, 2001; Sugai et al., 2000). Some examples of classroom activities improved by establishing procedures include the following:

- Student transitional periods
- Entering the classroom
- Gathering materials
- Preparing for the end of an instructional period
- Preparing for a laboratory activity
- Individual and group work
- Instructional periods
- Teacher-led small groups
- Room and equipment use
- Class presentations and discussions
- Student feedback

As described in the previous chapter, for procedures to work most effectively, teachers must guide each student through the process of learning how to perform a procedure; teaching each procedure by modeling, allowing opportunities for practice, and providing feedback. If students receive good, intense instruction on classroom procedures at the start of the year, they are more likely to spend more time on instructional activities and less time on transitional activities during the rest of the year (Cameron, Connor, & Morrison, 2005). In fact, Cameron et al. (2005) found that teachers spending the most time on procedures during the start of the year were able to spend the most time delivering instruction the remainder of the year.

Of course, it is important to reteach procedures when new students enter the class or when the students begin deviating from a procedure. When teaching expectations, teachers should overcorrect or overteach their procedures to ensure that students perform them with minimal cognitive resources. This allows teacher expectations to become student habits.

When devising procedures, it is important to break down the task into small steps. For example, when Amy, a fifth-grade student, lines up to go to lunch, there are several intermediary steps she must follow:

- She puts away all materials from the previous project.
- She quietly backs out her chair and stands up.
- She pushes back her chair underneath the table.
- She walks (walks, doesn't run!) and stands by the door immediately behind the person who is in front of her.
- She waits until all students are lined up.
- She folds her hands in front of her.
- When the teacher gives the instruction for the line to begin moving, she walks with the rest of her class.

Most of us who are educators were probably able to line up without following a detailed list. Students today are no different. If your current practices are effective in eliciting the behaviors you expect, then trying to "fix something not broken" doesn't make much sense. However, many classes will have one or more students not responding well to the current classroom structure or procedures. To those teachers and classes, the recommended offerings within this book are likely to further enhance the learning environment. Let's return to Susan and the steps she takes in getting into line without instruction:

- She leaves her materials from her reading class on her desk. When it is time to begin social studies after lunch, her reading material is still on her desk.

- When she backs out her chair, she waits until a student is right behind her, and backs it into his leg, causing a bruise.
- Her chair remains in the middle of the aisle, causing her teacher to replace it.
- She runs to the door, and in doing so inadvertently bumps into the same boy whose leg was bruised when she backed her chair into him.
- While waiting in line, she attempts to cut in front of other students. She subsequently gets into an argument and calls each of them "teacher's pets" (only she also inserts certain unpublishable adjectives).
- When she finally gets into line, she pulls the hair of the student in front of her.
- She walks before the teacher gives her permission and runs into other students walking down the hallway.

All of us know students like Susan who find ways to act out. All of the steps that Amy performed naturally were merely seven opportunities for Susan to get into trouble. Ms. Green, who teaches Susan and Amy, managed to break the task of lining up for lunch into these seven discrete steps. Ms. Green had effective and clear instructions for each of these steps with good examples of appropriate and inappropriate behavior. She then had the students practice lining up. Because she wanted to minimize the amount of time that students were in transition, she encouraged her students to perform each of these tasks fluently. After several practice sessions, she was able to get the students in her class to line up quietly for lunch in 45 seconds—with chairs pushed in.

Note on Planning

Our experience suggests that unengaged students are more likely to talk and demonstrate behaviors that may distract other students. Adequate planning should minimize idle time or "downtime" in the class. *Downtime* includes free time, students finishing their assignments early, or other periods of time when the expectations for students are not explicit. Note that students are more likely to finish early if the work is too easy or too difficult for them. Student on-task behavior, which is incompatible with problem behaviors, increases when students have many problems that are within their instructional range (Gilbertson, Witt, Duhon, & Dufrene, 2008). Thus, material that is delivered at the students' instructional levels will be more likely to lead to on-task behaviors (Gickling & Armstrong, 1978). However, students may have no academic expectations for the start of class. Starter assignments, sometimes known as *bell ringers*, consist of some review tasks that students complete quickly. Teachers may also use wrap-up assignments for the end of a session—those review assignments that students can do prior to a transition period.

Arranging Student Seating

A literature review by Wannarka and Ruhl (2008) examined research on the relationship between classroom seating arrangement and student behavior. Their review shared several crucial findings: The first is that a teacher needs to consider the types of behavior that he or she expects from students during class. If students are expected to brainstorm and interact with one another, certain seating arrangements involving clusters of chairs foster interactive communication (see Figure 5.3). However, classrooms requiring high degrees of independent work with minimal interaction benefit from rows of seats that minimize disruptions (see Figure 5.1). Sprick (2006) also indicated the importance of allowing students to be spread apart from one another—especially if a propensity toward disruptive behavior exists (see Figure 5.1). Thus, a classroom layout that promotes individual work and discourages students from talking and interacting will include clear rows and columns with spaces between the desks. Of course, that does not mean that students should be forbidden from moving if they are assigned group work. Keep in mind that moving from rows to groups may require a highly structured transition that students will need to practice to perform quickly, efficiently, and without accompanying behavior problems.

Proximity

Proximity is a behavior management strategy whereby a teacher moves close to a student. Students are less likely to act out if there is an adult within the immediate vicinity, and are more likely to stay on task and move smoothly from one activity to the next (Lampi, Fenty, & Beaunae, 2005). In a large class, a teacher needs to have the opportunity to move about the classroom easily. Typically, it is best if the teacher delivers instruction while moving throughout the classroom. A teacher moving in a random fashion may prevent those students who are prone to disrupt the classroom from being able to plan their disruptions.

Figure 5.1   A seating arrangement that promotes independent work. This arrangement has several advantages for encouraging independent work while preventing student interactions because all students face the same direction and are unable to reach each other without making movements that will be apparent to the teacher. This arrangement also allows a teacher to move freely and quickly among students and provides some privacy that will enable the teacher to deliver quiet redirection, reprimands, and praise without other students becoming involved. This arrangement is not conducive to group work or other situations where student interaction is encouraged.

Time In

Time in (TI) is the deliberate creation of an environment rich with activities that students find rewarding. Instead of simply catching students being good, a teacher using the TI technique will make frequent use of positive reinforcement for not only students who are exceptionally good but also those students who are simply complying with expectations. Even those students who have previous histories of behavior problems have opportunities to receive frequent and consistent reinforcement for following classroom expectations and rules. Research has also shown that using a TI procedure in the classroom can be effective in increasing compliance by recognizing and praising

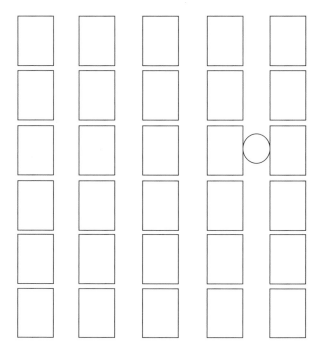

Figure 5.2   Problematic seating arrangement. Some classroom arrangements may actually make misbehavior easier and hinder a teacher's ability to interact with other students. This arrangement allows students to hide behind other students and also prevents a teacher, who is working with a student on the right side of the classroom, from easily moving to the left side of the room.

a student for engaging in appropriate behaviors (Marlow, Tingstrom, & Olmi, 1997; Oswald, Safran, & Johanson, 2005). By providing this kind of reinforcement, the student learns which behaviors result in teacher attention and other positive consequences. TI reinforcement can be in the form of praise, rewards, access to preferred activities, tokens, or other reinforcers. A positive classroom is an environment rich in positive reinforcement (e.g., verbal praise or time in).

Some ways to reward positive behaviors include using frequent praise, learning activities that students enjoy, and giving students opportunities to earn access to privileges or other rewards that frequently have educational value.

Characteristics of Effective Praise

One of the simplest and least expensive interventions involves praise, an intervention that most teachers understand as being

Figure 5.3   Group work seating arrangement. Other class arrangements either position students too close to one another, allow students to hide their actions from the teacher's line of sight, or prevent the teacher from moving easily about the classroom. This arrangement does support students working together in groups and providing answers to one another.

vitally important. After all, students who try hard on their assignments should get some form of recognition for what they are doing.

Researchers have long studied the impacts of teacher praise on student behavior (e.g., Madsen et al., 1968). This intervention has been recommended for use in managing both students with behavior difficulties and whole-class situations. The relationship between teacher praise and improved student behavior has been observed in multiple studies as teachers who increase the amount of contingent praise in the classroom reduce student disruption and increase on-task behavior (Matheson & Shriver, 2005; Reinke, Lewis-Palmer, & Merrill, 2008). Thus, researchers have indicated that teachers have increased the use of praise and are, in many instances, more likely to praise students than to issue disapproving comments (Beaman & Wheldall, 2000). However, this contingent praise occurs more frequently for instructional or academic behaviors (for example, "You did a great job on your reading"). Regarding behaviors for social interactions, responding to teacher requests, or procedural matters, teachers have continued to issue significantly more disapproval than approval (Beaman & Wheldall).

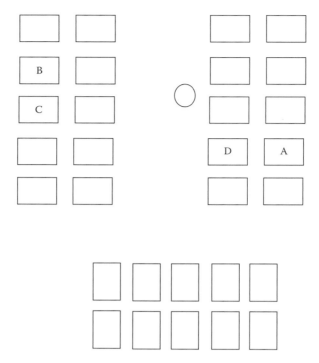

Figure 5.4   Horseshoe-shaped seating arrangement. While this format allows the teacher to move in the middle of the classroom, it still allows Student A to hide behind Student D. If the teacher wants to talk with Student A, he or she will have difficulty moving back to him. Also, Students B and C are able to talk easily and put their hands on each other which may create an unsafe opportunity for physical contact to occur. They are hidden by virtue of being in the second row.

Students need feedback and instruction on both academic and social behaviors. Students following the behavioral rules and expectations of classes should receive positive feedback. However, a common error is that some educators praise only students more likely to demonstrate effective behaviors. Students demonstrating higher levels of misbehavior often receive negative feedback for a higher percentage of misbehaviors compared to other students (Maag, 2001; Sprick, Knight, Reinke, & McKale, 2006). To improve student behavior, the opposite approach must be used: **Students prone to behavioral problems need praise *more often* than other students.**

How to Praise

Although praise is important, there are a few issues to keep in mind. The first is that some students, even though they may appreciate the recognition, find the praise to be uncomfortable. These students may be embarrassed, or they may be targeted by other students as being a "teacher's pet." Second, praise may appear to be insincere, and should be descriptive in nature. Finally, praise has a teaching component. A student may receive praise, but not know exactly why he or she is receiving it.

Praise should:

- Be descriptive in nature
- Be delivered in close proximity
- Include the student's name
- Be genuine and sincere
- Be specific—tell the student what he or she has done well

The following are examples of effective praise:

- Chris, I appreciated how you raised your hand.
- Kiara, I can tell that you have put a lot of thought into this assignment.
- Maria, I liked how you asked for help politely.
- Jerome, I liked how you remembered to put your backpack away when you entered the classroom.

Opportunities to Respond

Just as opportunities to respond (OTR) are an effective strategy in helping students acquire new skills, their use in behavior management is similarly effective. An OTR refers to any chance that a student has to correctly answer a question or to provide academic feedback. There are different ways that students respond to a teacher's prompt. In lecture formats, a student can give an oral answer individually, as part of a small group, or as part of the whole class. A student may also write an answer on a whiteboard or a piece of paper, or may tell his or her partner an answer. Sometimes, students are asked to provide a nonverbal response.

For a teacher to receive maximal benefit from the use of OTR, at least half of the prompts will need to be answers that students have already learned. If students give too many incorrect answers, they may feel reticent to give answers, and will be less likely to be maximally engaged with the process.

Typically, lessons should occur in short bursts as minilessons, whereby students receive portions of the necessary information they need (Trussell, 2008). These instructional periods should be short as students are more likely to display disruptive behaviors during extended lessons. Also, only one or two essential new components need be included in these lessons. This should be followed by a mini-review of the lesson whereby the students are asked to give relevant responses related to the lesson.

Example of Opportunities to Respond

Mr. Blue was teaching a science lesson focusing on photosynthesis. He began by asking multiple questions. First, he asked the whole class to pronounce *photosynthesis* in a choral response. He then asked Jarvis what types of living things used photosynthesis. Each student in the class was then asked to write down which gases were used in human respiration. All students held up their answers, and Mr. Blue reminded everyone that humans inhale oxygen and exhale carbon dioxide. Mr. Blue then began his mini-lesson. In his mini-lesson, he introduced the equation for photosynthesis showing that plants take carbon dioxide and the sun's energy and convert these things into oxygen molecules and sugars. He then asked the students several questions. Which gases does a plant take in as part of photosynthesis? After a choral response, he asked the students to write down the equation that he placed on the board. He then asked a more difficult question—what are the ways that photosynthesis helps humans? Students mentioned that it creates sugar that humans need to burn, takes carbon dioxide out of the air, and provides people with oxygen. The instruction continued with brief lessons followed by students having frequent opportunities to provide answers.

Pace of Instruction

Just as student behavior improves when students are verbalizing correct answers, student behavior also improves when the rate of instruction increases (Munk & Repp, 1994). Certainly, the pace of instruction does not mean that a teacher talks quickly, nor does it mean that a teacher covers more material at an inappropriate rate. However, it does mean that students need to have many opportunities to provide academically relevant information quickly. Pace of instruction overlaps with many of the concepts described earlier. Rapid, well-rehearsed transitions certainly aid in the reduction of opportunities for students to act out. Most typically, when students have multiple, shorter tasks to complete, overall behavior problems will decrease. For these purposes, we recommend that behaviorally challenging

students have two to three opportunities to respond (or opportunities to practice) per minute. Keep in mind, of course, that
these opportunities to respond do not have to be individual,
but may involve the entire gambit of responses.

Effective Reprimands

Reprimands are not a preferred means of preventing problem behaviors. Reprimands are an indicator of high levels of
acting-out behaviors in many classrooms (Reinke et al., 2008).
However, there may be occasions when a teacher needs to
give feedback to a student regarding the student's behavior.
The goals of a reprimand are simple: encouraging a student to
stop performing a disruptive behavior and to begin performing an on-task behavior. Unfortunately, teachers who issue
reprimands ineffectively run several risks. The first is that all
time spent on reprimands is time spent away from delivering
instruction. If a teacher spends too much time with one child,
the other students lose the opportunity to receive praise, feedback on their work, and the behavioral benefits of proximity. A
reprimand may also serve as a catalyst or trigger for acting-out
behaviors. Whether a student is embarrassed by the attention
or enjoys verbal combat with teachers, a poorly delivered reprimand may actually cause more classroom disruption.

How should a reprimand be delivered? Ironically, many
principles of praise are also principles of reprimands. To avoid
embarrassing a child, a reprimand should be delivered quietly
and individually. The first author must take this time to admit
that when he was first learning to deliver reprimands, he left his
desk, walked up to a student, and reminded the student of his
responsibilities. Unfortunately, he was usually a "sit at the front
of the room" teacher. So, the movement toward the student was
sufficiently embarrassing, and the student reacted loudly. Thus,
remember that if you are consistently working with students and
delivering quiet praise, quiet reprimands are a means of limiting
student embarrassment. In fact, students perceive quiet reprimand and praise as effective discipline techniques (Infantino &
Little, 2005). O'Leary, Kaufman, Kass, and Drabman (1970) found
that teachers issuing loud reprimands during two phases of a
study had higher levels of disruptive behavior. When they began
issuing quiet reprimands in the other two phases, classroom
behaviors improved. A reprimand must also be behavioral in
that it describes the infraction rather than describing the student's character (Gable, Hester, Rock, & Hughes, 2009). The best
reprimands, however, include a phrase that cues the student

Table 5.1 Examples of Ineffective Reprimands

Statement	Reason for the Problem
Ms. Yellow approaches Juan and loudly tells him to put his comic books away. Juan tells the teacher, "You can't talk to me like that!"	The reprimand is delivered loudly, and Juan's response is loud and disruptive.
Mr. Red whispers to Michelle, "I really wish that you would stop playing that game because it disrupts the whole class, and I don't have an opportunity to teach. If I can't teach, other students can't learn, and it's not fair to them."	Although delivered quietly, the reprimand is too long and runs the risk of slowing down the pace of the teacher's instruction.
Ms. Green whispers to a kid, "Why don't you ever work?"	The statement is too sweeping, and criticizes the child's character.

about the appropriate behavior and are delivered quickly to prevent other disruptions (Gable et al., 2009). (See Table 5.1.)

CONCLUSION

Managing a classroom of students who are prone to demonstrating disruptive behaviors is exceedingly challenging. A teacher needs to demonstrate two almost contradictory mind-sets—being exceedingly active and finding ways to ensure every student has an opportunity to feel success while, at the same time, maintaining composure. Most importantly, in the most stressful situations and with the most challenging students, a teacher's calm is all the more critical. Positive classrooms require teachers to be highly prepared, focused, and effective. Teachers must be able to quickly react to changing classroom environments while maintaining their composure. These behavior management techniques will diminish problem behaviors, and provide more opportunities for effective instruction. Ultimately, our goal is to create a relaxed, enriching environment whereby the teacher is able to move freely about the room, and engage students through a series of lessons. The teacher should also be able to ask questions that permit students to respond actively, praise students often, and deliver the occasional reprimand as needed. In this way, a teacher can create a relationship with each individual student in his or her classroom. This relationship provides the core of both active learning and positive behavior management.

CHAPTER 5 TASKS

Classroom management is a process that teachers may never fully perfect. We recommend following these procedures as a means of helping all teachers improve their classroom management practices.

- Conduct an in-service that gives an overview of teacher praise, rules and expectations, opportunities to respond, and seating arrangements.
- Provide teachers with the coach cards on basic classroom management, opportunities to respond, and procedure instruction.
- Introduce teachers to the Classroom Self-Monitoring Form. Indicate that this is only for teachers' purposes, and will not be used to evaluate the teacher's performance.
- After one week of implementation, the Classroom Self-Monitoring Form (located in Appendix A) should be completed by each teacher to self-evaluate the effectiveness of his or her individualized classroom procedures.
- The teachers should again complete the classroom self-monitoring form in October, January, and March to determine areas where their management is strong, and areas that can be improved.
- If desired, a teacher can ask another school staff person to observe his or her class and complete the self-monitoring form. This will allow an observer to provide more potentially objective feedback.

6

Implementing a Schoolwide Token Economy

INTRODUCTION

Previous chapters addressed the inherent value of creating a structured academic environment and use of systematic procedures for teaching appropriate social behavior. In particular, Chapter 2 described the theories underlying the successful use of tangible items and activities to reinforce positive behavior. This chapter details how to successfully develop and implement a schoolwide token economy, an integral component of a PBS system. A token economy system (TES) is a cornerstone of a positive behavior support (PBS) system. A TES offers direct means for school staff to reward and provide positive incentives for students engaged in approved and desirable behaviors.

The conceptual basis for a TES was described briefly in Chapter 3 and will be further developed later in this chapter. A fundamental understanding of the rationale for selection of a PBS strategy is that PBS systems help children to understand what behavior is expected and then reinforce those desired behaviors as well as aid school staff in maintaining a data-based understanding of why techniques and operations are or are not effective.

A token economy system is a set of tangible reinforcements for increasing the frequency of select behaviors while reducing the frequency of others. Tokens, which can come in various forms such as paper tickets, are earned by students for complying with previously taught school and classroom rules. The value of the tokens comes from the ability to exchange them for rewards (e.g., candy, toys, free time, and homework passes) or submit them for a daily, weekly, monthly, or annual drawing for a large prize. Students are rewarded for "being good" (matching their behavior to established, explicitly clear expectations), which, in turn, increases teacher-approved behaviors and reduces behaviors leading to discipline referrals.

The central intent of a TES is to strengthen the relationship between engaging in appropriate behavior and reinforcement. Research and practice show that reinforcement:

- Increases student engagement in the curriculum.
- Enhances school as a pleasant location.
- Increases the probability of students exhibiting appropriate behavior.
- Reduces resources allocated to disciplinary procedures.
- Increases successful academic outcomes for both students and schools (Lassen, Steele, & Sailor, 2006).

Another concern voiced by teachers resistant to participating in a PBS TES pertains to the reasonability, given time restraints and class size, of expecting teachers to distribute tokens. This valid question might be best answered when viewed through a different lens. An alternative question to ask might be "Do we have time not to reinforce behaviorally challenging students for appropriate behavior?" Teachers already spend a significant amount of time correcting undesirable behaviors. The modeling of inappropriate behavior by one student allows observational learning of inappropriate behavior by other students. Rewarding positive behavior decreases the time spent correcting undesirable behaviors and disciplining students (Swinson & Knight, 2007).

The preceding pages' argument has provided a brief overview of the position that TES can be an effective component of a PBS system that focuses on eliciting appropriate behavior and replacing inappropriate with appropriate behavior. It is not, however, a foregone conclusion that PBS, TES, or any newly introduced program or component will be embraced by personnel within a school or school system. It is human nature to resist the unknown and to cling to that which is familiar and comfortable. How, then, do we increase integrity and implementation fidelity?

One option is to threaten punishment for noncompliance, but this approach conflicts with the central tenets of PBS. There is little rationale for using aversive and intrusive techniques when more positive options are available. In building an effective reinforcement system, it is often helpful to provide teachers with incentives to participate. This might include providing reinforcement to teachers who distribute a winning student ticket or intermittently awarding reinforcers to teachers who are caught handing out tickets for good behavior. Administrators or problem-solving teams may model reinforcement by providing a meaningful token of recognition, such as flowers, dinners, or merely an extra planning period though the course of the day, for a faculty member who demonstrates positive behavior management practices.

In our introduction to TES, we provided a general overview, explained the rationale, identified key variables influencing behavior, and concluded by providing answers to questions that have previously limited "buy-in" and thus negatively impacted student, school, and district outcomes. We now move from broader concepts and generalizations to the fine points and procedures that collectively work in unison to create a successful TES. We begin by addressing schoolwide reinforcement surveys, reward acquisition, ticket procedures, and raffles, and end with a discussion on the school store.

FORM TO BE INTRODUCED

Form 6.1: Positive Behavior Ticket Template

MATERIALS NEEDED

- Tokens
- Prizes
- Annual prize
- Ten monthly prizes
- Abundant prizes of varying value for the school store
- Tables for school store
- Recording mechanism for number of tickets received
- Collection bins for monthly and annual raffle drawings

PEOPLE NEEDED

- PBS token economy coordinator. This person is responsible for the following:
  - Collecting and tracking tickets
  - Generating and maintaining grade-level lists reflecting the number of earned tickets
  - Serving as the school store manager
  - Determining the ticket values of each store item
- Assuring the store has adequate supplies

CRITICAL INFORMATION

Schoolwide Reinforcement Survey

What do politicians, blue chip companies, and token economy systems have in common? If you said they are all full of corruption, well, we hope you are wrong at least about that. Actually, all three use surveys for the same purpose; they want to know exactly what you (the voter, consumer, or student) want. The reason is simple. People will do what you ask when you offer them something they strongly desire. Politicians get votes, companies get customers, and a TES gets students to demonstrate appropriate behavior. The TES survey is simply a systematic means of determining which rewards students find reinforcing.

The process is straightforward and can be efficiently initiated and completed in a nominal amount of time when a small investment of human resources is paid on the front end. Although the survey can be conducted on an individual or small-group basis, a streamlined and comprehensive approach allows any sample size from randomly selected grade-level representatives to an entire student body to participate. Remember that an increase in the sample size tends to suggest that findings are more representative of the student body as a whole.

Initiating the process involves the PBS team developing a questionnaire asking students to select and rank from a list the 10 things they would like to earn. To get an idea about what 10 items to include in the survey, observe the types of things students have, the activities that they do, or the things they talk about. They can be categorized in terms of edibles (i.e., things to eat), tangibles (i.e., thing to own), academics (i.e., get out of one homework assignment), or socials (i.e., things to do). The forms are disseminated, completed by students at a designated time, collected by teachers, and returned to the PBS team. Afterward, the results are calculated and rank-ordered. A variation involves allowing the students to "write-in" preferences. This variation provides a greater number of, and possibly identification of, stronger reinforcers. Once results are available, the PBS team possesses a greater degree of confidence that students will find the rewards and reinforcers they identified motivating.

Surveying is a quick and easy way to learn what students want. Often, though, an assumption results in more than just a mistake, but also loss of time and money that could have been used better elsewhere. A recent situation helps illustrate the point. A concerned first-grade teacher appeared distressed at a teacher support team meeting. When queried, she told of her student who was not responding to an intervention that had historically been very effective with her students. A team member later observed the intervention and reported that the teacher was implementing the treatment with a high degree of integrity. After correctly answering a set of math facts, the student was praised and awarded several small pieces of candy. No improvement was noted through the course of the intervention. When interviewing the student, a team representative tactfully approached the topic of intervention failure to bring about improvement. The student eventually revealed to the interviewer that every time she did as she was asked and answered the questions correctly, the teacher encouraged her to eat candy. "What's so bad about that?" the confused interviewer asked. "I don't like candy," the student confided. Sometimes we forget how unique we each are and make assumptions that unnecessarily lead us astray. The survey allows the opportunity to reduce the errors by verifying or failing to verify what we believe to be true. In the end, as should typically be the rule, the data guide the decision making.

Acquiring Rewards

A TES without rewards or reinforcers is equivalent to competing at the Kentucky Derby without a horse. You can try, but do not expect much success. The reward is what the child wants, what he gets up for in the morning, and the reason he grits his teeth, turns, and walks away rather than engaging in a fight. If your reward is not strong enough to bring out appropriate behavior, it may not be as powerful as you desire.

Rewards come in varying shapes and sizes, and range from high dollar amounts to no price tags at all. Some of the rewards even include activities such as playing basketball after school, having lunch with a teacher, or getting a free homework pass. One school in which we have come in contact was known for giving away scooters at their end-of-the-year finale drawing. The power of potentially winning a scooter can have great influence on a child. But expensive prizes are not required for a TES. A few years ago, a high school teacher asked for a consultation regarding a disruptive student in her class. Having conducted a functional behavior assessment, the consultant hypothesized that the function or purpose of the disruptions was to gain peer attention. In a follow-up interview, the young man was asked what items would motivate him. His response was immediate. He wanted a piece of gum at the end of each day. This surprised the consultant, but he and the teacher signed an agreement with the student. The next day, having exhibited appropriate behavior, he was offered a piece of gum by the instructor. Slowly, he walked to the front of the class, smiled at his classmates, put the gum in his mouth, and returned to his seat. It quickly became apparent that acquisition of the gum itself was not the function of the behavior, but instead the vehicle by which to gain peer attention. The price for implementing the intervention was a "staggering" 43 cents per week. No more disruptions, and no more referrals to the principal's office; instead, each day only a little attention from peers and a single stick of gum. The strength of a reward, therefore, comes not from a price tag but from its intrinsic reinforcing value to the individual.

In the TES, rewards generally fall in one of two categories: access to preferred activities and tangibles. Access to preferred activities can be provided at no direct cost to the school. There is usually *something* a student wishes she could do or have more time participating in (e.g., computer, recess, P.E., or lunch with friends or staff). Use of preferred activities allows a win–win situation for all participants. The student engages in highly desirable activities while the school reduces discipline problems without expending capital. The second category, tangibles, is not necessarily more effective, but does receive a bulk of the discussion in TES literature. Tangibles can be touched (e.g., candy, movie tickets, toys, pencils, or bicycles). Student selection of tangible rewards is an effective but often more expensive option leading to the same outcome.

Rewards can be purchased at local retail stores but may also be, and are frequently, obtained through donations. The PBS team typically works together or designates a representative to contact stores, businesses, restaurants, theaters, and foundations for the purpose of requesting consideration for donations. The number one reason that PBS schools fail to receive meaningful donations is not because they are turned down, but because they never ask. Often, you get what you ask for. So, if you're asking for donations from a grocery store, expect groceries. If you are asking for donations from a dollar store, expect trinkets. If you want something nice, ask for it, and if you are turned down at the first location, go to a second, and then a third. Regardless of mood during the seasons of economic bliss and distress, will help fill a need when they know one exists. Give potential benefactors the opportunity to be generous.

Distributing Tickets

Meaningful ticket dissemination practices play a pivotal role in determining levels of PBS success. A page of tickets that can be cut out and distributed has been included in the accompanying CD (see "Form 6.1: Positive Behavior Ticket Template" in Appendix A).

The richness and variety of school cultures make it impossible to provide a one-size-fits-all answer as to the number of tickets to administer. Before discussing ticket procedures, it is important to discuss a concept called *schedules of reinforcement*. These schedules refer to the frequency in which a reinforcer is provided following a particular behavior. Students may receive incentives on a seemingly random basis. Although it may make intuitive sense for a student to receive a reward every time a positive behavior exists, both practical and behavioral principles suggest otherwise. Table 6.1 describes examples of schedules of reinforcement that indicate that behaviors that are rewarded every time they occur are subject to a principle called *extinction* (Skinner, 1938). Through extinction, a behavior stops occurring when reinforcement is removed (O'Reilly, Lancioni, & Taylor, 1999). Because those of us working with children want ideal behaviors such as walking carefully down the hallway or being helpful and respectful to others to occur regardless of the existence of a reward, a more irregular type of reinforcement schedule is preferred. This slot machine-like reward schedule, called *intermittent reinforcement*, is a very powerful method of providing incentives (Slavin, 2006). An example of this kind of intermittent reinforcement is holding weekly raffle drawings for students who have tickets. The point of this kind of intermittent reinforcement is that it amplifies the value of the tokens (e.g., tickets), thereby heightening the incentive for students to work for these tickets.

Although continuous reinforcement results in more tickets being awarded and helps students acquire new skills quicker, it has long been established that it is also more vulnerable to extinction (Eckerman & Vreeland, 1973; Ferster & Skinner, 1957; Skinner, 1969). For instance, rewarding a child each time he raises his hand before being called upon to speak produces

Table 6.1 Schedules of Reinforcement

Type of Reinforcement	Reinforcement Frequency	Example	Effect on Student Behavior	Resistance to Extinction
Continuous	Every time the behavior occurs.	Tanisha receives a positive behavior token every time she turns in her homework on time.	Student learns quickest when this method is implemented first; can use prior to switching to an intermittent schedule.	Weakest resistance to extinction.
Partial or Intermittent	Only some of the time a behavior occurs.	Vance receives an occasional smile from the teacher if he raises his hand to answer a question.	The response is acquired slower.	Behavior becomes more resistant to extinction.
Fixed Ratio	Reinforced after a set number of responses.	Marge receives a positive behavior token every third time she walks into the classroom without talking.	Behavior is acquired slower than with continuous reinforcement.	Most resistant to extinction.
Variable Ratio	Reinforcement occurs after an undetermined number of responses.	A student is reinforced by teacher attention, but the teacher gives attention only occasionally when the child throws a spitball.	Behavior is acquired slower than with continuous reinforcement.	Most resistant to extinction.
Fixed Interval	Reinforcement is available only after a set amount of time.	A teacher decides that every 15 minutes, she will hand out tickets to students who are demonstrating on-task behaviors.	Desired behaviors increase as the moment of reinforcement approaches, but suddenly decrease again after receiving the reinforcer.	More resistant to extinction than continuous reinforcement; less resistant than variable reinforcement schedules.
Variable Interval	Reinforcement is only available at variable times.	A teacher decides that at certain times during the class, she will hand out tickets to students who are demonstrating on-task behavior.	Students will demonstrate slow and steady responding.	Highly resistant to extinction.

a timely pairing, and subsequent learning, of reinforcement for speaking after raising one's hand and being granted speaking permission by the teacher. The risk becomes the potential extinction, in fewer trials, of the desired behavior (i.e., hand raising and waiting for permission to speak) when permission is not given to speak. Thus, a continuous reinforcement schedule is not recommended in the vast majority of instances addressed under a PBS model. Yet, there may be a select number of isolated cases in which a continuous reinforcement schedule is selected in order to more rapidly elicit a specific behavior or set of behaviors and create behavioral momentum for success prior to shifting to a more extinction-resistant schedule. Such strategies should typically be implemented when consulting with a professional well versed in the science of behavioral shaping.

For the majority of cases, an intermittent reinforcement schedule offers a nice balance between research findings and practical application. This type of scheduling allows students to be frequently, but not continuously, awarded tickets for appropriate behavior. As such, the learning rate is less pronounced, but once the behaviors are learned they become more difficult to extinguish. Unless there is a clear reason why an alternative reinforcement schedule should be implemented, the intermittent schedule is likely to be the better selection as a predetermined default selection. Fortunately, an intermittent schedule of reinforcement is also more manageable.

How Many Tickets Do We Need?

Finding an estimate for the number of tickets needed is individualized and up to the school problem-solving team. As discussed earlier, we recommend administering tickets on an intermittent schedule, and recommend that they be used in the times and places where behavior problems are most likely. At one school, the team decided that most students, on average, should earn a minimum of two tickets per day. To make that occur, during any day, a teacher with 30 students distributes a minimum of 60 tickets to her students. A school of 500 students distributes 1,000 or more tickets per day. In streamlining the process, the problem-solving team issues 1,200 or more tickets each month to each teacher with the teacher's name preprinted on the back of his or her tickets. In addition, the problem-solving team provides at least 600 tickets to other school staff including paraprofessionals, bus drivers, cafeteria personnel, custodial staff, and office staff. Tickets should include a place for the school staff members to write both the student's and school staffer's name. Thus, a total of 20,000 tickets per month may be necessary! Tickets are most easily managed when their size approximates that of half of a business card. They can be acquired in bulk at office supply stores, at local print shops, or through e-commerce for as little as 4 cents per page. An alternative is to print and photocopy the sample ticket sheet on the accompanying CD (see "Form 6.1: Positive Behavior Ticket Template" in Appendix A).

Raffle

School TES raffles help maintain interest in appropriate behavior and ticket acquisition. The raffle maintains a lottery format in which each ticket has an equal chance of being selected. In its most traditional form, principals have used a wire hopper and literally spun the tickets about the device before making a selection. Others have used buckets or garbage bags to hold the tickets. One of the newest options has been to incorporate technology and electronically enter the number of tickets obtained by each student. This serves a dual purpose as data can also be used for tracking purposes. The computer then selects a ticket or name, and the prize is awarded.

Raffles often occur at various levels and different venues. For instance, classroom teachers may hold a raffle at the end of the day or week. Grades may combine tickets and offer grade-level rewards to those with winning tickets. Most impressive are the school-level drawings that can occur daily, each semester, or yearly. One district, having discovered the "secrets" of TES, brought students to the auditorium at the end of each 9 weeks for the Finale, a gathering where music was played, snacks could be eaten, speakers were heard offering praise and encouragement, and public drawings were held in sight of the entire student body. Prizes included radios, tickets to ballgames, sought-after brand name clothing, and more. Students looked forward to the event, and both behavior and morale improved as the event neared.

Having changed the atmosphere of the school to a large extent, the administration and staff ran an experiment to see whether the Finale concept could provide even greater returns on student behavior. The following year, the school announced an end-of-the-year Finale Finale. Signs were occasionally posted, morning announcements were sprinkled with references, and suspense was soon built toward the event. The unveiling came during the first 9-week Finale, when the principal announced that an end-of-year spectacle would be held with unrivaled prizes. On stage, assistants brought video game consoles with an assortment of games, season passes to professional ballgames, gift certificates, and iPods and coupons for downloads, and the grand prize of ... the principal left the stage to return only a few moments later riding a bright red scooter. The students were ecstatic, and improvements were noted in even the most behaviorally challenged students. The school had found a recipe for success, and the Finale Finale became the most anticipated event of the year.

A "secret" this school discovered is that everyone will work for something, and if you find that something that almost everyone really wants—almost everyone will really work for it. Naysayers will argue that people will not contribute, or that the plan will not work, or that anyone could get kids to listen if they gave away scooters. They will find an excuse for their failure to be successful, whereas the problem solvers, those who see obstacles not as problems but as opportunities to become stronger and make even greater gains, are the ones demonstrating success year after year.

Store

The TES store quickly becomes a favorite destination within the school. Younger and older students alike look forward to visits when they can exchange their tokens or tickets for items carried in the store. Skills to run the store are equivalent to those used to sell hot dogs and soft drinks at a little league ball field. Items are neatly displayed with prices clearly marked. The store requires little time to set up and can be located in a media center, empty classroom, gymnasium, school office, or large storage closet.

To encourage structure and routine, the store is open the last academic day of the week. Each grade and class has a designated time in which students visit the store and make their respective purchases. The store should contain a wide range of prizes to include tangibles (e.g., school supplies, sporting equipment, clothing, and stuffed animals), tickets to social events (e.g., dances, movie and popcorn day, and office work for a day), and edibles (i.e., things to eat that are preferably healthy).

The store monitor should also maintain electronic records (i.e., a spreadsheet or database) that allow each student the opportunity to deposit his or her tickets into a store savings account. A collateral benefit is teaching early in one's academic career the value of saving and delayed gratification.

A critical point to note is that students *should not* lose tickets they have earned or be denied access to the school store. This is not saying that inappropriate behavior should not be addressed. What we are expressing is that when a student earns a ticket, it is his ticket: not the teacher's ticket, not the principal's ticket, but the student's ticket. It is acknowledged that using response costs can be effective in some instances. However, students most in need of PBS services are those refractory cases for which other interventions have not resulted in adequate behavioral improvements. Students with moderate to severe behavior problems have been noted to respond negatively when previously earned points, tokens, or tickets are taken from them. This has the potential to exponentially exacerbate the problem, which then requires significantly more time to stabilize and remediate.

CHAPTER 6 TASKS

- Identify an individual to be in charge of maintaining the school store. This is a big task, and we would recommend that the individual gets some release time to be able to perform these tasks.
- Create tickets.
  - These can be purchased at an office supply store, created by the team themselves, or photocopied from the ticket sheet provided.
- Create ticketing guidelines.
  - What types of behaviors should teachers give tickets for?
  - How will tickets be authenticated (not shared or plagiarized)?
  - What happens when tickets are given to a student—who should maintain possession of them?
- Create procedures for raffles.
  - Encourage students to place their tickets with their names into a hopper.
  - Have a public drawing at the end of each week to give out desirable prizes.
  - Include a grand-prize drawing for the end of each semester.
- Identify prizes for the students.
  - See Appendix D for a list of possible rewards.
  - Include free rewards that students can earn.

- Identify those who can donate prizes.
  - Parents
  - Teachers
  - Organizations
  - Local businesses
- Create a school store.
  - Determine hours when it is open.
  - Determine when students have access.
  - Determine where the store will reside.
  - Determine the price of prizes—how many tickets will earn different prizes.
- Determine how students will get prizes (directly from the store, or delivered to student at the end of the day).

Creating Procedures for Office Discipline Referrals

S chool problem-solving teams function best when access to multiple sources of meaningful, reliable, and valid data is available. This chapter provides the start of a process that schools need teams to follow to ensure their data are collected in a standardized and systematic manner. More specifically, the chapter will explain the aggregation and examination of office discipline referrals (ODRs), which can then be used to differentiate between schoolwide, classwide, and student behavioral problems. Subsequent sections of the chapter will explain formal and informal data collection techniques.

CONCEPT TO BE INTRODUCED

- Database of ODRs

LINKS TO OTHER CHAPTERS

The systematic collection of office discipline referrals helps school problem-solving teams:

- Identify physical locations within the school and times within the day and year that problem behaviors are most likely to be present (Chapter 8).
- Identify classrooms with low, moderate, and high levels of student misbehavior (Chapter 9).
- Identify students "at risk" of behavioral difficulties and in need of intense interventions (Chapters 10 and 11).
- Evaluate how well an intervention is working by monitoring the student's progress (Chapter 11).

FORM TO BE INTRODUCED

Form 7.1: Office Discipline Referral Form.

CRITICAL INFORMATION

Meetings

A goal of the meeting should be to reduce the likelihood of "data hoarding," or the collection of data simply for collecting data. Through this meeting, the facilitators can help define clear and viable means to enhance outcomes. In order for ODRs to be useful tools for schools, a problem-solving team must help the faculty agree upon which student behaviors should necessitate office referrals, and which student behaviors the classroom teacher should manage (Irvin, Tobin, Sprague, Sugai, & Vincent, 2004). Effective and systematic tracking of ODRs can be useful data for schools to use when identifying problems throughout various school settings (Irvin et al., 2006). Prior to the start of the school year, the *entire* school faculty should attend a meeting addressing ODRs. At this meeting, the school staff:

- Creates clear and observable definitions of student behaviors of concern.
- Creates categories of behaviors of concern (e.g., major and minor types of behavioral infractions).
- Establishes consequences for each behavior of concern and class of concerning behavior (Irvin et al., 2004) (e.g., the teachers address minor behaviors while referring major behavior violations to the school office).

An advantage to holding this meeting is that it allows and encourages greater teacher participation. Increasing teacher participation is critical because when faculty members fail to buy into school discipline policy and as a result communicate a message inconsistent with the established policy, students demonstrate high levels of behavior problems (Reinke & Herman, 2002). Additionally, these meetings offer opportunities for school staff to modify, customize, and simplify forms for addressing specific student behaviors. Schools in residential treatment or day treatment settings may target more unusual behaviors (e.g., head banging or other forms of self-abuse), whereas public elementary schools may seek to reduce the rates of more common behaviors (e.g., running in the hall-way and fights in the playground).

Creating Categories for Behaviors

When categorizing unacceptable behaviors, it is important for faculty to assess the severity of each behavior or group of behaviors. For example, behaviors that violate the basic civil rights of other students (e.g., assaults and stealing) are highly serious, whereas behaviors that merely disrupt the classroom instructional flow (e.g., talking without permission), although still problematic, are less serious.

Determining Appropriate Consequences for Behaviors

As the faculty work through this process, they decide which behaviors the teacher manages in class and which behaviors require an office referral. For example, teachers may be given a high degree of flexibility in managing students speaking loudly in class without permission, failing to turn in their homework, violating a school dress code, or chewing gum. However, behaviors categorized as serious or unsafe require an ODR.

Faculty Meeting Example

Table 7.1 identifies the results of a meeting between team members of a middle school faculty who were trying to determine appropriate responses to rule infractions. The following example identifies behaviors selected by a middle school faculty, the consequences of the behaviors, and the logic for the categorization. This faculty chose to place the behaviors into four different categories:

1. Definite "referral"
2. Probable "referral"
3. Probable "no referral"
4. Definite "no referral"

The faculty divided behaviors into two categories when they could not come to a consensus regarding definitions of specific behaviors. Because students create novel means by which to exhibit socially unacceptable behaviors, faculties should proactively plan to update their lists as the needs and characteristics of the student body change.

Table 7.1   Example of Rule Infractions and Subsequent Disciplinary Action

Definite Referral	Probable Referral	Probable No Referral	Definite No Referral
Fight	Verbal threat	Misuse of technology	Getting out of seat without permission
Physical assault toward another student	Verbal assault on other student	Cheating	Failing to finish assignments
Physical assault toward faculty or staff	Verbal assault on teacher	Horseplay	Violating dress code
Severe vandalism (Vandalism resulting in destruction of property in excess of $30)		Mild vandalism (Vandalism resulting in destruction of property less than $30)	Arriving late to class 3 or fewer times
Arson	Truancy (chronic: more than 7 unexcused absences)	Truancy (occasional: 7 or fewer unexcused absences)	Talking in class
Bringing contraband to school (weapons, drugs, and other dangerous materials)	Arguing with teacher	Teasing	Bringing materials not related to school curriculum but not dangerous
Drinking alcohol on campus	Smoking on campus	Public displays of affection	Chewing gum in class
Hurting oneself or self-abuse (unless child is on a behavior plan)	Being in an unauthorized area where students have been explicitly forbidden (severe)	Being in an unauthorized or dangerous area (mild)	
Stealing from peers (in excess of $20 in value)		Not following teacher directives	
Stealing from school staff (in excess of $20 in value)		Talking back	

Office Discipline Referral Form

An office discipline referral form should allow a teacher or staff member to quickly catalog the time, date, location, and nature of infractions (McKevitt & Braaksma, 2008). A sample form is included in Appendix A ("Form 7.1: Office Discipline Referral Form") and on the accompanying CD.

The information from these ODRs can then be used to identify areas and/or times when student behavior is most problematic (Clonan, McDougal, Clark, & Davison, 2007), and to identify areas in need of more intense monitoring (McKevitt & Braaksma, 2008). Perhaps the most critical and beneficial components of the forms for ODRs is that they may be used to track and identify behavioral trends within a school. Thus, one individual must be responsible for entering ODR data into a database each time a behavioral infraction requiring administrative help has occurred.

Other Considerations

ODRs are commonly used indicators of emotional and behavioral functioning (Irvin et al., 2004). However, when schools use only ODRs to identify problem behaviors, individuals with depression or anxiety who frequently do not disrupt the classroom fail to receive attention or benefit from needed services (Nelson, Benner, Reid, Epstein, & Currin, 2002). Thus, additional indicators designed specifically for the identification and progress monitoring of internalizing problems may be considered.

For example, tracking student absences may help in identifying students with emotional rather than behavior difficulties. The school problem-solving team may utilize absences and grade point averages to gain an understanding of how individuals are progressing throughout the school system (McKevitt & Braaksma, 2008). It is important to reiterate that individuals with emotional and behavioral disorders frequently demonstrate academic deficits. Thus, a team wanting to improve a child's behavior should also consider taking steps to improve his or her academic performance.

CONCLUSION

To prevent and reduce behavior problems, schools should use data to identify areas of need and determine intervention effectiveness. Although many schools already track ODRs, the data become less useful without a systematic and consistent enforcement of behavioral expectations. Fortunately, clear and observable definitions and universal criteria for behavior management help the school more easily adopt meaningful forms to track the progress of students, classes, grade levels, and the collective student body.

CHAPTER 7 TASKS

- Conduct faculty meetings to establish universal criteria for making office referrals.
  - Identify categories of behavior problems.
  - Identify appropriate consequences for most behaviors.
  - Identify which behaviors should be managed in the classroom.

- Create an office discipline referral form.
- Teach all staff how to complete an office discipline referral.
  - Create procedures for tracking office discipline referrals.
- Create a database to track office discipline referrals. (See Appendix C for a tutorial.)

8

Identifying Schoolwide Problems

INTRODUCTION

Most everyone (or at least anyone who attended an elementary school as a child) intuitively understands that being "sent to the office" is a dire punishment. This intuitive "gut feeling" that being sent to the office is an aversive experience is moderately more difficult to explain than one might guess. Despite the theoretical complexity involved in explaining why receiving an office discipline referral (ODR) is unpleasant, we can all agree that generally speaking, an ODR is an experience that *most* children wish to avoid. What is much easier to explain, and more directly useful for our purposes, is unpacking the principal theoretical elements that drive behaviorism. Behavioral psychology, when simplified, suggests two rules: (a) An observed behavior will occur with greater frequency, intensity, and for a longer duration when reinforced (rewarded); and (b) an observed behavior will occur less often, with a lower degree of intensity, and for a diminished duration without reinforcement or when followed by a punishing stimulus. What is clear based upon this boiled-down version of behavioral psychology is that the typical intent of an ODR is to reduce the frequency, intensity, or duration of a student's inappropriate behavior by following it with an unpleasant stimulus.

The success of the ODR intervention should be measured by the degree to which the student's behavior reduces in frequency, intensity, or duration. If a subsequent referral is not necessary, we then assume the experience was unpleasant for the child, or that the school team has put into place effective intervention strategies for students who are sent to the office to prevent the reoccurrence of any misbehavior. However, some schools may become overwhelmed with students receiving

multiple ODRs. These occasions call for a school-based problem-solving team to systematically analyze schoolwide and
classwide problems.

CONCEPTS TO BE INTRODUCED

- Reviewing ODRs in order to identify problems
- Reviewing ODRs in order to evaluate interventions
- Other means of identifying problems

LINKS TO OTHER CHAPTERS

Previous chapters (Chapters 4, 5, and 6) have discussed how to
implement procedures to decrease the likelihood of experiencing problems at school. Chapter 7 outlined the work that a school
staff must undertake to ensure that ODRs occur on a regular
basis. However, even when those procedures are in place, there
may still be issues that require the attention of the school-based
problem-solving team. This chapter provides procedures to
determine whether schoolwide problems exist and also decide
on appropriate response strategies. Chapter 9 will address identifying and providing intervention for classwide problems.

FORMS TO BE INTRODUCED

Form 8.1: Elementary Student Schoolwide Assessment
Form 8.2: Middle School Student Schoolwide Assessment

INFORMATION NEEDED

Lists of all ODRs from previous years and the current year
need to be sorted in the following ways:

- By the number of infractions committed by each student (e.g., how many physical fights was Justin involved
  in last year?)
- By the number of infractions occurring at each location (e.g., how many fights occurred in the cafeteria
  last month?)
- By the number of referrals made by each staff member
  (e.g., how many referrals did third-grade teacher Ms.
  Jones write last year?)

- By the number of each infraction type (e.g., reported incidents of willful disobedience)
- By the number of infractions occurring on particular days (e.g., how many fights are reported on Fridays as compared to Wednesdays?)
- By the number of infractions occurring by time of day, and date

PEOPLE NEEDED

- Members of the problem-solving team
- School staff that monitor nonclassroom areas (this may include everyone on the school staff or at least a representative—e.g., from cafeteria staff, custodial staff, bus staff, and library staff)

CRITICAL BACKGROUND INFORMATION

Norms for ODRs

Many problem-solving team members find it useful to compare their ODRs to those of other schools across the country. Not only does it provide perspective on what other schools may be experiencing, but also it may help a school recognize an area of concern. The School-wide Information System (SWIS; 2008) is a computerized method of entering, integrating, and reporting ODR data and can be purchased by individual schools to support this effort (www.swis.org). For the school year 2007–2008, SWIS collected ODR information from all schools that had purchased the software and tracked the ODRs for major events such as fighting during the course of the school year. They found that for elementary schools (kindergarten through fifth grade), there was an average of .34 ODRs per 100 students per day. For middle schools, the average was .92 ODRs per 100 students per day. For high schools, it was 1.05 ODRs per 100 students per day (SWIS, 2008). Although this information is useful, it is important to keep in mind that it only represents those schools that have systematically chosen to track ODRs through the SWIS system, and may not be a representative sample of schools across the country or the world. In Chapter 7, we highlighted the procedures a school can undertake to bring its disciplinary referral systems in line with those of many of these "SWIS" schools.

Good Data Analysis

An important first principle of data management is that a systematic and regular review of the data is crucial. By regularly and systematically reviewing your data, you will overcome the common pitfall of responding intuitively to hot spots and subsequently missing important trends. However, it is important not to oversimplify the data. For example, simply knowing that many office discipline referrals are generated by hallway behaviors may not be enough to inform an effective intervention. Inflation in hallway ODRs may occur due to any number of different reasons or a combination of several factors. It may be that five or six students are frequently getting into trouble in the halls or that one class of students is having difficulty following procedures. The inflation of ODRs may be the result of significant congestion in the front hallway or students getting into conflicts near the end of the school day. Interviews and more in-depth reviews will help clarify problems and provide clues for effective interventions. The organization of your data will inform your team's ability to make use of the collected information. You and your team must be able to efficiently evaluate your data sets for the information critical to the development of your interventions.

CRITICAL INFORMATION

A good start to forming a behavioral response plan to school-wide issues identified by an examination of ODRs is for the problem-solving team to examine the data. To access the information necessary to make intervention decisions, data must be arranged to efficiently identify trouble spots, problematic times of the day, and students who are frequently referred to the school office. We have described in Chapter 7 that any ODR must include the date, day, time, offending student, referring teacher, location, and infraction type. Your data aggregation system should let you sort by each of these categories or by multiple categories. By being able to arrange and rearrange your data, you can quickly compile any number of lists. These lists are organized by category (referring teacher, location, type of infraction, referred student, etc.) and then arranged in rank order from most to least referrals. For example, if you want to know which teacher has made the most referrals in November, your system should be responsive to those search parameters and generate a listing of all the teachers who made referrals in November arranged in rank order. A flexible system will allow you to reorder the list chronologically or rearrange the November ODRs by type of infraction or by student referred.

Preferably, the individual in charge of maintaining data will enter ODR information the same day a student receives the referral.

Problem-Solving Process Steps

Step 1: Problem Identification and Verification

The Office of Special Education Programs, Center on Positive Behavior Interventions and Supports, recommends that teams evaluate ODRs once per month (Clonan, McDougal, Clark, & Davison, 2007).

The problem-solving team will record (i.e., input into a spreadsheet or data collection system) and review the following data at least once per month. Schools with many referrals may need frequent reviews of their ODRs. Clonan et al. (2007) recommended that school teams collect the following data:

- ODRs by date, day, and time
- ODRs by infraction
- ODRs by location
- ODRs by student
- ODRs by classroom and teacher

Review ODRs by Month

By reviewing ODRs on a monthly basis, the problem-solving team will be able to learn exactly when during the year behavior problems are more likely to increase or decrease. Although regular yearly evaluations of the data may reveal important trends, a monthly examination will reveal behavior patterns quicker. From month to month, the problem-solving teams may notice that behavior varies during the course of a year. If a team is noticing an increase in the rate of ODRs during a month, targeted schoolwide interventions may be necessary.

Note: To get accurate data, one must calculate a monthly rate. Calculate a rate by dividing the number of ODRs by the number of school days in that month. For example, in October the students may have been in school for 20 school days, whereas in November students attended school for only 15 days. When reviewing behaviors each month, it may be useful to compare your data to SWIS norms. For example, in an elementary school of 500 students, one would expect to see

not all mths have same amount of school days

5 * .34 = 1.7 referrals per day for major behavior problems. If an elementary school of this size consistently has a daily rate of more than three major ODRs per day, schoolwide and class-wide interventions may be necessary.

Review ODRs by Infraction

Reviewing ODRs by infraction can help schools to identify and focus social-skills teaching efforts. For instance, if a school's problem-solving team is observing an increase in dress code violations or fights throughout the entire student population, schoolwide assemblies and trainings may need to be sched-uled to help students review expectations and consequences.

Review of ODRs by Location

Understanding which locations generate the most ODRs will help the problem-solving team allocate its attention to the most problematic areas of the campus. For instance, if there are fre-quent problems in the hallways, they may decide to change how and when students transition between class periods. The problem-solving team reviews the following data, and deter-mines that most of the problems are presenting in the main hallway. Of course, it is important to consider how much time students spend in various locations. Classroom referrals will likely be the highest source, but students spend at least 75% of their day in a classroom. Attempts to regulate this data may include determining the number of minutes that students spend in each location and determining a per-minute ratio when looking at these data.

Example

During the month of March, a middle school team collected the following data:

    Main hallway: 36 ODRs
    Playground: 15
    Hallway outside of cafeteria: 10
    Front of school: 7

The team determined that students spent only 10 minutes per day in the main hallway, 30 minutes per day on the play-ground, and 10 minutes per day in the hallway outside of the cafeteria. The team identified the main hallway as a place where many problems occurred and decided to examine the problem closer.

Reviewing ODRs by Classroom and Teacher

The problem-solving team should also review the number of discipline referrals made by each staff member. The team should look closest at classrooms that generate many referrals on multiple students. In these types of situations, it is important to note that some teachers may be in locations where multiple disciplinary infractions occur. In the previous example, there were multiple incidents of main hallway violations that resulted in ODRs, and one teacher observed many fights and other major rule violations that occur in front of her classroom. Also, a hallway, lunchroom, or playground monitor may be more likely to write ODRs. Thus, a teacher writing many ODRs does not necessarily indicate that he or she would benefit from targeted classroom behavioral interventions. However, if a team has ruled out many of these other factors, it may be possible that a particular classroom is in need of receiving supports in classroom management. Chapter 9 will discuss classroom interventions in more depth.

Review of ODRs by Student

If there are no schoolwide and classwide problems, then the problem-solving team should target the behaviors of students receiving the most ODRs. Subsequent chapters address how to identify students in need of individualized interventions.

Collection of Student Observations Data

In addition to collecting data from ODRs, a school team should also collect data directly from students (Safran, 2006). Collecting student opinions has many advantages over ODRs. The first is that students can provide information on occurrences when adults are absent. Although this may sound obvious, we have firsthand knowledge of only what we observe. For example, when in high school, one of us observed other students playing dice games with high cash stakes in the bathroom. The students had a lookout and would stop and put their dice and money away in their pockets when any teachers came close by. As a student, I was able to see gambling taking place on school grounds! Obviously, the teachers were unaware of this. The second advantage of collecting student input is that some teachers may view events from only an adult perspective, and as such may not be aware that events are frightening for children. For example, younger students may be frightened by an aggressive game of tag that older students play on the playground.

This chapter includes a schoolwide student assessment form for elementary schools and middle schools (see Appendix A, Forms 8.1 and 8.2).

We recommend collecting these data once during the school year—either the middle of the fall or the middle of the spring semester are appropriate times to collect data. The survey is designed to help problem-solving teams understand times of the day and places where behavior problems may occur. There is also an opportunity for a student to write a comment about something that makes him or her feel unsafe. There are several ways to look at these data:

- Where do students feel unsafe?
- What time of day do most students worry about?
- What grades of students feel most unsafe?

It is also useful to look into the data more closely by looking at interaction effects. For example, are certain grades more likely to feel unsafe on the playground than other grades? Are there times of day and places where students feel unsafe? All of these data may be useful for a problem-solving team.

Step 2: Plan Design and Implementation

Once the problem-solving team has identified the area(s) and times of concern, it should intervene. The team writes a plan describing a desired change (i.e., a goal) and what action will be taken to achieve the goal (i.e., the intervention), and then assuring plan implementation. The following are intervention examples:

- Assemblies to review the rules
- Review of the school's implementation of PBS
- Teaching stations whereby school staff teaches students how to behave in various locations on the campus (e.g., hallway or cafeteria)
- Increased staff visibility in problem areas
- Schoolwide bullying interventions (e.g., No Name Calling Week or Bullyproofing)
- Social-skills lessons in all classes

Step 3: Intervention Evaluation

Once the intervention begins, the problem-solving team assesses implementation integrity and plan effectiveness. One means of assessing integrity is unannounced observations.

Form 4.1, "Schoolwide Integrity Checklist Form," should record the observation information.

One can assess the effectiveness of an intervention by counting the number of ODRs before and after the intervention begins to examine changes in the amount and/or type of ODRs. Modify the intervention if the school staff members perform it with high integrity but the student's behavior does not improve (e.g., choose a different intervention or intensify the current intervention). However, if the intervention proves effective, the problem-solving team may decide to continue or end it.

Step 4: Process Review

In a response to intervention (RTI) model, a team's actions serve, in part, to provide information about future intervention possibilities. At year's end, the team reviews data to answer several questions. Over the course of the school year, did the number of ODRs and other behavioral indicators increase or decrease? When the problem-solving team implemented an intervention for an area, was the intervention effective or ineffective? What needs to happen differently to solve a particular problem? What is working effectively that should not change? It is also important to note that, as student bodies change, the behaviors of concern change. Thus, the team attempts to prevent and solve problems.

These following examples provide data-based vignettes of problem-solving teams attempting to address their school system problems.

EXAMPLE 1

Problem Identification

The problem-solving team was reviewing data from their ODRs as arranged by month and identified the following data trend:

August: 27 ODRs
September: 43
October: 59
November: 47
December: 85

The problem-solving team calculated a rate of ODRs per day by dividing the ODRs by the number of days the students were in school (not including professional development days). The students were in school for 10 days in August, 19 in September, 20 in October, 15 in November, and 17 in December. Thus, the data revealed the following.

Month	Rate of ODRs per Day
August	2.7
September	2.3
October	2.9
November	3.1
December	5.0

When reviewing these data, the team notices that December has shown a marked increase in the number of ODRs.

Intervention Planning

The team enacted a schoolwide intervention to reteach the rules. With the entire school staff, the problem-solving team reviewed the procedures that the school staff needed to follow in order to implement the PBS plan, and encouraged all teachers to review their classroom rules and reteach the procedures in their classes.

Evaluation

The team reviewed their average ODRs per day for the months of January and February. They noticed the following:

January: 3.5 ODRs per day
February: 3.8 ODRs per day

The team believed the interventions were working, but planned a more intensive intervention involving an increase in the amount of precuing, more active supervision, and a more systematic review of the data to determine which students may have been most actively involved in these problematic behaviors.

EXAMPLE 2

The following data were collected from Alpha Middle School. The program recorded a total of 227 ODRs in one academic year. Review of those data revealed that 11 students were involved in generating 60% of the referrals. Stated differently, fewer than 5% of the students were responsible for 60% of the discipline referrals.

Teacher	Students	Referrals
Mr. Red	2 students	7 of 17
Ms. Yellow	1 student	17 of 41
Mr. Blue	2 students	12 of 22
Ms. Green	1 student	14 of 30
Mr. Black	3 students	66 of 76
Ms. White	2 students	21 of 41
Total	11 students	137 of 227

The data were valuable in identifying students who were most likely to benefit from intensive, individualized interventions. By remediating these students or a majority of these 11 students, discipline referrals might significantly decline if other variables were held constant. Further examination of ODRs provided data for school and district. (See Figure 8.1.)

Initially, the team looked more closely at Mr. Black's ODRs, and noted that three students were responsible for 66 of his referrals. In looking more closely, the team also noted that most of these referrals occurred during transition periods. Thus, a two-pronged intervention was recommended. Mr. Black decided to implement the strategies described in Chapter 9 to help manage his entire classroom in a more structured format. Also, the three students responsible for the lion's share of the referrals were recommended for Tier II interventions.

The school-based problem-solving team also reviewed the percentage of school ODR referrals by month to gain an understanding of whether discipline problems were increasing or decreasing over the course of the year. The team reviewed data from the previous 4 years to gain an understanding of when possible discipline problems were more likely to occur. (See Figure 8.2.)

Through this example, the team noted that October, January, and April appeared to be months when students had frequent difficulties with office discipline. After looking more closely at the data, they realized that students were frequently referred for defiance and occasional fights—especially during the month of April. Thus, the team decided to hold assemblies and schoolwide training days to remind students about the important of following directives and helping students remember the procedures they were expected to follow. The team also

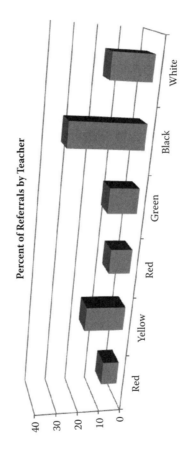

Figure 8.1   Percentage of referrals by teacher.

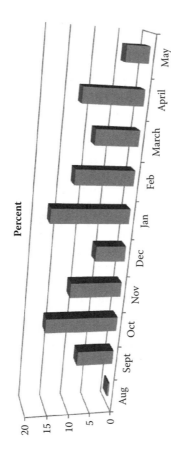

Figure 8.2 Percentage of referrals by month.

increased the number of positive behavior tokens given to students during the months of October, January, and April to provide more tangible incentives for desirable behaviors.

The team then began to investigate ODRs over the course of the week to determine whether some days generated more ODRs. They learned that Fridays were days when students were most often referred. When reviewing Friday's school structures, they noted that teacher absences were highest on Fridays, and that students were spending more time on the playground as teachers sent their students for recess more frequently. Often, there was more than one class on the playground at a time, resulting in more crowding. Thus, the problem-solving team began to offer trainings for regular substitute teachers on Fridays to make sure they understood the importance of following the PBS guidelines. The team also modified the recess schedule to ensure that only one class was out on the playground at one time. (See Figure 8.3.)

The problem-solving team then looked at times of the day when different infractions occurred. Infraction times appeared to be relatively equally distributed across times, though more than one in five referrals failed to contain this information. Again, absence of important data impaired the team's effectiveness. This not only helps illustrate the importance of completing ODRs but also acts as a reminder to teams developing ODRs that they should be adequate but as succinct as possible. Thus, the problem-solving team reminded all school staff to record the time an incident occurred when completing an ODR form. (See Figures 8.4 and 8.5.)

Finally, types of infractions conveyed the types of violations. For our reviewed district, it was clear that aggression or violence as well as noncompliance were behaviors most in need of team attention. These data, along with the time of year when infractions occurred, helped the problem-solving team to help teachers develop further procedures, increase staffing levels in common areas, and ensure that active supervision was occurring.

CONCLUSION

This chapter has provided a rationale for a school-based problem-solving team to assess whether its school has any schoolwide behavior problems. When a team identifies problems, the chapter gave procedures to resolve them. Once the schoolwide problems have been resolved, the team should review its ODRs

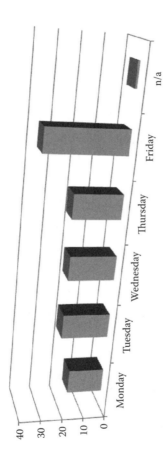

Figure 8.3 Comparison of referrals by day of week.

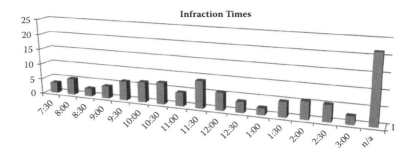

Figure 8.4   Infraction times.

again to determine whether there are still certain classrooms generating many referrals. If so, the next chapter will guide the team as to how it should provide additional attention and support to those classrooms.

CHAPTER 8 TASKS

- Monthly tasks
  - Review previous interventions.
    - Ensure intervention integrity.
      - If intervention is not being implemented correctly, make appropriate adjustments.
    - Review data to understand effectiveness.
      - If intervention is implemented correctly, determine whether the intervention is correctly targeted.
    - Determine whether it is time to continue, alter, or end the schoolwide intervention.
  - Problem identification.
    - Administer the schoolwide student opinion survey once during the fall and once during the spring semesters.
    - Review ODRs and student opinion surveys for patterns. Review for the following:
      - Monthly patterns of increase or decrease.
      - Infractions that occur frequently.
      - Locations where frequent incidents occur.
      - Classes or grades whose students demonstrate frequent behavior problems.
      - Individual students who may be demonstrating frequent behavioral problems.

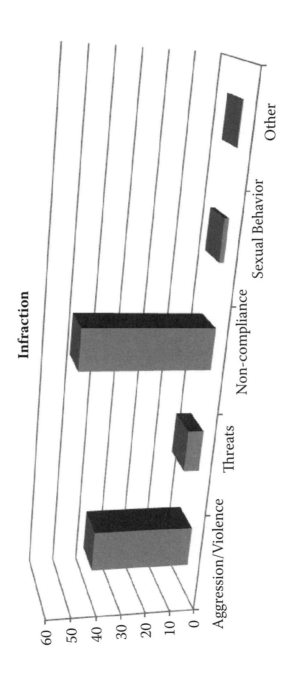

Figure 8.5   Types of infractions.

- Design interventions.
  - Consider staffing changes.
  - Consider possible schedule or traffic changes.
  - Consider schoolwide assemblies.
  - Consider intensifying administering PBS tickets in problem areas.
- Semiregular tasks
  - At the end of each semester, review the team's process.
    - Are decisions objective and data based?
    - Are the numbers of behavioral problems decreasing?
    - What additional information would make the problem-solving process more effective?
    - What are the strengths of the team?
- What are the weaknesses within the school's process?

9

Identifying Classwide Problems

INTRODUCTION

Previous chapters focused on ensuring that schools and classrooms meet the basic needs of students by creating a positive culture. However, some classrooms need additional supports. Before the problem-solving team identifies students needing support, it must first ensure that classrooms are operating effectively. If a classroom is not operating effectively, the problem-solving team may become overwhelmed by a disproportionate number of referrals from that classroom. Furthermore, individual interventions will show limited effectiveness when effective classroom management practices are not consistently implemented. Students demonstrating challenging behaviors are more likely to misbehave in classrooms lacking the necessary behavioral structures.

This chapter provides steps for maximizing classroom time that students spend on tasks and receiving instruction.

FORMS TO BE INTRODUCED

Form 9.1: Classroom Observation Form
Form 9.2: Classroom Intervention Form

CRITICAL INFORMATION

This section provides a brief overview of common pitfalls made by educators in managing student behavior. A common error made by parents and teachers is not being clear about behavioral expectations. Too often, behavioral expectations are poorly described; as a result, children are uncertain about what behaviors are desired and expected. Offering children simple, clearly understandable operational descriptions of desired behavior is often a solution to more than half of the problem.

Consider the example of a supervisor at your job site. This supervisor routinely issues unclear directives. Unfortunately, the stated expectations for your professional position are murky at best. Occasionally, this supervisor will extend a favorable remark concerning your job performance, whereas on other days (truth be told, more frequently than not) this supervisor seems unreasonably controlling and demanding, asking that you justify your time and offering criticism for devoting time to tasks that he or she doesn't seem to see the relevance of or understand. Later, you are reprimanded for not completing a new form. When you explain that you had not heard about or seen the new form, your supervisor inquires why you seem to need extra assistance. This series of events would create a stressful situation for any of us. The same principle holds true for students. In some classes, the rules and expectations for behavior are more ambiguous than clear. Thus, students are forced to guess how loud they can talk, whether they were supposed to use cursive or print, or where they are expected to sit.

A second problem is relying on reactive disciplinary measures for eliciting changes in student behavior. Chapter 1 delineated many of the problems with punishment-based systems. Consider working with a supervisor whose chief method of direction involves providing feedback only after you make a mistake. In such a situation you might become resentful, act passive-aggressively, or become defiant. You may also become accustomed to the reprimands and begin negative internal dialogue such as "My supervisor needs mental help. He gets angry because I can't read his mind, and I have to wait for him to calm down before I can even talk to him." The same is true for students. When teachers acknowledge only student errors, they foster situations where students may begin ignoring or resenting the instructor (Nelson, 1985). Worse yet, many power struggles occur when teachers resort to reprimanding students or giving directives to students when misbehavior is occurring. Although some misbehaviors do require a response from the teacher, simply waiting for the misbehavior to occur before correcting the misdeed places a teacher in a difficult position.

Unscheduled idle time is another factor with the potential of contributing to student misbehavior. Students completing assignments early or ceasing their engagement on a presented task will typically seek means for occupying their minds and hands. Teachers not prepared for these possibilities will gain experience in dealing with problematic student behavior.

Finally, unnecessarily slow pacing is related to student misbehavior. Excessive transition times, extended attendance periods, or prolonged reprimanding allows added opportunities for students to engage in undesirable behavior.

COMMON INDICATORS OF EFFECTIVE CLASSROOM MANAGEMENT

Analyses of effective teaching practices have identified several characteristics of well-managed classrooms. Two important variables include the amount of time students are on task and the amount of time teachers spend delivering academic instruction (Stronge, Ward, Tucker, & Hindman, 2007). Classroom management is a means to an end, or a tool for helping teachers deliver academic instruction. During effective delivery of academic instruction, students are actively absorbing the knowledge transferred from the instructor. However, the definition of *delivering academic instruction* may differ among consumers. To minimize confusion, we define *providing instruction* as occurring when a teacher is working with a student or group of students on content related to the current curriculum. When a teacher is conducting class business such as collecting papers, grading papers, redirecting a student, or helping students work through a transition, he or she is not, by this definition, providing instruction. These behaviors are all important and necessary, because teachers fluently performing those tasks have more time for classroom instruction. Table 9.1 describes examples of behaviors considered related or unrelated to academic instruction.

2 impt. variables

INITIAL PROCEDURES

Identifying Classrooms in Need of Support

In the second month of the school year, a member of the problem-solving team, usually a behavioral expert with training on classroom observation, should complete a classroom observation form (COF) on every classroom in the building. (See Form 9.2, "Classroom Observation Form.")

If time is no object, members of a team should strive to collect two (or three when time allows) data points for each classroom over the course of a week or so. During the first few weeks

Table 9.1   Examples of Teacher Behaviors That Are Related and Not Related to Academic Instruction

Behaviors Related to Academic Instruction	Behaviors *Not* Related to Academic Instruction
Lecturing	Pausing a lecture to reprimand a student
Asking academic-related questions	Taking attendance
Checking students to assure they are making progress on group work	Conversing with another adult
Working with an individual student	Sending students to the office and completing relevant paperwork
Delivering individualized academic intervention	Teaching procedures or reminding students about procedures
	Collecting student papers

of class, a teacher often spends a great deal of time teaching expectations and procedures to students. Also, many students may temporarily demonstrate more compliant and less disruptive behavior early in the school year than would be typical for that child; this is often called a *honeymoon period*.

DIRECTIONS FOR COMPLETING CLASSROOM OBSERVATION FORM

When completing the COF, the evaluator observes teacher behaviors and the behaviors of three randomly selected students in the classroom. To complete the COF, a member of the problem-solving team serves as the observer and guarantees that the following conditions are met. Formal observation should begin once the students have settled down from any transitions:

1. Randomly select three students from different locations in the class, reflecting gender and ethnic differences when possible.
2. The observation begins with the observer focused on the teacher for 10 seconds. If the teacher delivers instruction for the entire 10 seconds, the observer should check the box. If the teacher is not delivering instruction for the duration of the 10 seconds, the observer should not check the box, but should leave it blank.
3. During the next 10-second interval, the observer shifts attention to the first student. If the student is on task for the entire 10-second period, the observer checks

the box, and if the student is not on task, the observer leaves the box blank. Steps 2 and 3 include the first 20-second portion of a one-minute interval.

4. The observer then observes the teacher again. If the teacher is delivering instruction for an entire 10-second period, the box is checked. If not, the box is left blank.

5. The observer then observes student 2. If the student is on task, the box is checked. If not, the box is left blank. The second 20-second interval has just been completed.

6. The observer then observes the teacher again. If the teacher is delivering instruction for an entire 10-second period, the box is checked. If not, the box is left blank.

7. The observer then observes student 3. If the student is on task, the box should is checked. If not, the box is left blank. The third 20-second interval has just been completed.

8. The observer then returns to step 2, and completes steps 2–7 until the 20-minute observation is completed.

The form provides the following information:

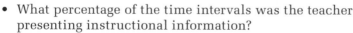

- What percentage of the time intervals was the teacher presenting instructional information?
- What percentage of the observed intervals was the student on task?

The problem-solving team gathers this information from every class in the building.

The following criteria help the problem-solving team identify classrooms likely to benefit from instructional support:

- If time on task is less than 50% of the intervals, the classroom will need intervention (Sprick, Knight, Reinke, & McKale, 2006).
- If a school has all classrooms with more than 50% of its students on task, consider supporting classrooms with less than 70% of on-task behavior.
- If more than 50% of classes have low rates of student on-task behavior, the problem-solving team addresses the issue on a schoolwide basis.

Table 9.2   Observations of Teachers and Classrooms

	SO 1	TO 1	SO 2	TO 2	SO 3	TO 3	Student Average	Teacher Average
Ms. White	50	54	48	40	68	61	55.3	51.7
Ms. Black	91	79	85	73	81	83	85.7	78.3
Mr. Red	31	39	47	53	41	49	39.7	47.0
Mr. Green	75	61	65	70	49	50	63.0	60.3
Ms. Blue	70	61	64	69	71	79	68.3	69.7
Ms. Yellow	40	53	71	74	65	55	58.7	60.7
Ms. Purple	81	71	82	71	84	78	82.3	73.3

Key: SO = student observation; percentage of time students were on task. TO = teacher observation; percentage of time the teacher was providing instruction.

For example, the following elementary school has seven teachers. The school psychologist gathered the data in Table 9.2 by conducting three observations of each classroom.

After reviewing the data, the team notices that Mr. Red is likely to benefit most from classroom support. The problem-solving team determines to also offer classroom support to Ms. White and Ms. Yellow.

INTERVENING WITH CLASSROOMS IN NEED

It is important to make clear that these procedures are designed to support rather than evaluate teachers. By clearly establishing that some teachers have a higher percentage of students with challenging behaviors, problem-solving teams will minimize teacher defensiveness. Second, problem-solving teams must understand that providing individualized direction in each classroom is time intensive, and whole-class interventions represent an investment in the staff and the school's students. Class-by-class analysis can lead to whole-class interventions effective for addressing and improving the behavior of many children. Additionally, there is evidence to suggest that this sort of classwide intervention may be effective in increasing the compliance of a single difficult student (Fairbanks, Simonsen, & Sugai, 2008). These environmental changes may remove triggers or antecedents to problematic behavior. Thus, it is reasonable to create individual plans containing whole-class solutions.

It is also important to discriminate whether frequent classroom referrals or frequent off-task behaviors result primarily from the behaviors of one or two students, or the behaviors of a broader group of students needing interventions. There are many occasions when one or two students significantly and frequently disrupt an entire classroom. If only a few students are the source of most of the ODRs, then those students should receive Tier II interventions as highlighted in Chapter 11. If a classroom needs additional support, several components should be considered. One member of the problem-solving team observes the classroom and completes the classroom intervention form (CIF). (See Form 9.1, "Classroom Intervention Form.")

The CIF enables an observer to determine to what extent a classroom has enacted the features described in Chapter 5. The problem-solving team may also determine whether the majority of the ODRs are for one student or for multiple students. If multiple students are the source of the difficulties, classwide interventions should begin.

PROCEDURES

- If the observer identifies an area for teacher improvement, that teacher and the observer create a goal to help the teacher better manage student behavior. For example, if the team obtains data indicating that praise is not consistently used in a classroom, the teacher's goal might read, "The teacher will administer four times as many praising statements as reprimands," and, "The teacher will find a way to recognize every student in the class."
- Within one week, the member of the problem-solving team should complete another COF to evaluate the effectiveness of the intervention.
- These observations and interventions continue weekly until 70% on-task behavior for students is achieved and the teacher is able to deliver instruction 70% of the time. If the classroom is already above 70%, the problem-solving team may set their own criteria for determining if a teacher would benefit from assistance.

ADDITIONAL INTERVENTIONS

Additional staff or schedule changes may provide relief for teachers with exceptionally difficult groups of students. Oftentimes, however, scheduling problems may prevent a teacher from receiving much-needed support from other adults. Thus, if a classroom continues to have multiple students demonstrating challenging behaviors, they may benefit from group contingency interventions such as the Good Behavior Game (Barrish, Saunders, & Wolf, 1969; and see Appendix B) and the Classroom Point System (Fabiano & Pelham, 2003; and see Appendix B).

Group Contingencies

Group contingencies are powerful means of eliciting desirable behaviors from groups of students and can support behavior plans for individual students (Hulac & Benson, 2010). However, they must be implemented with great care as improperly implemented group contingencies may actually harm students. There are three types of group contingencies: independent, dependent, and interdependent (Litow & Pumroy, 1975). Independent group contingencies require every student to meet the same criteria to receive a reward. However, the behavior of others in the group does not impact whether another student earns a reward. In a system of dependent group contingencies, if a few individuals meet certain criteria, the entire classroom gets a reward. For example, a teacher may decide to draw three names from a hat. If all three of those students have met certain behavioral criteria (i.e., have completed assignments), then the entire class earns a reward. In an interdependent group contingency, the entire group receives a reward if all group members perform some task. For example, if every member of the student body is able to avoid being suspended from school for a designated month, then the reward might be that the principal will kiss a pig (Skinner & Skinner, 1999). Because all the students enjoy the reward of the principal kissing a pig and every student met the established criterion, this is a good illustration of an interdependent group contingency.

An area of potential concern when using interdependent and dependent group contingencies is that one student, or a small group of students, may be subjected to intimidation by others in the classroom if the intervention is not closely monitored and one student's or the small group of students' behavior prevents others from receiving a reward. This negative peer attention may in some cases be detrimental and result in other than the hoped-for effects (Romeo, 1998). Thus, we offer considerations for implementing group contingencies:

(handwritten margin note: consideration for implementing group contingencies *)*

1. If students are aggressive with each other, most interdependent group contingencies should be stopped or temporarily suspended and replaced with social-skills training.
2. Never use a group contingency to provide punishment to members of a class.
3. Announce students' names when their behaviors have helped the class obtain a reward or reach a goal.
4. Avoid naming students whose behavior has prevented other students from earning a reward.

Good Behavior Game

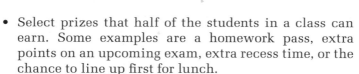

The Good Behavior Game (Barrish et al., 1969) is a method of helping students work closely together and reach behavioral goals. (See the coach card for this game in Appendix B.)

The steps include the following:

- Select prizes that half of the students in a class can earn. Some examples are a homework pass, extra points on an upcoming exam, extra recess time, or the chance to line up first for lunch.
- Establish rules.
  - The rules are observable and positively stated.
  - The teacher will post the rules.
- Divide the classroom in half with a visible mark.
- Place 10 tally marks on the board.
- When one team member breaks a rule, that team loses one tally mark.
- At the end of the class period, the team with the greatest number of points receives a prize. If both teams have more than six tally marks, the whole class may earn the prize.

These troubleshooting tips may be helpful: It may come to pass that one student is intentionally sabotaging his or her team. When this situation is suspected, that student should be the sole member of a third team. On rare occasions, classroom aggression has escalated in response to a game. If students approach or attempt verbal or physical abuse when trying to encourage other students to comply, the teacher should immediately and indefinitely pause the Good Behavior Game and use the experience as an opportunity to teach students about appropriate social interactions and norms. This opportunity should not be disregarded, as gaining mastery of societal expectation will likely benefit students as much as an academic lesson taught on any given day.

The Good Behavior Game is flexible insofar as the game's rules can easily be altered or modified to fit specific needs. Group contingency strategies can and should be utilized as a means of promoting desirable behavior. For example, by dividing a group into two halves, a teacher creates a command whereby she wants everybody's attention quickly. When she says, "Your attention, please," she waits and looks to see which half of the class is able to sit quietly and have their eyes looking directly at her. One group is awarded a point for following her command quicker. Soon, she begins whispering, "Your attention, please," which encourages students to remain quiet so that they may hear the command.

Classroom Points System

A classroom points system (Fabiano & Pelham, 2003; Fabiano et al., 2007) is a modification of an independent group contingency and a token economy. Through this system, every child begins with a certain number of points. Clear criteria are established for earning and losing points. At the end of a set time period, only those students with enough points earn a prize. The coach card (see Appendix B) describes a step-by-step process through which this points system can be established. However, it is important to note that this classroom points system does not replace other interventions and methods of good classroom management as described in Chapter 5.

CONCLUSION

One of the most common concerns voiced by teachers is managing classroom behavior. Some teachers feel defensive when observed. However, these recommendations are in the spirit of evaluation for support, and are by no means meant to be judgmental or used for any punitive or disciplinary action. Implementing these suggestions should provide meaningful results and help teachers effectively manage their classrooms.

10

Identifying Students for Tier II Interventions

INTRODUCTION

Schools that implement schoolwide preventative positive behavior systems (PBS) should encounter significantly fewer behavior problems than schools relying upon traditional discipline practices (Colvin, Kameenui, & Sugai, 1993; Horner, Sugai, Eber, Phillips, & Lewandowski, 2004; Taylor-Green & Kartub, 2000). True as this statement may be, even schools adhering closely to PBS guidelines (i.e., clear rules, well-taught procedures, and frequent opportunities for student success) will likely still have students who manifest behavioral difficulties (Anderson & Kincaid, 2005; Lewis-Palmer, Sugai, & Larson, 1999; Luiselli, Putnam, Handler, & Feinberg, 2005). By proactively identifying students demonstrating behavior problems or students who are at risk of becoming disruptive to the school environment, school personnel can intervene to reduce, minimize, or eliminate problems before they become difficult to manage. This chapter explores means that school problem-solving teams use to identify students most in need of support.

FORM TO BE INTRODUCED

Form 10.1: Tier II Student Questionnaire Form

INFORMATION NEEDED AT BEGINNING OF SCHOOL YEAR

- In the week before students come into school, the problem-solving team will gather a list of the students expelled the previous year.

- In the week before students come into school, the problem-solving team also needs a list of students sorted by number and kind of infractions.
- The data analyst sorts the data in rank order from most to least referrals.
- Each ODR needs to indicate the date, time, location, student's name, teacher's name, classroom number, and infraction committed.

CRITICAL INFORMATION

An expected constant in modern American schools is the continued presence of students who do not respond to typical primary behavioral prevention efforts. Every educator has encountered students who for one reason or another don't respond to popular first attempts at behavioral intervention. The first understandable reaction of many educators is frustration and confusion. These students often demonstrate their poor behavioral and social adjustment in even the best-run classrooms, causing disruption to other students' learning and consternation to even the most seasoned teachers. Tier II interventions are designed for these relatively few troubled and troublesome students.

The practice of operating a system to identify students for Tier II interventions should be thought of as having two discrete components. The first is identification of students who have an existing pattern of concerning behavior or students presently showing signs (e.g., absenteeism and declining grades) consistent with being at risk of developing social, emotional, or behavioral adjustment issues.

The second component is tracking the general student population to preemptively discover students who may have just begun to show signs consistent with risk of developing social, emotional, or behavioral problems. The difficulty of providing this sort of preventive intervention is the danger of false positives. The downside of responding to false positives is offering services and supportive intervention to students who may not need these services. That said, the net cost of failing to respond is greater than the cost of overresponding.

The science of preemptively identifying students in need of behavioral intervention continues to be in its infancy (Gresham, 2005). Thus, information provided in this manual, and any previous or current literature, is subject to modification as the professional research base evolves.

FINDING STUDENTS CURRENTLY IN NEED

Though it may sound strange, as an organization, your school may not have a mechanism in place to systematically identify and respond to students who are currently showing signs of trouble and of being at risk of developing behavioral health concerns. A good starting point in the process of identifying the students who may currently be in need of targeted Tier II intervention is to go to the data. By combing through the existing records, you and your team should be able to find the following:

- Students whose grade point averages are significantly below the median and those with the highest absence rates (Hallfors, Cho, Brodish, Flewelling, & Khatapoush, 2006).
- Students with a history of previous behavior problems—especially those suspended on multiple occasions or expelled the previous year.
- Students with multiple ODRs. As will be described later in more detail, it is important to understand how many ODRs are expected for each student. However, those students sent to the office more than twice per month are most likely demonstrating behavioral problems needing to be addressed before they worsen.

The advantages of using existing data about previous problem behavior, grade point averages, and absences are that these data are systematically tracked by most schools. The second advantage of employing these data is their strong positive relationship to future behavior problems (Hallfors et al., 2006). Despite the facts that each school is a unique setting and that all children are individuals, some data have proven to be universally suggestive of trouble brewing. For example, as referenced above, we know that students whose grade point average is chronically and significantly below the school mean are either currently behavioral concerns or at risk of becoming behavioral issues. It is also true that students whose grades take a sudden and precipitous decline are very likely to simultaneously experience a similar decline in social, emotional, or behavioral adjustment. These students must be systemically targeted for intervention—either academic, behavioral, or both.

use extant data!!

Chronically absent students should also be systemically targeted for intervention. At the elementary level, frequently absent students may have chronic illness, difficulty getting to school, or other family stressors. For secondary students, all of the above issues may be true, but school refusal and truancy are more frequent explanations of absenteeism.

Before we enter into a discussion of the next steps, let's take a moment to explore the second component of identifying students for Tier II intervention.

PREEMPTIVE IDENTIFICATION OF STUDENTS NEEDING TIER II INTERVENTION

The first step of preemptive identification of students needing Tier II intervention is tracking the general student population to discover students who may have just begun to show signs consistent with being at risk of developing social, emotional, or behavioral problems. This is done by consistently and closely reviewing ODRs. As mentioned in earlier discussions, ODRs must indicate the date, time, location, student's name, teacher's name, classroom number, and infraction committed. The frequency of ODRs is one method of targeting at-risk students. A common cutoff is to provide interventions for those students who have received at least two to five office discipline referrals over the course of a semester (Severson, Walker, Hope-Doolittle, Kratochwill, & Gresham, 2007; Walker, Cheney, Stage, & Blum, 2005). In addition to an examination of frequency of ODRs, looking for low-frequency, high-intensity infractions is a good method of identifying potentially at-risk students. Unfortunately, ODRs may miss many students who are at risk for developing future behavioral and emotional problems (Walker et al., 2005). Thus, additional means may help to supplement the information necessary to accurately identify those students whose behavior may become more problematic without early intervention. Severson et al. (2007) reviewed several possible tools that schools could use. These include the Systematic Screen for Behavioral Disorders (Walker & Severson, 1992). This is a multiple-tier assessment that includes a teacher nomination procedure, a critical events checklist, and, for those students who do not respond to early interventions, a systematic method of observing classroom and playground behavior. Currently, the screener is only designed for students who are in kindergarten to sixth grade. This measure is perhaps the most popular of its kind. Other measures include the Student Risk Screening Scale (SRRS; Drummond, 1993), the Revised Behavior Problem Checklist, the Eyberg Child Behavior Inventory, and the Brief Academic Competence Evaluation Scales System (BACESS; Elliott, Huai, & Roach, 2007). Finally, a school problem-solving team should never turn down a teacher's request for support in managing the behavior of a particular student or group of students.

So now you have assembled your first list of students who will be considered for Tier II services.... What now?

INITIAL PROCEDURES

- Formally invite the parents of the previously expelled students to the next meeting of the problem-solving team to discuss intervention possibilities.
- Identify the top 10–15% of students who received the most ODRs.
- Identify those students who are most frequently absent, and whose grade point averages fall below the school's mean.
- Formally invite the parents of the students who received the most ODRs to the next meeting of the problem-solving team to discuss intervention possibilities.
- Identify students with histories of high-intensity aggressive behavior such as fighting or assaults.
- These students should automatically be considered for Tier II interventions with parent approval.

PEOPLE NEEDED AT BEGINNING OF SCHOOL YEAR

- Members of the problem-solving team
- Parents

INFORMATION NEEDED

The problem-solving team needs a list of students receiving ODRs ranked by the number of ODRs each student received in the previous month.

SECONDARY PROCEDURES

- Identify those students who received four or more office discipline referrals in a month.

- Continue to acquire names of students who may be demonstrating conduct problems in the classroom or in other parts of the school. Of course, if a teacher nominates multiple students from one class (three or more can serve as a general rule of thumb), it may be worthwhile conducting a classwide intervention (see Chapter 9) to help increase the amount of structure and support that teachers can give to students.

Once a student has been identified:

- That student's teacher must fill out Form 10.1 the Tier II student questionnaire that is located in Appendix A.
- The problem-solving team reviews the student's discipline referrals to determine the behavior of concern.
- Once the problem-solving team is considering implementing an intervention for a student, the team *must* invite the student's parents or guardians to the next meeting of the problem-solving team.

CONCLUSION

By following the guidelines stated in this brief but important chapter, school problem-solving teams will be able to consistently and proactively take notice when students are having difficulties getting along well in the school system. Chapter 11 will discuss the data collection procedures and describe the interventions that these Tier II–identified students must receive.

11

Providing Interventions
for Students in Tier II

INTRODUCTION

The problem-solving team plays a critical role in recommending appropriate, empirically validated interventions and assuring those interventions are implemented with integrity. After identifying "at-risk" students (by *at risk*, we mean students needing additional support to overcome potential behavior difficulties), empirically supported treatments are selected, customized, and implemented, and student response is measured.

Because well-validated interventions are selectively applied and these strategies are individually tailored, most students respond by demonstrating behavioral improvements. These empirically supported Tier II interventions are only effective when the selected intervention plan is implemented consistently and with integrity. Because the issue of intervention integrity is so essential to the success of effecting behavioral change, the treatments here presented have been determined to have high levels of social validity.

An idea is socially valid when the people recommending and implementing the intervention understand and value the selected techniques (Winett, Moore, & Anderson, 1991). By ensuring that the teachers and school staff responsible for intervention integrity have both an interest in the success of the treatment efforts and a feeling of ownership and involvement in the process of treatment selection, the likelihood of the intervention being put into place correctly and consistently increases exponentially.

Of course, no intervention can elicit the degree of desired responses in every case. In these rare situations, a functional   f BㅏA behavior assessment (FBA) will be the next step. FBA helps to match more intensive intervention efforts to specific student needs by focusing upon the causes or functions for the student of the disruptive, maladaptive, or inappropriate behavior. Though FBA is the gold standard of assessment for behavioral intervention, conducting a complete FBA requires a great deal of time and resources (Ingram, Lewis-Palmer, & Sugai, 2005). The extreme time and resource commitment demanded by an FBA process dictates that only those children who do not respond to the individualized but standard sort of interventions that comprise Tier II are selected to receive comprehensive FBA.

These standard Tier II interventions are generic but may be adapted to address individual student needs. Though these Tier II interventions are always tailored to the students' presenting difficulties, Tier II is different in kind from Tier III interventions, which are most often created from the ground up to address a specifically identified behavioral function. Despite the fact that Tier II interventions are always slightly adjusted variations of a theme (i.e., a home school report card, and check-in and check-out), these treatments should have empirical evidence supporting their effectiveness in improving the challenging behavior of many students. To recap, the Tier II interventions offered below, when implemented with integrity, will in most circumstances positively influence the student–environment interaction.

CONCEPTS TO BE INTRODUCED

- Corrective teaching sequence (CTS)
- Effective instruction delivery (EID)
- Self-monitoring
- Behavioral contracting
- Daily behavior report card (DBRC)
- Check-in and check-out (CICO)

FORMS TO BE INTRODUCED

Form 10.1: Tier II Student Questionnaire Form (see Appendix A)

Form 11.1: Self-Monitoring Form

Form 11.2: Behavioral Contract Form

Form 11.3: Tier II Integrity Checklist

Form 11.4: Daily Behavior Report Card (Younger Students)

Form 11.5: Daily Behavior Report Card (Older Students)

Form 11.6: Intervention Tracking Form

PROCEDURES

Identifying Needs of a Student

The following procedures identify behaviors targeted for intervention.

1. Identify student needs and create goals.
2. The student's teacher, the teacher who refers the child to the problem-solving team, or the teacher most frequently referring the student to the office for discipline concerns completes the Tier II teacher questionnaire.
3. The team reviews the student's academic abilities. If the student has academic difficulties, intensive instruction must begin at the student's academic level to remediate academic deficiencies.
4. The problem-solving team will do the following:
   - Review the student's referrals.
   - Record the number of referrals.
   - Record the time of the referrals.
   - Record the behaviors resulting in office referral.
5. Members of the problem-solving team write *student behavioral contracts* with a maximum of three goals. Each goal will do the following:
   - Address behavioral concerns.
   - State behaviors positively.
   - Be observable.
   - Identify behaviors that are incompatible with the problem behavior.
   - Create a behavioral contract.
   - Create a self-monitoring form.
6. Communicate the interventions to the student's teachers.
   - Train the teacher to mastery on the effective instruction delivery (EID) system.
   - Teach the teacher, to mastery, the corrective teaching sequence (CTS).

TIER II INTERVENTIONS

Behavioral Contract Procedure

Behavioral contracts have proven to be an effective means of improving student behaviors for several decades. Contracting has helped improve behaviors of adolescents (Kelley & Stokes, 1982), elementary school students with disruptive behaviors

(De Martini-Scully, Bray, & Kehle, 2000), and students receiving special education services (Ruth, 1996). Behavioral contracts provide educators the opportunity to teach alternative, replacement behaviors that increase the likelihood of student success (e.g. Allen, Howard, Sweeney, & McLaughlin, 1993; Kelley & Stokes).

The problem-solving team and student guardians should work collaboratively to develop a behavior contract. Information from the ODRs and the Tier II teacher questionnaire aid in selecting undesirable behaviors to target for replacement; an important idea to note is that one of the most effective methods of effecting behavioral change is by reinforcing a desired behavior that is incompatible with the target undesirable behavior. A reason why this technique works so well is because often the targeted undesirable behavior will occur at a low or very low frequency. Low-frequency behaviors like physical aggression can be disruptive and destructive despite their infrequency; by focusing upon the reinforcement of an incompatible desired behavior, the intervention team (often the teacher) is presented with frequent opportunities to offer positive feedback, thus increasing the power of the intervention.

Another good idea is to design the contract to reflect positively stated goals and objectives. This practice is basically the same practice as described in Chapter 5 related to the establishment of classroom rules. The team writes positively stated student goals in response to the identified problematic behaviors. Observable and measurable positive behaviors are emphasized as behavioral goals. This practice helps increase agreement regarding student compliance by describing behavioral definitions in detail. Rather than target a reduction in talking out of turn, set speaking when called upon as the goal. Not only does the team strive to offer positively stated goals but also the contract must be carefully crafted so as to provide operationally clear definitions of the target behaviors, and use age-appropriate terminology. These contacts are most effective when the student can feel some buy-in and ownership over his or her own progress. School personnel should ensure that the student can feel some connection to the process, and every student should be able to read and understand his or her own behavioral contract.

❥ *Incompatible behaviors.* As briefly described above, whenever possible, assure the student's goals are incompatible with the problem behavior. For example, if a child is talking out of turn in class, a goal may read, "Prior to talking in class, Chris will raise his hand and wait for the teacher to call upon him."

- *Creating a student incentive.* A clear and definitive statement must be included as part of the behavioral contract indicating the minimum conditions under which the student will earn a reward. The reward system may include points, stickers, or any token that is a signifier of the student showing an adequate frequency of appropriate behaviors. For example, a contract may state, "Jim will earn a positive behavior token each time he arrives at school on time." Positive behavior tokens are an established component of existing schoolwide positive behavior support programming. Remember, if the incentive is not sufficiently rewarding for the student, the behavior plan will be ineffective.

- *Bonus clauses.* Bonus clauses can provide additional incentives for student compliance with the contract. A bonus clause offers a "reward" for consistently reaching behavioral goals. For example, if Keith earns a bonus point each day, Monday through Friday, he will earn an additional positive behavior token (Wright, 2000). Note that parents, as compared to schools, are often able to deliver more enriching rewards. When a student meets bonus clause requirements, parents reward them (e.g., pizza, a baseball game, or a trip to an amusement park).

- *Signatures.* The behavior contract includes spaces for both teacher and student signatures, as a sign that both parties agree to adhere to their responsibilities in the contract. Additionally, the instructor may want to include signature blocks for other staff members (e.g., school administrator) and/or the student's guardians.

Behavioral Contract (Sample)

Student name: _____
Teacher name: _____
Date of contract: _____

When Jayden gets into line, he will walk with his hands at his side, or will keep his hands behind his back until he arrives at his destination. Every time Jayden does this successfully, he will earn one positive behavior token from the teacher.

Bonus clause: If Jayden is able to go an entire week without an office referral, Jayden will be allowed to call his parents and tell them about his good week.
Signatures:

_____

Student

_____   Parent

_____

Teacher

_____

Other   Principal

_____

Other

Procedures for the Self-Monitoring Process

Self-monitoring strategies have proven effective at helping students gain awareness of their presenting behaviors. Elementary school students with attention deficit/hyperactivity disorder (ADHD) and oppositional defiant disorder (ODD) (Hoff & DuPaul, 1998), as well as those with serious emotional disabilities (Dunlap, Clarke, Jackson, & Wright, 1995), have benefited from self-monitoring in improving their behaviors. Miller, Miller, Wheeler, and Selinger (1989) demonstrated effective implementation of self-monitoring procedures with adolescents, and Mooney, Ryan, Uhing, Reid, and Epstein (2005) were able to improve student academic outcomes through self-monitoring.

Loftin, Gibb, and Skiba (2005) provided an effective outline for creating self-monitoring strategies. The five steps include the following:

- Identifying a target behavior
- Selecting the self-monitoring data collection system
- Choosing reinforcers and criteria for student success
- Teaching the student to use the system
- Fading prompts and reinforcers

Identify target behavior. The members of the problem-solving team should identify the target behavior (DuPaul, Stoner, & O'Reilly, 2008). The next step is similar to the procedure described above. The team must work to establish a well-defined, easy-to-understand, observable, and positively stated incompatible replacement behavior to substitute for the existing problem behaviors. A sample goal for a student verbally disrupting class upon his arrival might read, "John will enter the classroom, hang up his backpack, walk to his desk, and sit quietly." We have provided Forms 11.1, 11.2, and 11.3 in appendix A to aid in goal writing.

2. *Select self-monitoring system.* Methods of self-monitoring include a wide array of techniques spanning from the simplistic use of tally marks on paper to the use of more sophisticated commercially purchased computer-based monitoring systems. Self-monitoring forms should be appropriate for the student's age. For instance, K–2 student forms may have three faces (smile, neutral, and frown) printed on them to represent whether the student felt that he or she met the goals or came close to meeting them during the self-monitoring period. Older students may use more sophisticated forms. The problem-solving team should help identify a system that will be easiest for the child to employ.

3. *Reinforcer selection.* A reinforcer increases the probability of a behavior occurring. The more a child values the reinforcer, the more effective the intervention will be at modifying behavior. Common incentives include allowing the student to earn extra computer time, extra recess, and supplemental PBS tokens. See Chapter 3 for a more comprehensive explanation identifying effective rewards systems.

4. *Teach the student to use the system.* The teacher, a member of the problem-solving team, and the student will review the self-monitoring procedure together (DuPaul et al., 2008). Concerns and potential conflicts must be resolved before initiating self-monitoring practices. The student will track his or her behavior independently after establishing inner-observer reliability with the teacher on 2 consecutive days.

5. *Fade prompts and reinforcers.* Once the student demonstrates the ability to successfully and routinely exhibit appropriate behaviors, the problem-solving team addresses a new behavior or terminates the current intervention.

Example of Self-Monitoring Intervention

The problem-solving team identifies Rachel as "at risk" after she receives multiple ODRs for noncompliance.

- The problem-solving team develops a goal: Rachel will comply with teacher-administered class and individual directives.
- Rachel will place a tally mark on her sheet when she complies with a teacher directive. The teacher, with Rachel, compares aggregated tallies at the closure of the school day.
- On day 1, the teacher records 25 instances of compliance by Rachel, and Rachel records 40 instances of compliance. The teacher and Rachel identify causes for the large discrepancy.
- On day 2, Rachel records compliance with 33 teacher directives, and her teacher records compliance with 35 teacher directives.
- On day 3, the teacher and Rachel again report compliance scores in close proximity.
- On day 5, only Rachel records and reports compliance data. Rachel receives additional verbal praise after following directions 10 different times. Rachel receives a positive behavior token each day that she remains in class without an office referral.
- Rachel earns an hour playing basketball with her father when she completes a week without an office referral.
- The problem-solving team along with the teacher reviews Rachel's progress and decides to initiate a fading program after Rachel successfully meets her goals for 2 consecutive weeks.

Procedures for Corrective Teaching Sequence

The corrective teaching sequence (CTS: University of Southern Mississippi, 2007) is best utilized when the student's behavior disrupts the flow of instruction. When correcting students, the teacher provides immediate feedback in a manner that is minimally disruptive to instruction. Use the following CTS when correcting a student exhibiting inappropriate behavior.

1. Describe the inappropriate behavior.
   A. Be specific—do not force the student to interpret the meaning of your message.

2. Describe or demonstrate appropriate behaviors.
    A. Choose an appropriate alternative behavior, response, or skill.
    B. Clearly provide the student with alternative behaviors appropriate for similar incidences that are likely to occur in the future. This allows students to better understand how to engage their environment in the future.
    C. The goal is to teach the *replacement* behavior.
    D. Give a rationale for using the alternative behavior.
3. Point out the benefits, from *their* perspective, of using the skill.
    A. Help the student understand the relationship between the target misbehavior and its subsequent consequence. Offering reasons and rationales will increase compliance with new behaviors.
4. Ask the student for a verbal response.
    A. Throughout the process, inquire whether the student comprehends: "Do you understand?" or "Please repeat to me what I said."
    B. Require verbal confirmation and verbal summary by the student. Allow the student to participate.
5. Practice the alternative skill.
    A. Practicing the alternative skill begins a pattern of replacing the inappropriate behavior with the newer, appropriate skill.
    B. Recreate the situation when the student failed to earn points.
    C. Practice the skill as often as needed, but at least twice.
6. Use praise throughout the process. The formation and delivery of the praise are important. The praise must
    A. Be descriptive in nature.
    B. Be delivered in close proximity.
    C. Use the student's name.
    D. Be delivered without sarcasm.
7. Be specific when giving rewards, and tell the student exactly why he or she earned the rewards.

Example of Corrective Teaching Sequence (CTS)

Students in Ms. Red's second-grade class are engaged in small-group learning when she sees Steve throwing a pencil across the room. Ms. Red addresses the violation using CTS.

- Ms. Red walks to within arm's reach of Steve and bends down to allow closer face-to-face contact.
- "Steve, you broke the 'be safe' rule by throwing a pencil across the room."
- Ms. Red provides a consequence (e.g., timeout): "You must now sit in timeout quietly for 2 minutes" (offering a duration of the punishment increases the likelihood of compliance).
- When Steve has successfully entered timeout and remained quiet and still, he receives permission to return to his desk.
- Ms. Red walks to within arm's reach of Steve and physically lowers her body to allow for eye contact at the same level. She describes an alternative, appropriate behavior. "Steve, one way to be safe in the classroom is to hold your pencil properly and control its movements." Ms. Red demonstrates the proper technique for holding a pencil.
- Ms. Red provides a rationale for using the alternative behavior. "If we hold our pencil properly and use it only for its intended purpose, we can complete our work in less time and move on to other activities. It also helps us keep our friends safe by assuring that a pencil doesn't hit them in the eye."
- Ms. Red asks if Steve understands, and may have him repeat the rationale using his own words.
- Steve engages in overcorrection by demonstrating two or more times that he can hold a pencil properly and engage in safe classroom behavior.

Procedures for Daily Behavior Report Card

Often, a problem-solving team decides to implement additional interventions to provide support for students who are demonstrating behavioral difficulties. These procedures are more labor intensive, but may be extremely effective at helping provide students with behavior supports prior to implementing a functional behavior assessment and a highly individualized behavior plan.

A behavior report card is an efficient way for a teacher to provide feedback about a student's behavior at the end of an instructional period. The behavior report card is merely a sheet of paper with the student's behavioral goals written down and space for teacher endorsements of progress toward the stated goals.

how it works

Students with report cards (see "Sample Student Report Card," below) carry the report cards from class to class. After a certain time interval, the teacher is able to score the child on different behavioral goals. At the end of the day, a designated adult helps the student add up the number of points he or she received and provides the child a reward based on the child's performance.

Teachers frequently use the daily behavior report card (DBRC) in a wide variety of settings to help manage a broad range of behaviors (Chafouleas, Riley-Tillman, & Sassu, 2006). The popularity of the DBRC may be due to its flexibility and ease of use, and because it allows teacher an additional means to communicate behavior problems and successes with students and parents (Chafouleas, Riley-Tillman, & McDougal, 2002). Teachers have reported that it is more effective when used to provide positive reinforcements for positive behaviors rather than as a means of providing punishment for negative behaviors (Chafouleas et al., 2006).

The DBRC is most appropriate for use with behaviors that are not immediately dangerous, but instead occur frequently (more than once per day) and are more disruptive than dangerous (Chafouleas et al., 2002). Second, DBRCs will be most useful if the child is able to understand the feedback. In middle schools, a child may have to carry a piece of paper from classroom to classroom. A child who is incapable of such a behavior would not find success with a DBRC.

Process

process

- Define the problem behavior: See the section earlier in the chapter.
- Create goals: See the section earlier in the chapter.
- Create time intervals: How frequently should the child receive feedback? *Note*: Children who are younger or who are more impulsive will need feedback more frequently than will older and less impulsive children.
- Determine who will provide the child with a copy of the report card at the beginning of the day, and who will review the report card at the end of the day.
- Train student and teacher how to perform the intervention.
- Determine criteria for success.
- What must the child do to earn a reward?
- Should there be ways to determine if the child has been successful for an extended period?
- Determine rewards.
- What should the child receive for being successful?

Examples of Report Card Goals

- I will be respectful to adults.
- I will listen to adults without talking while they're talking.
- I will do what the teacher asks me to do right away (I will say "yes" or "okay" before asking questions or raising my hand).
- I will use a nice voice when talking to adults.
- I will follow my plan for dealing with my anger.
- I will tell my feelings and wants with "I statements" ("I feel … when … because … I would like …").

Complete Work

- I will begin doing my work when told.
- I will finish all classwork as given.
- I will focus on my own work until I finish it.
- I will ignore what my classmates are doing.
- I will ask for help when I need it.
- I will ask for any supplies I need to finish my work.
- While at P.E., I will do my exercise and play the game.
- I will be safe and responsible.
- I will speak nicely to my classmates and teachers.
- I will use words when I am upset or angry instead of acting out.
- I will stay in or near my seat.
- I will count forward and backward to 10 before answering when I feel upset or angry.

Procedures for Check-In and Check-Out

Frequently, behavior report cards are part of a larger check-in and check-out (CICO) system. The check-in and check-out system is more involved than a daily report card because a coordinator is involved rather than a classroom teacher. Using a check-in and check-out program that includes a daily behavior report card in conjunction with daily social-skills training is called the *behavior education program* (BEP; Crone, Horner, & Hawken, 2004); schools were able to improve the behavior of middle school students (Hawken, 2006) and elementary school students (Hawken, MacLeod, & Rawlins, 2007; Todd, Campbell, & Meyer, 2008) with this combined and integrated intervention plan. This system is a positive behavioral support for students who demonstrate moderate to severe behavior problems. This system is effective in large part because it provides frequent reinforcement for compliance with specific behavioral goals.

The classroom teacher with support from the problem-solving team sets the goals in clear, behavioral terms. The CICO coordinator is to meet twice daily with the student to individually provide social-skills training related to each of the designated behavioral goals. As discussed above, the student will review the goals each morning with the CICO coordinator in order to completely understand the established behavioral expectations and each of the goals. The CICO coordinator also has the opportunity to provide social-skills training or other needed supports for students who may be having difficulty understanding classroom expectations.

hav it works

Step 1: Daily Check-In

A student who is participating in CICO should meet with the CICO coordinator at the beginning of the school day. This staff person checks in with the student to help make sure that the student is ready for the beginning of the day.

- The CICO coordinator reiterates school rules.
- The CICO coordinator gives the child a daily behavior report card.
- The CICO coordinator asks if each child has all of the materials he or she needs for class.
- The CICO coordinator can provide a social-skills training lesson to students to make sure they understand the expectations or address necessary problems that arise.

Step 2: Daily Check-Out

- Students will check out with the CICO coordinator at the conclusion of the school day.
- The CICO coordinator collects daily report cards from students.
- The CICO coordinator provides tangible rewards or access to preferred activities to students reaching daily goals.
- The CICO coordinator determines if the student has all of the materials needed to do homework during the evening.
- The CICO coordinator enters the daily report card data into a spreadsheet.

EXAMPLE OF A MIDDLE SCHOOL
CHECK-IN AND CHECK-OUT SYSTEM

The problem-solving team identified the school counselor, Ms. Beige, to be the CICO coordinator. If Ms. Beige was to be unavailable, Ms. Magenta, the school psychologist, would back her up. Ms. White would provide a third backup, because Ms. White did not have a class in her room at the start of the school day. Because Ms. White's classroom was available during the homeroom period, the CICO students and the CICO coordinator gathered there to prepare for the day. At the end of the day, the students would meet in the empty lunchroom.

The problem-solving team agreed to use the template of the daily behavior report card included in this chapter. Goals were positively stated and written such that they were incompatible with identified problematic behaviors. The problem-solving team created a reinforcement system whereby each student earned points (tokens). A perfect score on a report card earned the student 20 points. By meeting any single goal, students were able to earn 5 points for each achieved goal. Initially, some students were not checking out at the end of the day because they did not have all of their points. When students returned their report card and came to both the beginning and the end of the day, they were able to earn 3 additional points. The students exchanged these points for a variety of rewards, or the awarded points could be used at the PBS store.

At the start of each day, the CICO students came 5 minutes before the bell rang to Ms. Beige's room. Ms. Beige greeted the students at the door and asked them how their day was going. Frequently, students would complain about being hungry because they did not have their breakfast. With parent permission and with help from the school principal, the CICO coordinator was able to provide students with some breakfast foods (breakfast bars). Ms. Beige also checked to see if students had their necessary school supplies, and reminded them about the school rules.

When the day ended, all of the students gathered in the cafeteria 5 minutes prior to the dismissal bell. During this time, Ms. Beige made sure that all children wrote their homework assignments in a calendar and made sure they had the proper materials. Students received points to cash in for prizes from the prize menu. The most popular prize was a chance to miss one class a month to play basketball with the gym teacher.

If a student met his or her goal for a period of 2 weeks, he or she earned the chance to graduate from the check-in and check-out program. Both the teacher and the student received a copy of the DBRC. If the student and the teacher's scores were different, the CICO coordinator helped the student understand the discrepancy. If the child continued to be successful for another week, he or she earned a final goodbye party, and graduated from the CICO program with behavioral contracts, the corrective teaching sequence, self-monitoring, and effective instruction delivery still in place.

SECONDARY PROCEDURE

Integrity Checks

A crucial variable heavily influencing the effectiveness of interventions is integrity or fidelity to the intervention. Stated differently, it is the compliance or degree of compliance to a specific intervention. Regardless of the quantity of research proclaiming the strength of an intervention, the probability of replicating research outcomes diminishes when procedures are not followed or when they are deviated from to a meaningful degree.

Members of the problem-solving team should complete integrity checks throughout the intervention process, but especially and with greater frequency when a student is failing to respond to a Tier II intervention. When an intervention fails to elicit the desired outcome or the desired degree of improvement, school personnel should review the integrity of the intervention prior to changing the intervention (Witt, VanDerHeyden, & Gilbertson, 2004). As a school begins to implement interventions, it can expect many mistakes, and integrity checks will be essential as a school works to perfect its problem-solving process.

Several real-life illustrations will aid in demonstrating why integrity checks play a vital role in assessing intervention effectiveness. The first example involves a school district with behavior programs established at several schools throughout the district. One school in particular was consistently reporting the failure of empirically validated behavioral interventions to remediate student behaviors. Consultants conducted informal observations and met with the school's staff members regarding the staff's concerns about implementation of behavioral interventions. These concerns voiced by the staff were reflected in the consultants' notes indicating that key interventions were not being implemented, whereas others appeared to lack integrity and fidelity. Interventions strategies were retaught, and an integrity checklist was distributed to the staff responsible for establishing and maintaining the selected interventions. The consultants established an agreement with the school administration and staff that random checks would be conducted the following week. Subsequently, the checks were conducted and staff compliance was recorded at less than 40% on each of two observations.

A follow-up meeting was held to discuss the results. Surprisingly, the class staff readily and correctly recited intervention steps. It was agreed that additional unannounced integrity checks should be conducted. Compliance remained low, and staff supervisors were eventually brought in to help overcome the compliance challenge. With the additional assistance of building administrative staff that offered incentives (gift cards) to staff for demonstrating commitment to intervention integrity, the culture started to shift and the fidelity of interventions began to improve as assessed by the continued compliance checks. Over the course of the next several weeks, students' scores began and continued to rise, with students' behaviors reported as much improved by class staff.

In an intervention team meeting held 6 weeks later, the consultants reported that their observations of students' behaviors reflected a significant reduction in behavioral disturbances and ODRs were down schoolwide. Teachers and school staff reflected that initially a substantial skepticism and resentment of the extra effort involved in establishing the interventions was a substantial barrier to staff compliance. Two factors were recounted as being instrumental to adjusting the trajectory of the intervention efforts: first, encouraging teacher and staff buy-in by offering rewards for becoming involved; and, second, the effectiveness of the behavioral interventions was described as being an incentive for the teachers to continue.

Not all instances of noncompliance or low compliance are acts of willful neglect. Often, performance feedback on low intervention integrity allows educators to pinpoint the areas in which they need to pay particular attention and thereby help students meet their goals. During a recent intervention integrity observation, it was noted that rather than providing hourly feedback on student behavior, the teacher was keeping the behavior sheet on her desk and returning it to the student at the end of the day. Without the frequent feedback built into the intervention, the student's behaviors were not improving.

A consultant working with the teacher included a review of integrity observations and discussion on how to follow more closely the intervention design. The following day the teacher instructed the student to maintain possession of his behavior point sheet while she, without interrupting the lesson, quietly passed by his desk each subject period and wrote a score in the appropriate box. With no other modifications to the intervention, the student's behaviors began improving and scores, both behaviorally and academically, began to rise. ODRs were still made, but were reduced for this student from an average of one every 3 school days to one every 14 school days. The intervention was proven effective at significantly improving classroom behavior. When effects appeared to plateau, a supplemental intervention was added to the initial intervention to continue reducing the problem behaviors. Upon successful implementation of both interventions, the referring problem behaviors were replaced with socially acceptable behaviors and a fading procedure implemented.

DETERMINING INTERVENTION EFFECTIVENESS

Review the number of ODRs weekly. Also review the permanent products created by the intervention—especially self-monitoring form data and behavioral report card data. Form 11.6, the "Intervention Tracking Form," provides an outline for tracking and evaluating the effectiveness of interventions.

Form 11.3 in Appendix A includes a sample of how the form may be used by school personnel.

- If a student is receiving more than one ODR during the course of one week, the child refuses to follow the intervention, or data from the self-monitoring form or daily behavior report card do not change, a member of the problem-solving team should complete a Tier II integrity checklist.

- If a teacher is expressing concern that the intervention is ineffective, a member of the problem-solving team should complete a Tier II integrity checklist.
- The teacher and the problem-solving team should use the goals described by the intervention checklist to develop a plan to help improve student behavior. The problem-solving team should review and correct any errors in the intervention.

- The team should continue to review the number of ODRs the student receives.
- The least desired option, if used at all (and not recommended), is a self-report integrity checklist.
- Tier II intervention integrity checklists continue as needed until the intervention runs as designed.
- If the teacher, with help from the problem-solving team, is implementing the intervention with integrity and the student continues receiving more than one ODR per week, the problem-solving team should look to further individualize the student's intervention, or consider a referral for a functional behavior assessment. At the very least, the team should consider implementing the check-in and check-out intervention to ensure that students are closely monitored.

CONCLUSION

This chapter addressed two important responsibilities of the problem-solving team, intervention selection and integrity and fidelity assurance. Easy-to-use, research-based intervention procedures effective at managing a spectrum of behavior problems were offered and recommended for consideration. The behaviors of many students will improve when these interventions are implemented with consistency, integrity, and fidelity. However, more intractable cases are certain to exist. That is, a small percentage of students will continue to have behavioral difficulties despite staff adherence to the interventions. The next chapter helps in objectively identifying students not responding to these robust interventions.

12

Understanding the Function of Behavior

INTRODUCTION

When Tier I and II interventions are unsuccessful at remediating problematic behaviors, more intensive, individualized interventions are required. This chapter describes techniques used to hypothesize reasons for serious behavior problems. Behavioral experts spend years learning and mastering functional behavioral assessment (FBA) and functional behavioral analysis (FBAn). It is not within the scope of this chapter to provide comprehensive instruction on FBA or FBAn. Rather, the intent is to provide a broad overview of FBA to an educational community that has not benefited from intensive training on behavioral theory, research, assessment, and modification. We begin with the premise that FBA is a means of gathering information related to the environment, antecedents, and consequences that cause or permit a problem behavior (Drasgow, Yell, Bradley, & Shiner, 1999; Gresham, Watson, & Skinner, 2001).

CONCEPTS TO BE INTRODUCED

- Functional behavioral assessment (FBA)
- Indirect and direct assessment methods
- Positive reinforcement
- Negative reinforcement
- Functional behavioral analysis (FBAn)

LINKS TO PREVIOUS DISCUSSIONS

Previous chapters delineated means for identifying students needing individualized interventions. This chapter details procedural necessities for FBA implementation. Conducting meaningful FBAs is time intensive and reserved for students for whom Tier II interventions were not effective, or whose behaviors are of a severity that they require immediate intensive attention. The FBA determines the function, or purpose, of a behavior and the interventions most likely to elicit prosocial behaviors from the target student.

FORMS TO BE INTRODUCED

Form 12.1: Target Peer Comparison Form for a Functional Behavioral Assessment (FBA)

Form 12.2: Conditional Probability Form

Form 12.3: Functional Behavior Assessment Form—Teacher Interview

Form 12.4: Antecedent–Behavior–Consequence (Narrative Version)

Form 12.5: Antecedent–Behavior–Consequence (Checklist Version)

MATERIALS NEEDED

Cumulative file
Previous records of interventions
Office discipline referrals
Academic data

PEOPLE NEEDED

- Student's teacher
- Student
- Student's parent or guardian
- Other informants who are knowledgeable about the student (e.g., bus driver, cafeteria worker, and people from the community)

INFORMATION NEEDED: UNDERSTANDING FBA

FBA information analyzes the reasons behind a student's specific problem behaviors. Within this analysis, pattern identification suggests the function of the problem behavior. To identify these patterns, FBAs generally approach problem behavior by analyzing a three-term relationship: antecedent, behavior, and consequence (A-B-C).

Example of an A-B-C relationship:

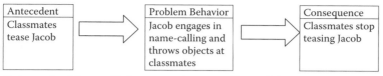

Outcome: Jacob is more likely to engage in name-calling and throwing objects when classmates tease him.

Figure 12.1 This chart demonstrates the A (antecedent), B (behavior), C (consequences) relationship.

Antecedents are precipitating events (e.g., person, time of day, place, or demand or request) occurring prior to the behavior of interest. A "triggering" antecedent typically occurs immediately before the behavior. "A"

Target behaviors are the observable and measurable inappropriate behaviors of interest that need to be suppressed, and the appropriate behaviors that should increase. "B"

Consequences are events (e.g., social, tangible, activity, and sensory stimulation) following the student's target behavior that increase or decrease the likelihood of the behavior occurring. (See Figure 12.1.) "C"

After examining the behavior chain, the problem-solving team concluded that an appropriate intervention would entail teaching Jacob to ignore, walk away, and/or tell an adult when classmates tease him. In other words, the desirable behaviors will produce the same result as the problem behavior but without the additional negative consequences (e.g., being sent to the office, or injuring others). Once Jacob learned to ignore classmates and get adult assistance, the classmates stopped teasing him. To ensure that Jacob was motivated to acquire the skill and fluently assimilate it as a means of getting his classmates to stop teasing him, the teacher rewarded Jacob when he exhibited the desirable behavior and admonished the offending students, thus further reducing the likelihood of teasing, name calling, and throwing projectiles within the classroom. (See Figure 12.2.)

Antecedents

As stated previously, antecedents are events or conditions that occur before the student behaves inappropriately, and they often serve as triggers. A particular set of questions, answered through interviews and observations, helps to identify trigger-ing antecedents. The questions are as follows:

*helpful
?s*

- When does the problem behavior usually occur?
- Where does the problem behavior usually occur?
- Who is present when the problem behavior occurs?
- What activities or events precede the occurrence of the problem behavior?
- What do other people say or do immediately before the problem occurs?
- What do other people say or do immediately after the problem occurs?
- Does the student engage in any other behaviors before the problem behavior?
- When, where, with whom, and in what circumstances is the problem behavior least likely to occur?

Behavior

As described earlier, behavior is the student's actions—what the student says or does. Defining the behavior in observable and measurable terms is the most critical component of the FBA process. If the target behaviors lack clear and accurate definitions, the entire FBA process can be invalidated. For instance, an ambiguous definition may result in overreport-ing a single behavior that actually represents multiple behav-iors. In addition, antecedents and consequences of the poorly defined behavior become less meaningful. The following are characteristics of clear behavioral definitions:

> *Active verbs:* Behavioral definitions describe what a stu-dent is *saying* or *doing*.
> *Unambiguous:* There should not be multiple interpreta-tions of a behavioral definition. For instance, a behavior

Example of an A-B-C relationship following successful intervention:

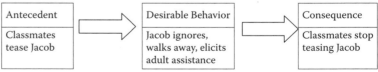

Antecedent		Desirable Behavior		Consequence
Classmates tease Jacob		Jacob ignores, walks away, elicits adult assistance		Classmates stop teasing Jacob

Outcome: Jacob is more likely to walk away, ignore, and get adult assistance when classmates tease him.

Figure 12.2   This chart provides an example of an A-B-C relationship following a suc-cessful intervention.

described as *unsportsmanlike conduct* in baseball could mean yelling obscenities, throwing the bat at someone, refusing to shake hands, or kicking the dirt.

Observable: Internal states such anger, sadness, or apathy cannot be directly observed and should be excluded from behavioral definitions. Similarly, perceived intentions should also be excluded from behavior definitions.

Describe one or two behaviors: Target the most problematic behaviors. It becomes logistically more difficult to track increasing numbers of problematic behaviors. Once the first targeted problem behavior improves, the team can redirect its focus to challenging secondary problem behavior.

Examples of well-defined behaviors:

- Sean's *tantrums* are recorded as occurring whenever he cries and sobs, lies on the floor and kicks the floor or wall, or pounds toys or other objects on the floor.
- Michael *hits* with his fists (versus "Michael is aggressive").
- Keisha is *studying* whenever she is observed underlining sentences in the text, completing math or physics workbook exercises, copying notes from class, or outlining chapters from the text.
- Lisa *takes* money from her classmates (versus "Lisa is delinquent").
- Alison is *sharing* whenever she passes or hands material to another classmate, when she exchanges materials with another classmate, or when she uses the same material at the same time with another classmate (e.g., she and another classmate color on the same piece of paper).
- Byron *arrives 10 minutes late* (versus "Byron is irresponsible").
- Danielle is *out of her seat 75% of the time* (versus "Danielle is hyperactive").

Consequences

A consequence describes what happens as a result of the student's behavior. It helps to maintain the behavior. To determine a behavior's consequence, ask the following questions:

helpful Qs

- What happens after the problem behavior occurs?
- What do the school staff members do when the problem behavior occurs?
- What do other students do when the problem behavior occurs?
- What changes in the environment after the problem behavior occurs?
- What does the student receive after the problem behavior?
- What does the student get out of or avoid after the problem behavior?

The consequences of behavior generally fall into one of four categories.

4 CONSEQUENCES

 ### Positive Reinforcement

Positive reinforcement increases the probability of a behavior and occurs when a target behavior is followed by a positive stimulus. For instance, a student turning in a lost wallet may receive a reward or recognition for his honesty. A second example is receiving a cola after pressing a button on a soda machine. Positive reinforcement involves the presentation of a stimulus that increases the likelihood of a behavior.

 ### Negative Reinforcement

Negative reinforcement also increases the probability of a behavior and occurs when a target behavior is followed by removal, escape, or avoidance of an aversive stimulus. For instance, a student with poor reading skills may act out before his turn to read orally and be sent to the office without reading aloud to the class. A second example is changing TV channels from an undesirable channel. Negative reinforcement involves the removal of a stimulus that increases the likelihood of a behavior.

 ### Positive Punishment

Positive punishment decreases the probability of a behavior and occurs when a target behavior is followed by presentation of an aversive stimulus. For instance, a student is caught talking during a test and receives a grade of F as a consequence. A second example is getting bit when attempting to pet an angry dog. Positive punishment involves the presentation of a stimulus that reduces a behavior.

Negative Punishment

Negative punishment decreases the probability of a behavior and occurs when a target behavior is followed by removal of a positive stimulus. For instance, a student may lose recess for not completing an in-class assignment. A second example is taking away a teen's cell phone for exceeding his or her plan's monthly minutes. Negative punishment involves the removal of a stimulus, which decreases a behavior.

Identifying Problem Behaviors, Antecedents, and Consequences

Multiple steps are necessary to complete an FBA. Although these are presented in a linear order, one should understand that the steps may not fall in lockstep with one another. An indirect assessment may lead to a direct assessment, but an evaluator may need to conduct more interviews after watching the child. Throughout the entire process, remember to evaluate the environment—what is happening around the child that is both eliciting problem behaviors and preventing desirable behaviors.

✳ mostly interviews

Indirect Assessment

Indirect assessment refers to file reviews and interviews that provide background information about a child's behavior. The advantage of indirect assessment is that a great deal of information can be collected quickly. However, the information may not contain adequate specificity and is subject to interviewee bias. We recommend the following steps:

- Review the child's file. Form 12.1 may be used when reviewing comprehensive files. Pay close attention to ODRs, previous special education forms including previous FBAs and behavior intervention plans (BIPs), medical history, grade history, and academic or other assessment information.
- A member of the problem-solving team completes the Functional Behavior Assessment Form—Teacher (FBAF) with the child's teacher. The form is located in Appendix A (see Form 12.3). Middle school problem-

solving teams complete this form with the teachers identifying the student's most challenging behaviors.

- A member of the problem-solving team interviews the student to get his or her perspective on the problematic behavior, and then identifies reinforcers when conducting a preference assessment.
- The parent interview records the parental perspective of the problem behavior and any relevant background information.
- Interview other relevant personnel (e.g., a bus driver or outside service provider).
- Review the student's cumulative folder (e.g., grades, test scores, health record, and discipline record).
- Review Tier II intervention data in addition to any other interventions that may have been implemented informally.

The indirect assessment component of an FBA involves gathering, in a written format, information from the student and people familiar with the student. A structured interview is the best method to obtain information from the student, parent(s), teacher(s), outside service providers, bus driver, and others who are able to provide meaningful information about the student and behaviors of concern.

The Functional Behavior Assessment Form—Teacher (FBAF) is an instrument used to interview the teacher. It requires a behavioral intervention expert to meet with the teacher and ask questions regarding the behaviors of concern, possible antecedents, and possible consequences. The student interview will involve asking the student a series of questions to ascertain why he or she is engaging in the behavior(s) of concern. In addition, the interviewer can conduct a preference assessment to learn what is rewarding for the student so that effective reinforcers can be identified for the intervention plan. Jim Wright delineates a method involving a reward deck (Wright, n.d.). A *reward deck* is a tool that teachers can use in collaboration with the problem-solving team representative and parent to quickly select and regularly update student reward menus. This strategy involves five steps:

1. The teacher reviews a list of reward choices typically available in school settings. (Teachers can use the comprehensive sampling of possible school rewards

that appears in Appendix D.) From this larger list, the teacher selects only those rewards that she or he approves of using, believes would be acceptable to other members of the school community (e.g., administration and parents), and finds feasible and affordable. The list should include rewards that allow a student access to preferred tangibles, access to student or teacher attention, or avoidance of difficult assignments and difficult relationships. (*Note*: Sometimes a student may be reluctant to volunteer items that he or she enjoys or wants. It is also reasonable to observe the student's behavior when there are no expectations, and watch the types of behaviors he or she demonstrates. Is the student trying to get adult or peer attention? Is he or she playing alone? Are there some activities he or she seems to enjoy doing? What are the high-frequency behaviors during free time?)

2. From the initial list, he or she "screens" the reward choices for any reinforcers that seem inappropriate for the particular student. For example, the teacher may screen out the reward "pizza party" because the magnitude of the reinforcer is too great (and too expensive) when paired with a minor difficulty involving homework completion.

3. The teacher writes out the acceptable reward choices on index cards to create a master "reward deck."

4. The teacher sits with the student and presents each of the reward choices remaining in the reward deck. For each reward option, the student indicates whether he or she (a) likes the reward a lot, (b) likes the reward a little, or (c) doesn't care for the reward. The teacher sorts the reward options into three piles that match these rating categories. The teacher can then assemble that student's reward menu using the student's top choices ("like a lot"). If the teacher needs additional choices to fill out the rest of the menu, he or she can pull items from the student's "like a little" category as well. Periodically (e.g., once a month), the teacher should meet with the student and repeat the above procedure to make sure the rewards are still reinforcing to the student. At this point, some rewards may need to be removed and replaced with others.

5. Finally, the problem-solving team representative reviews the archival data in the student's cumulative

folder (e.g., grades, test scores, health record, and discipline record).

Direct Assessment

＋mostly observations

The direct assessment component of an FBA utilizes school staff personnel with experience in conducting structured observations (e.g., a behavior specialist or school psychologist). The problem-solving team representative records each instance of problematic behavior along with its antecedents and consequences. The data from the indirect assessment component help to determine which behaviors to target along with the possible antecedents and consequences. The next step involves selection of an observational method. Recommended methods may include conditional probability assessments and A-B-C records.

The conditional probability method involves tracking when behaviors occur and what happens before and after the behavior. Next, the observer calculates what percentage of the time a certain event precedes or follows the problematic behavior. If an event or condition consistently precedes a behavior, then it is likely that the event or condition is sustaining the problematic behavior. A procedure for using the conditional probability method is located in Appendix A (see Form 12.3).

The A-B-C method has three possible formats: descriptive, checklist, or interval record. The descriptive format involves recording observations as a narrative under the columns for antecedent, behavior, and consequence and time it occurred.

The checklist format has columns for antecedents, behaviors, and consequences based on the indirect assessment data. If the observer puts many possible antecedents, behaviors, and consequences into the form, he or she will do less writing than with the narrative format. The possible antecedents, behaviors,

descriptive format →

Date/Time	ANTECEDENT What happened just *before* the behavior?	BEHAVIOR What behavior happened? Be specific.	CONSEQUENCE What happened just *after* the behavior?
7/7/09 10:00 a.m.	Teacher asked the class to take out their reading books to prepare to take turns reading aloud.	Robert pushed back his chair, stood up, and kicked the chair over.	The teacher told Robert to go to the principal's office. The other students gasped.

Figure 12.3   Example of A-B-C narrative format (see Form 12.4).

Person	Time	Antecedents		Behavior			Consequences		
		Reading Lesson	Group Activity	Screams	Hits another person	Kicks his desk	Peers Give Attention	Sent out of the Classroom	Teacher Gives Attention
J.W.	10:00 a.m.		X	X					
J.W.	10:05 a.m.	X				X		X	X

Figure 12.4   Example of A-B-C checklist format (see Form 12.5).

and consequences are already listed, and the observer simply records the identity of who is being observed, notes the time the observation starts, and places a mark under which antecedent, behavior, and/or consequence occurs. (See Figure 12.4.)

The interval format involves dividing an observation period into brief time intervals and recording whether a particular behavior, antecedent, or consequence occurred during that interval. It is a more detailed form than the above described checklist in that it yields information about the frequency, duration, and sequence of behaviors. (See Figure 12.5.)

The reading lesson was the sole antecedent during the observation. It occurred 60% of the time (i.e., 6/10, because the observation ended when the student left the room). The student left his seat, talked to a peer, and kicked his desk during the reading lesson. The teacher redirected the student twice— once after he got out of his seat and once after he talked to another peer. After the second redirection, the student kicked his desk and consequently was sent out of the room by the teacher. The student engaged in problematic behaviors in 30% of the observation periods.

- A problem-solving team representative identifies in measurable and observable terms the problematic behaviors and their possible antecedents and consequences based on the indirect assessment data.
- A problem-solving team representative identifies, based on indirect assessment data, when and where to observe the problematic behavior.
- A problem-solving team representative chooses an observational method that will yield information about the behavior and its antecedents and conse-

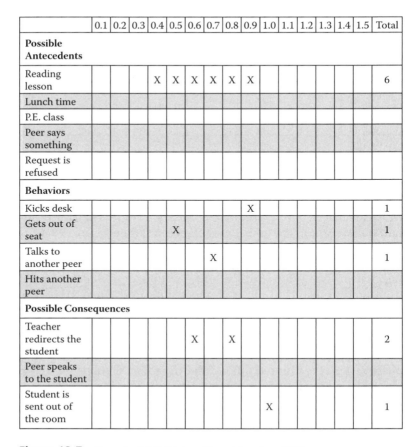

	0.1	0.2	0.3	0.4	0.5	0.6	0.7	0.8	0.9	1.0	1.1	1.2	1.3	1.4	1.5	Total
Possible Antecedents																
Reading lesson				X	X	X	X	X	X							6
Lunch time																
P.E. class																
Peer says something																
Request is refused																
Behaviors																
Kicks desk								X								1
Gets out of seat				X												1
Talks to another peer						X										1
Hits another peer																
Possible Consequences																
Teacher redirects the student					X		X									2
Peer speaks to the student																
Student is sent out of the room									X							1

Figure 12.5   Example of A-B-C interval format (see Form 12.6).

quences (conditional probability observation form or program; A-B-C records).

- A problem-solving team representative evaluates observational data and develops hypotheses about the function of the behavior.

Hypothesis Testing

Once the behavioral analyst determines the hypothesized function of a behavior, a hypothesis statement should be written. This statement includes the following pieces of information: the child, the problematic behavior, a statement of the settings where the behavior occurs, and a function of the behavior. Some hypothesis statements include the following:

- When Jordan is given directions to start his work by his teacher, he begins to yell back at his teacher to escape engaging in the assignment.
- In all class settings, Michelle calls other students names because she gains peer attention.
- When given work that is difficult for him, Jonathan throws chairs in the class because he is able to escape the task.
- As lunchtime approaches and Charla's Ritalin begins to lose its effect on her concentration, Charla begins to shout out answers to questions in order to gain teacher attention.

These hypothesis statements give clear indications about the antecedent, the behavior, and the consequence of that behavior.

Functional Analysis (FBAn)

The FBAn involves the deliberate manipulation of variables to determine the effect those variables have on a student's behavior. The functional analysis helps to confirm a hypothesis, or helps to choose between two or more possible functions of behavior. In schools, this process, normally called *brief functional analysis*, can greatly reduce the amount of time spent on interventions that are ineffective because they address the wrong functional needs for a child. Sterling-Turner, Robinson, and Wilczynski (2001) described a functional analysis of a child who was throwing spitballs. Following the functional assessment, the team hypothesized that the child's behavior was motivated by attention. However, they were unsure whether he sought teacher attention or peer attention. They then ran two separate experiments. In the first experiment, the teacher was asked to ignore the child's spitball throwing. The behavior persisted despite the removal of teacher attention. Next, Sterling-Turner et al. (2001) recruited a cohort of students and asked them to ignore the child's spitball-throwing behavior. When the students were able to successfully ignore the behavior of the student demonstrating the problematic behavior, that child's spitball behavior quickly extinguished. Thus, the researchers determined that the behavior was motivated by peer attention, and created interventions designed to alleviate that concern.

Setting Analysis

A type of experimental analysis that is closely related to functional analysis includes a setting analysis. Behavior specialists utilizing experimental analysis alter environmental triggers to determine which setting events are most likely serve as a catalyst for a behavior. For example, members of a behavior team may guess that a teacher's directives are triggering a child's verbally explosive behaviors, but they are unsure which types of directives provoke this behavior. They ask the teacher to give the child directives in close proximity to the child but find that the child's behavior persists. Next, the team has the teacher give nonverbal directives whereby both she and the student are trained to give signals for "Get back to work," "Turn and face forward," "Thank you," and "You're doing a good job." They found that nonverbal directives substantially reduced the occurrence of the child's disruptive behaviors.

Either form of experimental analysis can provide valuable information about which interventions may be effective, which setting events trigger problematic behaviors, or what events can make a desirable behavior more likely.

CONCLUSION

Functional assessments yield correlational rather than causal data, but allow for greater levels of objective data to be collected and utilized. Correlational data allow one to develop a strong hypothesis about the antecedents and consequences of behavior. When a behavior consistently precedes or follows a particular event, condition, or behavior, it becomes clear where to intervene. If a student's calling out in class always results in laughter from his peers, then the intervention should focus on extinguishing the reinforcing laughter while teaching the student alternative and appropriate ways to gain peer attention. Members of the problem-solving team should review all FBA data and generate a hypothesis regarding the function of the behavior, which typically falls into one of two broad categories: obtain something, or avoidance or escape.

After identifying the function of a behavior, the team creates a BIP designed to decrease the problematic behavior and increase the student's use of an acceptable alternative behavior that serves the same function.

13

Providing Tier III Behavioral Interventions

INTRODUCTION

Most of this manual articulated clear, step-by-step procedures for implementing positive behavioral interventions (PBS). As behavior becomes more challenging and when other methods have not elicited the desired outcomes, the process of providing further interventions requires individualization. This means the problem-solving team or, in cases of students identified with educational handicaps, the IEP team will work closely with a behavioral specialist to design and implement the interventions. Finally, the team should acknowledge that no one intervention will be successful for all students.

To successfully provide individualized interventions to students receiving Tier III services, an understanding of behavior and its function(s) is necessary. However, working knowledge of behavioral concepts is not sufficient for the selection of appropriate Tier III interventions. Risks of misidentifying behavioral functions are higher when targeted students are not evaluated using information acquired through functional behavior assessment (FBA) (e.g., interviews, data-based observations, academic assessment, rating scales, and cumulative folder review) practices described in Chapter 12. The FBA provides the context that problem-solving teams use when intervening with students demonstrating severe and/or chronic behavior problems. For example, the team may find that after reviewing the FBA, the student's behavior occurs only in certain places, at certain times, or when the student of concern is near certain individuals. It is also important to note that Tier III interventions occur alongside Tier I and Tier II interventions. Removal of Tier I or Tier II interventions occurs only when a preponderance of objective, data-based evidence supports a position that documented interventions are ineffective or aversive to the student. This chapter introduces how to use FBA data and techniques for intervention implementation.

FORMS TO BE INTRODUCED

Form 13.1: Functional Behavior Summary Chart
Form 13.2: Behavior Plan Worksheet

MATERIALS NEEDED

- Results from the FBA
- Cumulative folder
- Observation records

INFORMATION NEEDED

General Guidelines for Intervening with Students Displaying Behavior Problems

The following guidelines should be considered for nearly every behavior plan. Although a team may choose to remove one due to information learned during the FBA process, these interventions are frequently effective for students with more challenging behaviors.

Highly Structured Teaching Environment

High structure includes many of the features described in Chapters 5 and 9 when describing how a good classroom works. Thus, clear rules, expectations for each period of the class, and specifically taught procedures are all crucial elements for a highly structured classroom. Similarly, room setup, schedules, seating arrangements, and other physical features are crucial in creating a safe, structured setting. Used in conjunction with the steps outlined below, it is a powerful tool for increasing academic and behavioral success.

Clear Expectations and Directives

Ambiguously stated rules are more likely to elicit problem behaviors (Colvin, Sugai, Good, & Lee, 1997; Colvin, Sugai, & Patching, 1993). Establishing a collection of rules that are interpretable in only one way increases instructional time by preventing or reducing undesirable rule-violating behaviors.

Planned Transitions and Limited "Downtime"

Engaging in preplanned academic activity is less likely to bring about challenging behaviors when compared to "downtime" in the classroom. This time is most often used for temporary, scheduled academic breaks. However, downtime is also the time between academic lessons (i.e., in-class transition time). When not mentally engaged in a task, some students will find unhealthy or unproductive means by which to entertain themselves. A preoccupied teacher, working to prepare everyone for the next lesson, is less prone to monitor the classroom as effectively as she would when fewer immediate demands are placed upon her. Yet, this situation can readily be improved with preplanning and practice. Transition interventions may not show drastic improvements immediately, but fewer problems during transitions should be noted as the teacher improves the skill and as the class adjusts to the new, more efficient procedures.

Patient Teachers

When teachers become angry, threatening, or agitated, they model inappropriate behavior. Some students become more agitated when a teacher yells, and their behavior gets worse. Disruptive student behavior in the classroom has shown to be a primary factor in high levels of stress amongst teachers (Axup & Gersch, 2008). With added stress, teachers' ability to maximize their teaching potential is jeopardized and learning environments are weakened (Hawe, Tuck, Manthei, Adair, & Moore, 2000). In turn, regretful modeling of unwanted behavior is shown by the teacher in moments of frustration, despair, or anger. This behavior typically conflicts with the guidelines and expectations created by the teacher themselves, offers students insights into "hot buttons" that can be used to manipulate teacher behavior, and will, in many instances, escalate rather than deescalate current problematic students' behavior.

Delayed Consequences

Frequently, a teacher may become involved in a power struggle with a student who has a significant behavioral difficulty. These power struggles often involve the teacher making a demand of a student, and that student not following the demand immediately. When something like this happens, we as educators may become nervous, and fear that we are losing our own credibility. Soon, the power struggle escalates, the student ends up in big trouble, and the teacher feels embarrassed. One method to avoid this power struggle is the use of a delayed consequence when the student is not an immediate threat (Fay & Funk, 1995). The teacher tells the student that choosing not to follow the directive may result in some later consequence. This delayed consequence technique can alleviate many power struggles that are not imminently dangerous, and prevent disruptions to the classroom. For example, Jamie refused to complete an assignment in a class despite the teacher's frequent reminders about the importance of staying on task. Using a delayed consequence, the teacher said, "Are you sure you don't want to follow the directive? I'm afraid you may not be happy with your choice." When the student refused, the teacher waited until she had access to something the student wanted. The next day, the teacher decided to allow some of the students to work on computers. When Jamie asked if she could work on the computer, the teacher was able to provide a consequence by saying, "Unfortunately, I can only allow students who complete their assignments on time to use the computer."

Regular and Frequent Reinforcements

Because students with behavior difficulties often have difficulty delaying gratification, a reinforcement schedule should be frequent—and in some cases, reinforcements should be given every few minutes. Frequent reinforcements will help a student be more present and able to learn from the curriculum.

Principles for Functionally Based Interventions

As described in Chapter 12, most student behaviors are motivated by two general functions: to gain access to something, or to avoid something. Generally, students may behave in such a way as to gain the attention of others, have the opportunity to do something they want to do, or get the chance to have something that they want. Similarly, a student may be trying to avoid something he or she does not like, escape a social interaction, or avoid a painful stimulus. If a student's behavior is motivated by escape, using a timeout as a consequence may actually be rewarding for the student and may reinforce the behavior. In general, behavior plans should seek to ensure the student can get what he or she needs through desirable behaviors. If a student misbehaves, efforts should focus on ensuring the student's environment does not provide the necessary reinforcement.

Managing Behaviors Designed to Elicit Adult Attention

Behavioral interventions should provide students with adult attention when they are demonstrating appropriate behaviors. To achieve this, a teacher or adult may need to use a reminder to provide praise or some form of attention for students when they are completing their work quietly, when they answer a question correctly, or when they follow the expectations given to them. Similarly, students who crave adult attention may be motivated by a token economy system that rewards them with one-on-one adult time.

When a student demonstrates a behavior that is unacceptable, removing access from reinforcement can be a good strategy. A teacher ignoring the student's behavior may be an effective means of reducing the positive reinforcement a student had been receiving. Through this extinction procedure, a student's undesirable behavior will decrease if the reinforcement is removed. It is important to keep in mind, however, that the student's behavior may exhibit an extinction burst whereby the undesirable behavior increases before it decreases (Lerman & Iwata, 1995).

possibility of an extinction burst

Other options include the following:

- Increasing the ratio of positive to negative interactions.
- Social-skills training for the student to learn more effective means of eliciting adult attention.
- Planned ignoring.
- Token economy system with rewards that include adult attention.
- Allowing the student to be an office helper.

Managing Behaviors Designed to Elicit Peer Attention

Peer attention is more difficult to manage than adult attention for the obvious reasons that we as adults can control our own behaviors, but cannot directly control the behaviors of others. In fact, many of those who demonstrate undesirable behaviors find that peer conversations, comments, laughter, and even reprimands are enjoyable. Thus, a behavior plan for a student whose behavior is designed to increase access to peer attention must be able to provide the student with effective and appropriate strategies to gain peer attention, and must remove access to peer attention when the behaviors are more problematic.

challenge

Some methods for accomplishing these goals may include the following:

- Opportunities to do group work.
- Social-skills training to teach friendship-making skills.
- Rewards that include access to peer attention.
- Opportunities to gain peer attention such as telling jokes in front of the class.
- The use of group contingencies whereby a teacher rewards all members of the class when a student completes a particular task. Of course, it is important to complete such a task spontaneously to make sure the student does not become a victim of aggression from his or her peers (see, e.g., Hulac & Benson, 2010; Skinner, Cashwell, & Dunn, 1996).
- Using "group ignore" procedures. Through this procedure, the entire class is trained to begin ignoring the student's behaviors. Through a token economy system, the entire class receives points for successfully ignoring the targeted student's behavior and remaining on task (Hulac & Benson, 2010).

Managing Behaviors Designed to Elicit Access to a Preferred Item or Activity

- *Timeout from reinforcement.* Timeout is often understood to be a place where a student goes so he or she does not receive social attention. However, timeout from reinforcement simply means that we remove the item or activity that the student finds to be reinforcing. This idea is known as *stimulus control.* For example, a student may want to get a pencil and may be demonstrating behaviors designed to get a pencil. A timeout may merely mean removing the pencil from the student's sight and putting the pencil in "timeout." Some procedures that have been proven to be effective for small groups of students involve the use of a "yellow ribbon" to indicate that a student is on timeout from reinforcement (Alberto, Hefflin, & Andrews, 2002). Thus, timeout techniques are more easily performed when we control the reinforcer the student wants without getting into a power struggle by having the student move to a different place.
- *Token economy systems.* Token economy systems that allow a student to earn access to a preferred activity are a natural fit in these situations.

Managing Behaviors Designed to Avoid an Undesirable Activity

The FBA process should identify what in the environment is aversive to the student. For example, students with sensory integration difficulties may simply find that classrooms have too many distractions on the walls, which make the classroom overstimulating for some students. Similarly, a student may be more disturbed by a fan or a furnace noise than other students who can naturally filter it out. If at all possible, a behavior plan should seek to remove stimuli from a student's classroom that are causing the student distress. However, in the case of classroom assignments, this is not always possible as some activities may be problematic or difficult for students who demonstrate challenging behavior. If a student is refusing to do an activity, it is commonly because the student does not know what needs to be done. However, there are some methods to increase the likelihood that an assignment will be completed.

- Make sure that the directions are clear for the student.
- Make sure the student has specific instruction related to the task—in other words, make sure he or she knows how to do the tasks on the worksheet.
- Create worksheets or assignments that include a high number of "known" items rather than unknown items. Including more known items has been demonstrated to increase the amount of time that students are on task (Calderhead, Filter, & Albin, 2006; Skinner, Hurst, Teeple, & Meadows, 2002).
- Remove the student from a stimulus that is uncomfortable.

INITIAL PROCEDURES FOR CREATING BEHAVIORAL PLANS

The problem-solving team should be able to answer the following questions after reviewing a comprehensive FBA:

- When is the behavior *most likely* to occur?
- When is the behavior *least likely* to occur?
- What is an appropriate replacement behavior?
- What is a hypothesis for the reasons this undesirable behavior occurs?
- Who is present when the behavior occurs?

- What appears to motivate the student to perform desired behaviors?
- How frequently does the student get a reward?
- Complete the functional behavior summary chart.
- Complete the behavior plan worksheet.

FOLLOW-UP PROCEDURES

A member of the problem-solving team completes an observation of the intervention on the first day, and prior to the first review meeting.

Is it working?

Is it adequate progress?

- Meet after one week to determine how effectively the intervention is working.
- At this meeting, the problem-solving team determines if the student is making adequate progress.

If the student is not making acceptable progress:

- Determine if the plan is being implemented with integrity.
- Determine if the plan needs more time to work effectively.
- Consider changing the plan.
- Schedule the next review meeting.

If the student is making progress:

- Determine if the plan should be discontinued, continued, or revised.
- Schedule another review meeting.
- At subsequent review meetings, the team will need to do the following:
  - Determine if the plan is effective or ineffective.
  - Decide if the plan should be continued, changed, or discontinued.
- If the team decides to discontinue the plan, they must then make a plan to gradually remove the behavioral supports already in place.

BEHAVIOR PLAN EXAMPLE 1: JOEY

Ms. Willis, a third-grade teacher, expressed concern at a recent problem-solving team meeting. Joey continued to have difficulty with two specific behaviors: (a) staying in his seat, and (b) complying with teacher directives (i.e., willing noncompliance). Joey had been through a check-in and check-out program, but his out-of-seat behaviors continued. Similarly, the teacher used effective instruction delivery techniques to improve Joey's compliance, but the noncompliance continued. The problem-solving team initiated a functional behavior assessment to create an individualized behavior plan.

The behavior interventionist, using the data-based problem-solving model, divided the task into three steps.

Step 1. Problem identification
Step 2. Plan development and implementation
Step 3. Plan evaluation

In Step 1, the behavior interventionist defined the problem by establishing the specific, observable, and measurable components of the behaviors. The behaviors were written in concrete terms:

1. Joey frequently leaves his assigned class seat without permission.
2. Joey chooses not to comply when given specific instructions (e.g., "Take out your math book," "Stop teasing your classmate," and "Do not play paper football when you are given an assignment") issued to him.

The behavior interventionist then confirmed that the referral problems existed and were severe enough to warrant the level of intensive involvement requested. At this step attendance records, discipline records, grades, and cumulative records were reviewed. Many keys to solving the behavior riddle were found in this documentation. These components were synthesized together to verify the presence and severity of the referred problem. In Joey's case, a records review revealed regular attendance with no unexcused absences, eight discipline referrals for noncompliance, and poor scores in key academic areas. An A-B-C observation checklist (see Figure 13.1) confirmed out-of-seat behavior during academic assignments. The observer also noted fidgeting that occurred through much of the observation. When given directives, Joey was noncompliant on multiple occasions. Consequences for his behavior(s) included attention, redirection, and ultimately a discipline referral.

Student Name: <u>Joey Anderson</u>   Date & Time of Observation: <u>09/20/2010</u>

Teacher name: <u>Catherine Willis</u>   **PORTION OF SAMPLE A-B-C**

OBSERVATION

Time	ANTECEDENT (What happened just *before* the behavior?)	BEHAVIOR (What behavior happened? – Be specific)	CONSEQUENCE (What happened just *after* the behavior?)
8:35	Board work	Joey fidgets with watch	Assignment continues
8:37	Board work	Joey fidgets with collar	Assignment continues
8:40	Board work	Joey leaves his seat without permission	Teacher correction
8:47	Board work	Joey begins repeatedly tapping his foot against the desk	Assignment continues
8:58	Small group instruction; teacher assigns cooperative task	Joey refuses to work with peers	Teacher correction
8:59	Teacher correction	Joey engages teacher in verbal debate; remains non-compliant	Teacher lectures Joey on appropriate behavior and sends him to principal

Figure 13.1   Antecedent–Behavior–Consequence Narrative Form (Form 12.4).

Structured interviews helped to paint a better picture of Joey, his history, and the environments in which he operates. These data provided the behavior intervention specialist with some opportunities to observe the classroom to know when the problem behavior was most likely. After observing the referring behaviors, a series of data-driven observations was used to measure (a) how Joey compared to peers in regard to hyperactivity and (b) functions of the hyperactivity and/or noncompliant behavior. An interstudent behavioral observation, also known as a *target* or *peer comparison observation*, produced the results seen in Figure 13.2.

The data from the interindividual observation showed that the number of intervals in which Joey engaged in fidgeting, vocalization, and out-of-seat behaviors was significantly higher than that of randomly selected, same-gender peers in his classroom. A second interindividual observation produced a similar pattern of comparison behaviors. These findings, coupled with the subjective observation, teacher report, and behavior rating scale, supported a hypothesis that Joey engaged in more hyperactive behaviors compared to his peers. A conditional probability observation was conducted to identify possible antecedents and functions of the student's behavior. Given the specifics of this case, the conditional probability form (see Figure 13.3) targeted the following behaviors of interest for Joey:

Behavior 1. Vocalization (inappropriate vocalization)
Behavior 2. Out of seat
Behavior 3. Aggression
Behavior 4. Disrespect

The observer was unable to identify antecedents that routinely elicit the behaviors typically associated with out-of-seat behavior, nor were consequences for such behaviors identified. When evaluating the second concern, noncompliance, Joey complied with only 3 of 10 teacher directives, or 30% of the demands placed upon him by the authority figure. The behavior was usually followed by teacher attention. The data supported a hypothesis that behaviors were driven by a desire for attention because his out-of-seat behaviors were usually followed by teacher attention. No tangibles were available to act as reinforcers. The findings suggested that Joey was most likely to engage in out-of-seat behavior as a result of either gaining teacher attention or presenting with noncompliant behavior as a means to maintain or control an individual or situation.

Phase 2 of the problem-solving model is plan development and implementation. By the time this stage is reached, the problem has been identified and verified. It was now time to develop and create an individualized behavior plan. Given the multisource approach taken in collecting subjective perspectives and objective, empirical data, we were able to create hypotheses regarding Joey's target behaviors. A behavior intervention plan (BIP) can now be developed with interventions selected that will more likely bring about positive change (see Figure 13.4).

Phase 3 involves evaluation of the BIP. During implementation of the intervention, the team should have a time scheduled to evaluate its progress or lack thereof in remediating student behavior. The expectation should be that the vast majority of students will respond positively to appropriate interventions. By evaluating the team's effectiveness on each case, and then through data analysis from yearly aggregated success rates, it can maintain or modify its approach as needed.

	Student Name:	Class:
	Observer Name:	Teacher:
	Date:	Name of Observer:
	Time of day:	

		Frequency	
	Behavior	Target	Peer
Directions	1: Off-task	03/40 = 8%	04/40 =10%
	2: Fidgeting	17/40 = 43%	02/40 =5%
	3: Vocalization	10/40 = 25%	00/40 =0%
	4: Out of seat	05/40 = 13%	01/40 =3%
	5: Playing with objects	00/40 = 0%	01/40 =3%

Directions column:

Step 1: Determine which 4 behaviors to observe

Step 2: Observe the target student for 10 seconds.

Step 3: Record the behaviors for the next 5 seconds under the T column.

Step 4: Observe the student's peer for 10 seconds.

Step 5: Record the peer's behaviors for the next 5 seconds under the P column.

Step 6: Observe the target student again for 10 seconds.

Step 7: Record target student's behaviors for 5 seconds under the T column for 2nd half of the minute.

Step 8: Observe the peer again for 10 seconds.

Step 9: Record the Peer's behaviors for 5 seconds under the p column in the 2nd half of minute 1. The first minute is completed.

Step 10: Return to step 2 until the 20 minutes have elapsed.

Step 11: Add up the number of times a behavior was observed for the target student and for the peer. Record those numbers under the frequency column.

Figure 13.2   Student Behavior Observation Form.

| | Minute 1 | | | | Minute 2 | | | | Minute 3 | | | | Minute 4 | | | | Minute 5 | | | | Minute 6 | | | | Minute 7 | | | |
| | 1st | | 2nd | | 1st | | 2nd | | 1st | | 2nd | | 1st | | 2nd | | 1st | | 2nd | | 1st | | 2nd | | 1st | | 2nd | |
	T	P	T	P	T	P	T	P	T	P	T	P	T	P	T	P	T	P	T	P	T	P	T	P	T	P	T	P
Behavior 1									✓											✓								
Behavior 2			✓				✓		✓						✓			✓	✓		✓			✓				
Behavior 3	✓						✓				✓	✓					✓										✓	
Behavior 4													✓															
Behavior 5																												

| | Minute 8 | | | | Minute 9 | | | | Minute 10 | | | | Minute 11 | | | | Minute 12 | | | | Minute 13 | | | | Minute 14 | | | |
| | 1st | | 2nd | | 1st | | 2nd | | 1st | | 2nd | | 1st | | 2nd | | 1st | | 2nd | | 1st | | 2nd | | 1st | | 2nd | |
	T	P	T	P	T	P	T	P	T	P	T	P	T	P	T	P	T	P	T	P	T	P	T	P	T	P	T	P
Behavior 1			✓							✓												✓						
Behavior 2	✓				✓				✓				✓		✓		✓		✓				✓					
Behavior 3							✓		✓				✓		✓		✓					✓						
Behavior 4			✓								✓								✓								✓	
Behavior 5																												

| | Minute 15 | | | | Minute 16 | | | | Minute 17 | | | | Minute 18 | | | | Minute 19 | | | | Minute 20 | | | | Sum | | | |
| | 1st | | 2nd | | 1st | | 2nd | | 1st | | 2nd | | 1st | | 2nd | | 1st | | 2nd | | 1st | | 2nd | | 1st | | 2nd | |
	T	P	T	P	T	P	T	P	T	P	T	P	T	P	T	P	T	P	T	P	T	P	T	P	T	P	T	P
Behavior 1																									03		04	
Behavior 2	✓						✓						✓								✓		✓		17		02	
Behavior 3							✓												✓						10		00	
Behavior 4			✓				✓				✓				✓										05		01	
Behavior 5																									00		01	

Figure 13.2 *(Continued)* Student Behavior Observation Form.

		Student Behaviors					FX		Com				Student Behaviors					FX		Com	
		1	2	3	4	5	P	T	Q	E			1	2	3	4	5	P	T	Q	E
1	:00										8	:00									
	:10											:10									
	:20	X						X	1			:20									
	:30											:30	x							4	
	:40											:40									
	:50											:50									4
2	:00										9	:00									
	:10	X						X	2	2		:10									
	:20											:20									
	:30											:30									
	:40											:40									
	:50											:50	x							5	5
3	:00										10	:00									
	:10	X										:10									
	:20											:20									
	:30	X						x				:30									
	:40											:40									
	:50											:50									
4	:00										11	:00									
	:10											:10									
	:20	X										:20	X		x					6	
	:30	X					x					:30	X								
	:40	X										:40	x								
	:50											:50									
5	:00										12	:00									
	:10	X										:10	x							7	
	:20											:20									7
	:30											:30									
	:40	x							3			:40									
	:50											:50									
6	:00										13	:00									
	:10											:10									
	:20	X										:20									
	:30											:30									
	:40	x	X					x				:40									
	:50							x				:50			x				x		
7	:00			x				x	4		14	:00									
	:10									4		:10									
	:20		x									:20									
	:30											:30									
	:40											:40									
	:50											:50									

Figure 13.3   Conditional Probability Form (Form 12.2).

Define the student behaviors	Consequences	Compliance	Compliance rate
Student Behavior 1 = *Vocalization*	TA = Teacher attention	Q = Teacher directive	Total number of Qs: 7
Student Behavior 2 = *Out of seat*	PA = Peer attention	E = Student compliance	
Student Behavior 3 = *Aggression*	ES = Escape/Avoidance		Total number of Es: 4
Student Behavior 4 = *Disrespect*	PO = Power		
Student Behavior 5 =	TG = Tangibles		Compliance rate (E÷Q) = 57%

Directions:

Step 1: Determine negative or positive student behaviors to observe. Some examples include physical aggression, off-task, out of seat, talking with other peers, throwing items across the classroom, or on-task behavior. If the behavior occurs, mark an X in the box for that 10-second interval.

Step 2: After a student engages in a behavior, mark if the student's peers or teacher give the student attention.

Step 3: If a teacher makes a directive the student should follow, mark a number under the box marked "Q." Mark 1 for the first directive during the observation period, mark 2 for the second directive, and so on. If the student complies with the directive, make an X in the E column for the interval when the child complied.

Figure 13.3 *(Continued)* Conditional Probability Form (Form 12.2).

Behavior Plan Worksheet Student Name: <u>Joey</u>			*Non-compliance*		
		Antecedent		Behavior	Consequence
⇨ *How to avoid the problematic behavior?*	⇨	What triggers of the problematic behavior can be eliminated?	⇨	What is the problematic behavior?	⇨ What should occur after the behavior so that the student will not continue to choose to do the behavior?
		Tasks requiring sustained attention/ concentration can be broken into shorter sections and/or interspersed with other academic material currently being taught	⇨	*Hyperactive behavior including: Out of seat Fidgeting Inappropriate/ vocalizations*	⇨ *A nonverbal or verbal cuing procedure*
⇨ *How can we make the replacement behavior more likely?*	⇨	How can we trigger the replacement behavior?	⇨	What is the problematic behavior?	⇨ How can the student get his desires met by the replacement behavior?
		Positive reinforcement for remaining in seat; calling on Joey when his hand is raised; self monitoring	⇨	*In seat, appropriate/ reduced motor responses, speaking with permission*	⇨ *Allowed short breaks when he is allowed to move around the room more freely; calling on Joey more frequently to respond followed by a gradual decrease in the frequency in which he is asked to provide the appropriate verbal response*
		How can we teach the student the replacement behavior?			
		Joey has demonstrated mastery of the desired behaviors. This is a skill currently in his behavioral repertoire. The concern is underutilization of the replacement behavior.			
⇨ *How to avoid the problematic behavior?*	⇨	What triggers of the problematic behavior can be eliminated?	⇨	What is the problematic behavior?	⇨ What should occur after the behavior so that the student will not continue to choose to do the behavior?
		Teacher instruction, command or request.		*Non-compliance*	*Corrective teaching sequence or a delayed consequence*
⇨ *How can we make the replacement behavior more likely?*	⇨	How can we trigger the replacement behavior?		What is the desired behavior?	*How can the student get his desires met by the replacement behavior?*
		Provide student with the opportunity to follow directives that he enjoys prior to giving him a directive.	⇨	*Compliance*	⇨ *Selected or earn the privileges of leadership positions*
		How can we teach the student the replacement behavior?			
		Components of the corrective teaching sequence address specifically the modeling, student engagement, corrective feedback, and praise of teaching replacement behaviors			

Figure 13.4 Behavior Plan Worksheet (Form 13.2) for hyperactive behavior.

Student Name: Molly Sample					
	Antecedent		Behavior		Consequence
⇨ *What causes problem behavior?*	What triggers the problem behavior	⇨	What is the problematic behavior?	⇨	What happens after the student engages in the problematic behavior?
	The teacher asks Molly to do a difficult math assignment.	⇨	*Molly yells and swears at the teacher.*	⇨	*Several minutes go by when Molly does not have to work on the worksheet. The teacher and Molly's classmates either laugh or tell her to stop.*
⇨ *What causes replacement behavior?*	What happens in the environment when the desired behavior occurs?	⇨	What is the desired behavior?	⇨	What should occur after the behavior so that the student will not continue to choose to do the behavior?
	She completes addition and multiplication problems, her behaviors ..?.	⇨	*The team would like Molly to work on and complete her math worksheet. When she is frustrated, she should ask for help.*	⇨	*When she is quiet, her peers do not pay attention to her*

Figure 13.5   Functional Behavior Summary Chart (Form 13.1).

BEHAVIOR PLAN EXAMPLE 2: MOLLY

The problem-solving team referred Molly, a 12-year-old student in the seventh grade, for a behavior plan. The teacher reported that Molly would frequently yell obscenities at her peers and at the teacher. Mrs. White attempted many of the interventions described in the manual. She greeted Molly daily at the door, had clear rules posted in the classroom, and used the effective instruction delivery and corrective teaching sequence. By using the Daily Behavior Report Card, there was a slight improvement, but Molly quickly resorted to her old ways. Despite many of her best efforts, Mrs. White was unable to change the behavior, and was becoming aggravated. The behavior interventionist, Ms. Magenta, performed a functional behavior assessment.

The observer noted two things. The first was that the behaviors were the worst during math class. In particular, when the teacher gave Molly a difficult assignment, her behavior became much worse, and she began using profanity. The observer also noted that after Molly used profanity, the teacher would yell at

Student Name: Molly					
	Antecedent		Behavior		Consequence
⇨	What triggers of the problematic behavior can be eliminated?	⇨	What is the problematic behavior?	⇨	What should occur after the behavior so that the student will not continue to choose to do the behavior?
How to avoid the problematic behavior?	*Give Molly her assignments on a worksheet that includes 7 problems she can do for every 3 problems that are new or difficult for her.*				*When Molly yells and swears, the teacher and the students in the class will use a planned ignore whereby they will not talk to her while she is screaming. The class should get a point every time they ignore Molly's behavior for 15 seconds. If they earn 10 points, the class should get an additional five minutes of recess time at the end of the week.*
⇨	How can we trigger the replacement behavior?	⇨	What is the desired behavior?	⇨	How can the student get her desires met by the replacement behavior?
How can we make the replacement behavior more likely?	Unknown		*Molly completes her work*		*Molly's teacher should joke with her and compliment her privately when she is working well.*
	How can we teach the student the replacement behavior?				
	Molly needs direct instruction in identifying and using socially appropriate ways of anger expression. Molly also needs direct instruction in friendship-making skills.				

Figure 13.6   Behavior Plan Worksheet (Form 13.2).

her, and her peers would either laugh or yell at her telling her to stop. Thus, the team decided that Molly's behavior had two functions. The first was to get peer and teacher attention, and the second was to avoid a difficult assignment.

Figure 13.5 includes a sample of how the problem-solving team would organize its findings using the functional behavior assessment worksheet. From the functional behavioral worksheet, it became apparent that Molly receives peer and teacher attention when she swears and yells. She was also able to avoid the difficult

Communication	Who will be responsible for communicating the behavior plan to the appropriate staff members? The principal will send a memo to all of Molly's teacher outlining the behavior plan. The school psychologist, Ms. Magenta, will meet with each of Molly's teachers to explain the functions of the behavior plan. On the day after the plan begins, Ms. Magenta will meet again with each of Molly's teachers to answer questions. How will this communication take place? Through writing and oral communication When will this communication take place? This communication will begin tomorrow, the day after this meeting.
Social Skills Training	If any social skills training is needed for the student, who will be responsible for conducting that training? *Ms. Pink, the school social worker, will conduct a social skills training session with Molly to teach her friendship-making skills and to teach her to appropriately express her anger.* When will the social skills training occur? *The social skills training will begin next Monday.* How long will the skills training need to take place? *Initially, Molly will receive one session of training per week for 6 weeks.*

Figure 13.6 *(Continued)* Behavior Plan Worksheet (Form 13.2).

Plan evaluation	How will the behavior planning team know if the plan is effective? (e.g.; Review of ODRs; absence reports; systematic classroom observations?)
	Once per week, the school psychologist, Ms. Magenta, will observe Molly to record outbursts. The team will also review ODRs and will rely on the report of Molly's teachers.
	Who will be responsible for collecting that evaluation data?
	Ms. Magenta will collect the data.
	When will the team review the plan? (First review should take place within one week of the plan's implementation.)
	The team will meet one week from today to review the behavior plan.

Signatures: By signing, all participants agree to faithfully implement the portions of this behavior plan.

Parent	Molly's Parent
Student	Molly Sample
Classroom teacher	Ms. White
Problem solving team members	Ms. Beige
School principal	Ms. Magenta
Other participants	Ms. Pink

Figure 13.7   This form is used to assign responsibility for the different sections of the Behavior Plan.

math worksheet. The team decided to intervene in two areas as outlined in Figure 13.6 and described fully in Figure 13.7: making the math worksheets more rewarding to Molly, and limiting peer and teacher attention for her profane outbursts. The first addressed the difficulty she had with the math worksheet. Molly received a worksheet that includes seven arithmetic problems that she is able to do and three new problems that the rest of the class is working on (Robinson & Skinner, 2002).

The second intervention focused on teacher and peer behaviors when Molly would swear. When Molly would begin to swear, the classroom teacher was to instruct the students in her classroom to ignore the behavior and to continue to work on assignments. If the class successfully ignored the behavior for 15 seconds, they received a point. For each 15 seconds of ignoring the profane behavior, they received an additional point. The class was able to convert 10 of these points for 5 minutes of recess at the end of the school day. As the class got better at ignoring Molly's outbursts, the teacher would reward the class for 30 seconds of ignoring. The teacher was also encouraged to joke with Molly when she was behaving appropriately or to publicly praise her.

The team also used social-skills training to help her express negative emotions in an appropriate manner rather than using profanity. For instance, the school social worker taught Molly to approach her teacher for help when given a difficult assignment and taught her friendship-making skills.

References

Akin-Little, K. A., Eckert, T. L., Lovett, B. J., & Little, S. G. (2004). Extrinsic reinforcement in the classroom: Bribery or best practice? *School Psychology Review, 33*(3), 344–362.

Alberto, P., Heflin, L. J., & Andrews, D. (2002). The use of the timeout ribbon procedures during community-based instruction. *Behavior Modification, 26*(2), 297–311.

Alexander, K., & Alexander, M. D. (1998). *American public school law* (4th ed.). Belmont, CA: West/Wadsworth.

Allen, L. J., Howard, V. F. R., Sweeney, W. J., & McLaughlin, T. F. (1993). Use of contingency contracting to increase on-task behavior with primary students. *Psychological Reports, 72*, 905–906.

Anderson, C. M., & Kincaid, D. (2005). Applying behavior analysis to school violence and discipline problems: Schoolwide positive behavior support. *Behavior Analyst, 28*, 49–63.

Atkins, M. S., McKay, M. M., Frazier, S. L., Jakobsons, L. J., Arvanitis, P., Cunningham, T., et al. (2002). Suspensions and detentions in an urban, low-income school: Punishment or reward? *Journal of Abnormal Child Psychology, 30*(4), 361–371.

Axup, T., & Gersch, I. (2008). The impact of challenging student behaviour upon teachers' lives in a secondary school: Teachers' perceptions. *British Journal of Special Education, 35*(3), 144–151.

Bambara, L. M., Gomez, O., Koger, F., Lohrmann-O'Rourke, S., & Xin, Y. P. (2001). More than techniques: Team members' perspectives on implementing positive supports for adults with severe challenging behaviors. *Journal of the Association for Persons With Severe Handicaps, 26*, 213–228.

Barret, S. B., Bradshaw, C. P., & Lewis-Palmer, T. (2008). Maryland statewide PBIS initiative. *Journal of Positive Behavior Interventions, 10*(2), 105–114.

Barrish, H. H., Saunders, M., & Wolf, M. M. (1969, Summer). Good behavior game: Effects of individual contingencies for group consequences on disruptive behavior in a classroom. *Journal of Applied Behavior Analysis, 2*(2), 119–124.

Beaman, R., & Wheldall, K. (2000). Teachers' use of approval and disapproval in the classroom. *Educational Psychology*, *20*(4), 431–446.

Bear, G. G. (2008). Classroom discipline. In A. Thomas & J. Grimes (Eds.), *Best practices in school psychology V*. Bethesda, MD: National Association of School Psychologists.

Bondy, E., Ross, D. D., Gallingane, C., & Hambacher, E. (2007). Creating environments of success and resilience. *Urban Education*, *42*(4), 326–348.

Bradshaw, C. P., Sawyer, A. L., & O'Brennan, L. M. (2007). Bullying and peer victimization at school: Perceptual differences between students and school staff. *School Psychology Review*, *36*(3), 361–382.

Burns, M. K., & Gibbons, K. A. (2008). *Implementing response-to-intervention in elementary and secondary schools*. New York: Routledge.

Burns, M. K., VanDerHeyden, A. M., & Boice, C. H. (2008). Best practices in delivery of intensive academic interventions. In A. Thomas & J. Grimes (Eds.), *Best practices in school psychology* (5th ed.). Bethesda, MD: National Association of School Psychologists.

Calderhead, W. J., Filter, K. J., & Albin, R. W. (2006). An investigation of incremental effects of interspersing math items on task-related behavior. *Journal of Behavioral Education*, *15*(1), 53–67.

Cameron, C. E., Connor, C. M., & Morrison, F. J. (2005). Effects of variation in teacher organization on classroom functioning. *Journal of School Psychology*, *43*(1), 61–85.

Carr, E. G. (1977). The motivation of self-injurious behavior: A review of some hypotheses. *Psychological Bulletin*, *84*, 800–816.

Carr, E. G., Dunlap, G., Horner, R. H., Koegel, R. L., Turnbull, A. P., Sailor, W., et al. (2002). Positive behavior support: Evolution of an applied science. *Journal of Positive Behavior Interventions*, *4*(1), 16–20.

Carter, J., & Sugai, G. (1989). Survey on prereferral practices: Responses from state departments of education. *Exceptional Children*, *55*, 298–302.

Chafouleas, S. M., Riley-Tillman, T. C., & McDougal, J. L. (2002). Good, bad, or in-between: How does the daily behavior report card rate? *Psychology in the Schools*, *39*(2), 157–169.

Chafouleas, S. M., Riley-Tillman, T. C., & Sassu, K. A. (2006). Acceptability and reported use of daily behavior report cards among teachers. *Journal of Positive Behavior Interventions, 8*(3), 174–182.

Chalifant, J. C., Pysh, M. V. D., & Moultrie, R. (1979). Teacher assistance teams: A model for within-building problem solving. *Learning Disability Quarterly, 2*, 85–95.

Clonan, S. M., McDougal, J. L., Clark, K., & Davison, S. (2007). Use of office discipline referrals in school-wide decision making: A practical example. *Psychology in the Schools, 44*(1), 19–27.

Colvin, G., & Fernandez, E. (2000). Sustaining effective behavior support systems in an elementary school. *Journal of Positive Behavior Interventions, 2*, 251–254.

Colvin, G., Kameenui, E. J., & Sugai, G. (1993). Reconceptualizing behavior management and school-wide discipline in general education. *Education and Treatment of Children, 16*, 361–381.

Colvin, G., Sugai, G., Good, R. H., & Lee, Y-Y. (1997). Using active supervision and precorrection to improve transition behaviors in an elementary school. *School Psychology Quarterly, 12*(4), 344–363.

Colvin, G., Sugai, G., & Patching, B. (1993). Precorrection: An instructional approach for managing predictable problem behaviors. *Intervention in School and Clinic, 28*(3), 143–150.

Craig, W. M., Pepler, D., & Atlas, R. (2000). Observations of bullying in the playground and in the classroom. *School Psychology International, 21*(1), 22–36.

Crone, D. A., & Horner, R. H. (2003). *Building positive behavior support systems in schools.* New York: Guilford.

Crone, D. A., Horner, R. H., & Hawken, L. S. (2004). *Responding to problem behavior in schools: The behavior education program.* New York: Guilford.

Deci, E. L., Koestner, R., & Ryan, R. M. (2001). Extrinsic rewards and intrinsic motivation in education: Reconsidered once again. *Review of Educational Research, 71*, 1–27.

De Martini-Scully, D., Bray, M. A., & Kehle, T. J. (2000). A packaged intervention to reduce disruptive behaviors in general education students. *Psychology in the Schools, 37*(2), 149–156.

De Pry, R. L., & Sugai, G. (2002). The effect of active supervision and pre-correction on minor behavioral incidents in a sixth grade general education classroom. *Journal of Behavior Education, 11*(4), 255–267.

Doll, B., Zucker, S., & Brehm, K. (2004). *Resilient classrooms.* New York: Guilford.

Drasgow, E., Yell, M. L., Bradley, R., & Shriner, J. G. (1999). The IDEA Amendments of 1997: A school-wide model for conducting functional behavioral assessments and developing behavior intervention plans. *Education and Treatment of Children, 22*, 244–266.

Drummond, L. M. (1993). The treatment of severe, chronic, resistant obsessive–compulsive disorder. An evaluation of an in-patient programme using behavioural psychotherapy in combination with other treatments. *British Journal of Psychiatry, 163*, 223–229.

Dunlap, G., Clarke, S., Jackson, M., & Wright, S. (1995). Self-monitoring of classroom behaviors with students exhibiting emotional and behavioral challenges. *School Psychology Quarterly, 10*, 165–177.

Dunlap, G. L., Newton, S., Fox, L., Benito, N., & Vaughn, B. (2001). Family involvement in functional assessment and positive behavior support. *Focus on Autism and Other Developmental Disabilities, 14*, 215–221.

DuPaul, G. J., Stoner, G., & O'Reilly, M. J. (2008). Best practices in classroom interventions for attention problems. In A. Thomas & J. Grimes (Eds.), *Best practices in school psychology V* (pp. 1421–1437). Washington, DC: National Association of School Psychologists.

Dwyer, K. P., Osher, D., & Hoffman, C. (2000). Creating responsive schools: Contextualizing early warning, timely response. *Exceptional Children, 66*, 347–365.

Eber, L., Lewis-Palmer, T., & Pacchiano, D. (2002). *Schoolwide positive behavior systems: Improving school environments for all students including those with EBD* (ERIC Document Reproduction Service No. ED465253). Washington, DC: National Institute on Disability and Rehabilitation Research.

Eckerman, D. A., & Vreeland, R. (1973). Response variability for humans receiving continuous, intermittent, or no positive experimenter feedback. *Bulletin of the Psychonomic Society, 2*, 297–299.

Elliott, S. N., Huai, N., & Roach A. T. (2007). Universal and early screening for educational difficulties: Current and future applications. *Journal of School Psychology, 45*, 137–161.

Evenson, A., Justinger, B., Pelischek, E., & Schulz, S. (2009). Zero tolerance policies and the public schools: When suspension is no longer effective. *Communiqué, 37*(5). Retrieved March 16, 2009, from http://www.NASPonline.org

Fabiano, G. A., & Pelham, W. E. (2003). Improving the effectiveness of classroom intervention for attention deficit hyperactivity disorder: A case study. *Journal of Emotional and Behavioral Disorders, 11*, 122–128.

Fabiano, G. A., Pelham, W. E., Gnagy, E. M., Burrows-MacLean, L., Coles, E. K., Chacko, A., et al. (2007). The single and combined effects of multiple intensities of behavior modification and methylphenidate for children with attention deficit hyperactivity disorder in a classroom setting. *School Psychology Review, 36*(2), 195–216.

Fairbanks, S., Simonsen, B., & Sugai, G. (2008). Classwide secondary and tertiary tier practices and systems. *Teaching Exceptional Children, 40*(6), 44–52.

Fay, J., & Funk, D. (1995). *Teaching with love and logic: Taking control of the classroom.* Golden, CO: Love and Logic.

Ferster, C. B., & Skinner, B. F. (1957). *Schedules of reinforcement.* New York: Appleton Century-Crofts.

Fitzpatrick, J. L., Sanders, J. R., & Worthen, B. R. (2004). *Program evaluation: Alternative approaches and practical guidelines* (3rd ed.). Boston: Allyn & Bacon.

Fraznen, K., & Kamps, D. (2005). The utilization and effects of positive behavior support strategies on an urban school playground. *Journal of Positive Behavior Interventions, 10*(3), 150–161.

Friedman, R. M. (2003). Improving outcomes for students through the application of a public health model to school psychology: A commentary. *Journal of School Psychology, 41*, 69–75.

Gable, R. A., Hester, P. H., Rock, M. L., & Hughes, K. G. (2009). Back to basics: Rules, praise, ignoring, and reprimands revisited. *Intervention in School and Clinic, 44*(4), 195–205.

Gickling, E. E., & Armstrong, D. L. (1978). Levels of instructional difficulty as related to on-task behavior, task completion, and comprehension. *Journal of Learning Disability, 11*, 559–566.

Gilbertson, D., Witt, J. C., Duhon, G., & Dufrene, B. (2008). Using brief assessments to select math fluency and on-task behavior interventions: An investigation of treatment utility. *Educational and Treatment of Children, 31*(2), 167–181.

Gresham, F. M. (2004). Current status and future directions of school-based behavioral interventions. *School Psychology Review, 33*(3), 326–343.

Gresham, F. M. (2005). Response to intervention: An alternative means of identifying students as emotionally disturbed. *Education and Treatment of Children, 28*, 328–344.

Gresham, F. M., Watson, T. S., & Skinner, C. H. (2001). Functional behavioral assessment: Principles, procedures, and future directions. *School Psychology Review, 30*, 156–172.

Hallfors, D., Cho, H., Brodish, P. H., Flewelling, R., & Khatapoush, S. (2006). Identifying high school students "at risk" for substance use and other behavioral problems: Implications for prevention, *Substance Use & Misuse, 41*, 1–15.

Hawe, E., Tuck, B., Manthei, R., Adair, V., & Moore, D. (2000). Job satisfaction and stress in New Zealand primary teachers. *New Zealand Journal of Educational Studies, 35*(2), 193–202.

Hawken, L. S. (2006). School psychologists as leaders in the implementation of a targeted intervention: The behavior education program. *School Psychology Quarterly, 21*(1), 91–111.

Hawken, L. S., MacLeod, K. S., & Rawlins, L. (2007). Added effects of the behavior education program (BEP) on office discipline referrals of elementary school students. *Journal of Positive Behavior Interventions, 9*(2), 94–101.

Haydon T., & Scott, T. M. (2008). Using common sense in common settings: Active supervision and precorrection in the morning gym. *Intervention in School & Clinic, 43*(5), 283–290.

Hoff, K. E., & DuPaul, G. J. (1998). Reducing disruptive behavior in general education classrooms: The use of self-management strategies. *School Psychology Review, 27*, 290–303.

Horner, R. H., Sugai, G., Eber, L., Phillips, D., & Lewandowski, H. (2004). *Illinois Positive Interventions and Supports Project: 2002–2003 progress report.* Chicago: ISBE EBD/PBIS Network.

Hulac, D. M., & Benson, N. (2010). The use of group contingencies for preventing and managing disruptive behaviors. *Intervention in the School and Clinic, 45*(4), 257–262.

Hunter, L. (2003). School psychology: A public health framework III. Managing disruptive behavior in schools: The value of a public health and evidence-based perspective. *Journal of School Psychology, 41*, 39–59.

Individuals With Disabilities Education Improvement Act of 2004, 20 U.S.C. § 1400 *est seq.* (2004) (reauthorization of the Individuals with Disabilities Education Act of 1990).

Infantino, J., & Little, E. (2005). Students perceptions of classroom behavior problems and the effectiveness of different disciplinary methods. *Educational Psychology, 25*(5), 491–508.

Ingram, K., Lewis-Palmer, T., & Sugai, G. (2005). Function-based intervention planning: Comparing the effectiveness of FBA function-based and non–function-based intervention plans. *Journal of Positive Behavior Interventions, 7*(4), 224–236.

Irvin, L. K., Horner, R. H., Ingram, K., Todd, A. W., Sugai, G., Sampson, N., et al. (2006). Using office discipline referral data for decision-making about student behavior in elementary and middle schools: An empirical investigation of validity. *Journal of Positive Behavior Interventions, 8*(1), 10–23.

Irvin, L. K., Tobin, T., Sprague, J., Sugai, G., & Vincent, C. (2004). Validity of office discipline referral measures as indices of school-wide behavioral status and effects of school-wide behavioral interventions. *Journal of Positive Behavior Interventions, 6*, 131–147.

Iverson, A. M. (2002). Best practices in problem-solving team structure and process. In A. Thomas & J. Grimes (Eds.), *Best practices in school psychology IV* (pp. 657–669). Bethesda, MD: National Association of School Psychologists.

Johnson-Gros, K., Lyons, E. A., & Griffin, J. A. (2008). Active supervision: An intervention to reduce high school tardiness. *Education & Treatment of Children, 31*(1), 39–53.

Jolivette, K., Barton-Atwood, S., & Scott, T. M. (2000). Functional behavioral assessment as a collaborative process among professionals. *Education & Treatment of Children, 23*, 298–313.

Kelley, M. L., & Stokes, T. F. (1982). Contingency contracting with disadvantaged youths: Improving classroom performance. *Journal of Applied Behavior Analysis, 15*, 447–454.

Kohn, A. (1993). *Punished by rewards: The trouble with gold stars, incentive plans, A's, praise, and other bribes.* Boston: Houghton Mifflin.

Kounin, J. S. (1970). *Discipline and group management in classrooms.* New York: Holt, Rinehart & Winston.

Lampi, A. R., Fenty, N. S., & Beaunae, C. (2005). Making the three Ps easier: Praise, proximity, and precorrection. *Beyond Behavior, 15*(1), 8–12.

Lane, K. L., Barton-Arwood, S. M., Nelson, J. R., & Wehby, J. (2008). Academic performance of students with emotional and behavioral disorders served in a self-contained setting. *Journal of Behavioral Education, 17*, 43–62.

Lane, K. L., Gresham, F. M., & O'Shaughnessy, T. E. (2002). Identifying, assessing, and intervening with children with or at risk for behavior disorders: A look to the future. In K. L. Lane, F. M. Gresham, & T. E. O'Shaughnessy (Eds.), *Interventions for children with or at risk for emotional and behavioral disorders* (pp. 317–326). Boston: Allyn & Bacon.

Lassen, S. Steele, M., & Sailor, W. (2006). The relationship of school-wide positive behavior support to academic achievement in an urban middle school. *Psychology in the Schools, 43*(6), 701–712.

Leedy, A., Bates, P., & Safran, S. (2004). Bridging the research-to-practice gap: Improving hallway behavior using positive behavior supports. *Behavioral Disorders, 29*(2), 130–139.

Lerman, D. C., & Iwata, B. A. (1995). Prevalence of the extinction burst and its attenuation during treatment. *Journal of Applied Behavior Analysis, 28*(1), 93–94.

Lewis, T. J., Colvin, G., & Sugai, G. (2000). The effects of precorrection and active supervision on the recess behavior of elementary students. *Education and Treatment of Children, 23*, 109–121.

Lewis, T. J., & Sugai, G. (1999). Effective behavior support: A system approach to proactive school-wide management. *Focus on Exceptional Children, 31*(6), 1–24.

Lewis-Palmer, T., Sugai, G., & Larson, S. (1999). Using data to guide decisions about program implementation and effectiveness. *Effective School Practices, 17*(4), 37–43.

Litow, L., & Pumroy, D. K. (1975). A brief review of classroom group-oriented contingencies. *Journal of Applied Behavior Analysis, 8*(3), 341–347.

Little, S. G., & Akins-Little, A. (2008). Psychology's contributions to classroom management. *Psychology in the Schools, 45*(3), 227–234.

Loftin, R. L., Gibb, A. C., & Skiba, R. (2005). Using self-monitoring strategies to address behavior and academic issues. *Impact, 18*(2). Retrieved March 19, 2008, from http://ici.umn.edu/products/impact/182/over6.html

Luiselli, J. K., Putnam, R. F., Handler, M. W., & Feinberg, A. B. (2005). Whole-school positive behaviour support: Effects on student discipline problems and academic performance. *Educational Psychology, 25*, 183–198.

Maag, J. W. (2001). Rewarded by punishment: Reflections on the disuse of positive reinforcement in schools. *Exceptional Children, 67*(2), 173–186.

Madsen, C. H., Becker, W. C., & Thomas, D. R. (1968). Rules, praise, and ignoring, elements of elementary classroom control. *Journal of Applied Behavior Analysis, 1*(2), 139–150.

Marchant, M., Anderson, D. H., Caldarella, P., Fisher, A., Young, B. J., & Young, K. R. (2009). Schoolwide screening and programs of positive behavior support: Informing universal interventions. *Preventing School Failure, 53*(3), 131–143.

Marlow, A., Tingstrom, D., & Olmi, D. (1997). The effects of classroom-based time-in/time-out on compliance rates in children with speech/language disabilities. *Child & Family Behavior Therapy, 19*(2), 1–15.

Matheson, A. D., & Shriver, M. D. (2005). Training teachers to give effective commands: Effects on student compliance and academic behaviors. *School Psychology Review, 34*, 202–219.

McKevitt, B. C., & Braaksma, A. D. (2008). Best practices in developing a positive behavior support system at the school level. In A. Thomas & J. Grimes (Eds.), *Best practices in school psychology V* (pp. 735–747). Washington, DC: National Association of School Psychologists.

Metzler, C. W., Biglan, A., Rusby, J. C., & Sprague, J. R. (2001). Evaluation of a comprehensive behavior management program to improve school-wide positive behavior support. *Education and Treatment of Children, 24*, 448–479.

Miller, M., Miller, S. R., Wheeler, J., & Selinger, J. (1989). Can a single-classroom treatment approach change academic performance and behavioral characteristics in severely behaviorally disordered adolescents? An experimental inquiry. *Behavioral Disorders, 14*(4), 215–225.

Miltenberger, R. G. (2001). *Behavior modification: Principles and procedures* (2nd ed.). Belmont, CA: Wadsworth/ Thomson Learning.

Mooney, P., Ryan, J. B., Uhing, B. M., Reid, R., & Epstein, M. H. (2005). Targeting academic outcomes for students with emotional and behavioral disorders. *Journal of Behavioral Education, 14*(3), 203–221.

Munk, D. M., & Repp, A. C. (1994). The relationship between instructional variables and problem behavior: A review. *Exceptional Children, 60*(5), 390–401.

Nelson, J. (1985). The three R's of logical consequences, the three R's of punishment, and the six steps for winning children over. *Individual Psychology: Journal of Adlerian Theory, Research & Practice, 41*(2), 161–165.

Nelson, J. R. (1996). Designing schools to meet the needs of students who exhibit disruptive behavior. *Journal of Emotional and Behavioral Disorders, 4*, 147–161.

Nelson, J. R., Benner, G. J., Reid, R. C., Epstein, M. H., & Currin, D. (2002). The convergent validity of office discipline referrals with the CBCL-TRF. *Journal of Emotional & Behavioral Disorders, 10*(3), 181–188.

No Child Left Behind Act. (2001). Public Law 107-15.

O'Leary, K. D., Kaufman, K. F., Kass, R. E., & Drabman, R. S. (1970). The effects of loud and soft reprimands on the behavior of disruptive students. *Exceptional Children, 37*, 145–155.

O'Reilly, M., Lancioni, G., & Taylor, I. (1999). An empirical analysis of two forms of extinction to treat aggression. *Research in Developmental Disabilities, 20*(5), 315–325.

OSEP Technical Assistance Center. (N.d.). *OSEP Center on Positive Behavioral Interventions and Supports*. Retrieved April 12, 2010, from http://www.pbis.org

Oswald, K., Safran, S., & Johanson, G. (2005). Preventing trouble: Making schools safer places using positive behavior supports. *Education and Treatment of Children, 28*(3), 265–278.

Reinke, W. M., & Herman, K. C. (2002). Creating school environments that deter antisocial behaviors in youth. *Psychology in the Schools, 39*, 549–559.

Reinke, W. M., Lewis-Palmer, T., & Merrill, K. (2008). The classroom check-up: A classwide consultation model for increasing praise and decreasing disruptive behavior. *School Psychology Review, 37*, 315–332.

Robinson, S. L., & Skinner, C. H. (2002). Interspersing additional easier items to enhance mathematics performance on subtests requiring different task demands. *School Psychology Quarterly, 17*, 191–205.

Romeo, F. F. (1998). The negative effects of using a group contingency system. *Journal of Instructional Psychology*, *25*(2), 130–133.

Ruth, W. J. (1996). Goal setting and behavior contracting for students with emotional and behavioral difficulties: Analysis of daily, weekly, and total goal attainment. *Psychology in the Schools*, *33*, 153–158.

Safran, S. P. (2006). Using the effective behavior supports survey to guide development of schoolwide positive behavior support. *Journal of Positive Behavior Interventions*, *8*(1), 3–9.

Safran, S. P., & Oswald, K. (2003). Positive behavior supports: Can schools reshape disciplinary practices? *Exceptional Children*, *69*, 361–373.

Schanding, G. T., Tingstrom, D. H., & Sterling-Turner, H. (2009). Evaluation of stimulus preference assessment methods with general education students. *Psychology in the Schools*, *46*(2), 89–99.

School-wide Information System. (2008). [Home page]. Retrieved July 15, 2009, from http://www.swis.org

Schwanz, K. A., & Barbour, B. (2005). Problem-solving teams: Information for educators and parents. *NASP Communiqué*, *33*(8). Retrieved April 12, 2010, from http://www.naspon-line.org/publications/cq/cq338probsolve.aspx

Scott, T. M. (2001). A schoolwide example of positive behavioral support. *Journal of Positive Behavior Interventions*, *3*, 88–95.

Scott, T. M., & Barrett, S. B. (2004). Using staff and student time engaged in disciplinary procedures to evaluate the impact of school-wide PBS. *Journal of Positive Behavior Interventions*, *6*, 21–27.

Scott, T. M., & Hunter, J. (2001). Initiating schoolwide support systems: An administrator's guide to the process. *Beyond Behavior*, *11*(1), 13–15.

Sentürk, H. (2006). Student teachers' perceptions of classroom management models used by expert teachers. *Educational Administration: Theory & Practice*, *48*, 598–603.

Severson, H., Walker, H., Hope-Doolittle, J., Kratochwill, T., & Gresham, F. (2007). Proactive early screening to detect behaviorally at-risk students: Issues, approaches, emerging innovations, and professional practices. *Journal of School Psychology*, *45*, 193–223.

Simonsen, B., Fairbanks, S., Briesch, A., Myers, D., & Sugai, G. (2008). Evidence-based practices in classroom management: Considerations for research to practice. *Education & Treatment of Children, 31*(3), 351–380.

Skiba, R. J. (2008). Are zero tolerance policies effective in the schools? An evidentiary review and recommendations. *American Psychologist, 63*(9), 852–862.

Skiba, R. J., Reynolds, C. R., Graham, S., Sheras, P., Conoley, J. C., & Garcia-Vazquez, E. (2006). *Are zero tolerance policies effective in the schools? An evidentiary review and recommendations. A report by the American Psychological Association zero tolerance task force.* Washington, DC: American Psychological Association. Retrieved March 16, 2009, from http://www.apa.org/releases/ZTTFReportBODRevisions5-15.pdf

Skinner, B. F. (1938). *The behavior of organism: An experimental analysis.* New York: Appleton Century-Crofts.

Skinner, B. F. (1969). *Contingencies of reinforcement.* New York: Appleton Century-Crofts

Skinner, B. F. (1974). *On behaviorism.* New York: Vintage.

Skinner, C. H., Cashwell, C. S., & Dunn, M. S. (1996). Independent and interdependent group contingencies: Smoothing the rough waters. *Special Services in the Schools, 12,* 61–78.

Skinner, C. H., Hurst, K. L, Teeple, D. F., & Meadows, S. O. (2002). Increasing on-task behavior during mathematics independent seat-work in students with emotional disturbance by interspersing additional brief problems. *Psychology in the Schools, 39,* 647–659.

Skinner, C. H., & Skinner, C. F. (1999). Using interdependent contingencies with groups of students: Why the principal kissed a pig. *Educational Administration Quarterly, 35*(4, Suppl.), 806–820.

Slavin, R. E. (2006). *Educational psychology: Theory and practice* (8th ed.). New York: Pearson.

Sprick, R. S. (2006). *Discipline in the secondary classroom: A positive approach to behavior management* (2nd ed.). Hoboken, NJ: John Wiley.

Sprick, R., Knight, J., Reinke, W., & McKale, T. (2006). *Coaching classroom management: Strategies and tools for administrators and coaches.* Eugene, OR: Pacific Northwest.

Sterling-Turner, H. E., Robinson, S. L., & Wilczynski, S. M. (2001). Functional assessment of distracting and disruptive behaviors in the school setting. *School Psychology Review, 30*(2), 211–226.

Strein, W., Hoagwood, K., & Cohn, A. (2003). School psychology: A public health perspective I. Prevention, populations, and system change. *Journal of School Psychology, 41*, 23–38.

Stronge, J. H., Ward, T. J., Tucker, P. D., & Hindman, J. L. (2007). What is the relationship between teacher quality and student achievement? An exploratory study. *Journal of Personnel Evaluation in Education, 20*, 165–184.

Sugai, G., & Horner, R. (2002a). The evolution of discipline practices: Schoolwide positive behavior supports. *Child & Family Behavior Therapy, 24*, 23–50.

Sugai, G., & Horner, R. H. (2002b). Introduction to the special series on positive behavior supports in schools. *Journal of Emotional & Behavioral Disorders, 10*(3), 130–135.

Sugai, G., Horner, R. H., Dunlap, G., Hieneman, M., Lewis, T. J., Nelson, C. M., et al. (2000). Applying positive behavior support and functional behavioral assessment in schools. *Journal of Positive Behavior Interventions, 2*, 131–143.

Swinson, J., & Knight, R. (2007). Teacher verbal feedback directed towards secondary pupils with challenging behaviour and its relationship to their behaviour. *Educational Psychology in Practice, 23*(3), 241–255.

Taylor-Green, S. J., & Kartub, D. T. (2000). Durable implementation of school-wide behavior support: The high five program. *Journal of Positive Behavior Interventions, 2*(4), 233–235.

Thorndike, E. L. (1913). Animal intelligence; An experimental study of the associative processes in animals. *Psychology Review Monograph Supplement, 2*(8), 1–109.

Tidwell, A., Flannery, K. B., & Lewis-Palmer, T. (2003). A description of elementary classroom discipline referral patterns. *Preventing School Failure, 48*, 18–26.

Todd, A. W., Campbell, A. L., & Meyer, G. G. (2008). The effects of a targeted intervention to reduce problem behaviors: Elementary school implementation of check in–check out. *Journal of Positive Behavior Interventions, 10*(1), 46–55.

Trussell, R. P. (2008). Classroom universals to prevent problem behaviors. *Intervention in School and Clinic, 43*(3), 179–185.

Turnbull, A., Turnbull, H., Shank, M., Smith, S., & Leal, D. (2002). *Exceptional lives* (3rd ed.). Upper Saddle, NJ: Prentice Hall.

Tyre, A. D. (2003). State-level implementation of schoolwide positive behavior support: An evaluation of the Arizona Behavioral Initiative. *Dissertation Abstracts International, 64* (02),400. (UMI No. 3080893)

University of Southern Mississippi. (2007). *Therapeutic day treatment settings: Behavioral programming for change.* Hattiesburg: Author.

Walker, B., Cheney, D., Stage, S., & Blum, C. (2005). Schoolwide screening and positive behavior supports: Identifying and supporting students at risk for school failure. *Journal of Positive Behavior Interventions, 7*(4), 194–204.

Walker, H. M., Horner, R. H., Sugai, G., Bullis, M., Sprague, J. R., & Bricker, D. (1996). Integrated approaches to preventing antisocial behavior patterns among school-age children and youth. *Journal of Emotional and Behavioral Disorders, 4*, 193–256.

Walker, H. M., Ramsey, E., & Gresham, R. M. (2005). *Antisocial behavior in school: Evidence-based practices* (2nd ed.). Belmont, CA: Wadsworth/Thomson Learning.

Walker, H. M., & Severson, H. H. (1992). *Systematic screening for behavior disorders.* Longmont, CO: Sopris West.

Walker, H. M., Zeller, R. W., Close, D. W., Webber, J., & Gresham, F. (1999). The present unwrapped: Change and challenge in the field of behavioral disorders. *Behavioral Disorders, 24*, 293–304.

Wannarka, R., & Ruhl, K. (2008). Seating arrangements that promote positive academic and behavioural outcomes: A review of empirical research. *Support for Learning, 23*(2), 89–93.

Winett, R. A., Moore, J. F., & Anderson, E. S. (1991). Extending the concept of social validity: Behavioral analysis for disease prevention and health promotion. *Journal of Applied Behavior Analysis, 24*(2), 215–230.

Witt, J. C., Gilbertson, D., & VanDerHeyden, A. (2007). Instruction and classroom management: Prevention and intervention. In R. B. Rutherford, M. M. Quinn, & S. R. Mathur (Eds.), *Handbook of research in emotional and behavioral disorders.* New York: Guilford.

Witt, J. C., VanDerHeyden, A. M., & Gilbertson, D. (2004). Troubleshooting behavioral interventions: A systematic process for finding and eliminating problems. *School Psychology Review, 33*(3), 363–383.

Wright, J. (2000). *Behavior contracts.* Retrieved March 19, 2008, from http://www.interventioncentral.org/htmdocs/interventions/behavior/behcontr.php

Wright, J. (N.d.). *Creating reward menus that motivate: Tips for teachers.* Retrieved June 9, 2008, from http://www.interventioncentral.org

CD Contents

FORMS

Form 4.1: Schoolwide Integrity Check Form
Form 5.1: Classroom Self-Monitoring Form
Form 6.1: Positive Behavior Ticket Template
Form 7.1: Office Discipline Referral Form
Form 8.1: Elementary Student Schoolwide Assessment
Form 8.2: Middle School Student Schoolwide Assessment
Form 9.1: Classroom Intervention Form
Form 9.2: Classroom Observation Form
Form 10.1: Tier II Student Questionnaire Form
Form 11.1: Self-Monitoring Form
Form 11.2: Behavioral Contract Form
Form 11.3: Tier II Integrity Checklist
Form 11.4: Daily Behavior Report Card (Younger Students)
Form 11.5: Daily Behavior Report Card (Older Students)
Form 11.6: Intervention Tracking Form
Form 12.1: Target Peer Comparison Form for a Functional Behavioral Assessment (FBA)
Form 12.2: Conditional Probability Form
Form 12.3: Functional Behavior Assessment Form—Teacher Interview
Form 12.4: Antecedent–Behavior–Consequence Narrative Form
Form 13.1: Functional Behavior Summary Chart
Form 13.2: Behavior Plan Worksheet

INTERVENTION COACH CARDS

Coach Card of Opportunities to Respond
Coach Card for Active Supervision of Common Areas
Coach Card for Procedure Training
Coach Card for Basic Classroom Management
Coach Card for the Good Behavior Game (Barrish, Saunders, & Wolf, 1969)
Coach Card for the Classroom Point System (Fabiano & Pelham, 2003; Fabiano et al., 2007)

Coach Card for the Effective Instruction Delivery (EID)
    Procedure
Procedures for the Corrective Teaching Sequence
Coach Card for the Daily Behavior Report Card
Coach Card for Check-In and Check-Out

Appendix A: Forms

Note: The following forms are meant only to help school faculty better support and monitor the behaviors of students and staff. They are not designed to be used for teacher evaluation and should not be used in making high-stakes decisions about any faculty or staff members.

LIST OF FORMS

COPIES OF FORMS WITH DIRECTIONS
FOR COMPLETING THEM

Form 4.1: Schoolwide Integrity Checklist Form

School name: _____

Directions: A member of the problem-solving team should complete a schoolwide integrity checklist on four occasions during the year.

Interview Teachers and Principal to Determine if Procedures Have Been Set Up for the ...	Quarter
Start of the day.	
Office.	
Hallways.	
Common areas.	
Gym.	
School bus.	
Bathrooms.	
Lunchroom.	
Playground.	
Fire drills.	
End of the school day.	
Are the Rules ...	
Observable?	
Enforceable?	
Positively phrased?	
Understandable?	
Has a Training Day Taken Place for the ...	
Start of the day?	
Office?	
Hallways?	
Gym?	
School bus?	
Bathrooms?	
Lunchroom?	
Playground?	
Fire drills?	
End of the school day?	

(Continued)

	First Quarter
Are Staff Scheduled to Monitor the ...	
Start of the day?	
Office?	
Hallways?	
Gym?	
School bus?	
Bathrooms?	
Lunchroom?	
Playground?	
Fire drills?	
End of the school day?	
Pull 5 Students Aside and Ask Them the Following Questions	
1. Do they know the expectations for this area?	
2. Do they know the procedures they must follow in this area?	
At the start of the day?	
In the office?	
In the hallways?	
In the gym?	
In the school bus?	
In the bathrooms?	
In the lunchroom?	
On the playground?	
During fire drills?	
At the end of the school day?	
Randomly Select Teachers and Monitors on Duty and Observe Them Across a Variety of Common Area Settings	
Mark Yes if Staff Members on Duty ...	
Arrive on time.	
Stay until the end of their time.	
Walk toward students who are in groups.	
Help students move through areas that are congested.	
Move their heads back and forth to observe the area around them.	
Interact with students using praises and expectation reminders.	

Form 5.1: Classroom Self-Monitoring Form

Directions:
1. Review each question and answer *yes* or *no* under the corresponding column.
2. As a teacher, review this form as a checklist to plan procedures and classroom management strategies.
3. After the first week of school, complete this checklist to determine if there are any possible problems that may be managed by implementing these interventions.
4. Complete a separate form for yourself at the start of each semester and in the middle of each semester.

	End Week 1	Mid–Fall Semester	Start Spring Semester	Mid– Spring Semester
Classroom Rules				
Posted?				
Positively stated?				
Simple and observable?				
Procedures				
Do students have a short activity at the start of each class or period of the day?				
Do students have idle time during the class? When are students idle?				
Do students remain seated when the bell rings?				
Do students' transition times between activities last less than 2 minutes?				
Is the teacher able to get hold of important materials and papers to make the lessons work effectively?				
Is the classroom neat and orderly when the students have left at the end of the day or class period?				
Praise				
Does the teacher greet each student at the door?				

(Continued)

	End Week 1	Mid–Fall Semester	Start Spring Semester	Mid–Spring Semester
Does the teacher praise students four times as often as he or she reprimands students?				
Does the teacher praise students for following expectations or demonstrating behaviors?				
When giving praise, does the teacher make it clear to the student what he or she did well?				
Does the teacher praise each student?				
Is praise given individually and privately?				
Opportunities to Respond				
Do students have the opportunity to give correct answers two times per minute?				
Do all students have the chance give correct answers through individual or choral responding?				
Does the teacher acknowledge correct answers?				
Do the questions that the teacher asks include at least seven answers the students can answer correctly and quickly?				
Effective Reprimands				
When a teacher reprimands, is it done privately?				
Does the reprimand include a reminder of the expectation?				

(Continued)

(Continued)

	End Week 1	Mid–Fall Semester	Start Spring Semester	Mid– Spring Semester
Is the student praised or acknowledged as soon as he or she follows the expectation?				
Student Seating				
Are the students seated in such a way to minimize behavior problems?				
Does the student seating pattern allow easy access to the desired behaviors?				

Form 6.1: Positive Behavior Ticket Template

You've been noticed! You've been noticed! You've been noticed! You've been noticed!

Name: _____ Name: _____ Name: _____ Name: _____

You've been noticed! You've been noticed! You've been noticed! You've been noticed!

Name: _____ Name: _____ Name: _____ Name: _____

You've been noticed! You've been noticed! You've been noticed! You've been noticed!

Name: _____ Name: _____ Name: _____ Name: _____

You've been noticed! You've been noticed! You've been noticed! You've been noticed!

Name: _____ Name: _____ Name: _____ Name: _____

You've been noticed! You've been noticed! You've been noticed! You've been noticed!

Name: _____ Name: _____ Name: _____ Name: _____

Form 7.1: Office Discipline Referral Form

Student name: _____

Date of infraction: _____

Staff member issuing referral: _____

Time of infraction: _____

Location of infraction: Classroom   Hallway
Playground   Outside of school   Lunchroom
Gymnasium   School office
Other: _____

Infraction (see back for a description of each behavior):

Danger to Self or Others	Disruption of Learning	Destruction of School Property	Violation of School Rules
Fighting	Not following directives; severe defiance	Vandalism	Being in an unauthorized area
Drugs	Arguing with school staff member	Stealing from faculty or staff	
Weapons	Nonviolent bullying	Stealing from peer	
Threats of violence	Verbal abuse of peer		
Physical assault	Verbal abuse of faculty or staff		
Provoking other student	Excessive tardy		
Horseplay			
Other:	Other:	Other:	Other:

Please describe the incident below:

_____
_____
_____
_____
_____

Office Action Taken	
Parent–teacher conference	Referral to counselor or school psychologist
Violence prevention class	Referral to law enforcement
Expulsion	Detention (after school or during lunch time)
In-school suspension (number of days)	Out-of-school suspension
Reparation (describe)	Other (describe)

Danger to Self or Others	
Fighting	Multiple students involved in physical attempts to injure that include, but may not be limited to, punching, slapping, hair pulling, scratching, grabbing, or attempting to injure with a foreign object.
Drugs	Being in possession of or distributing any legal or illegal drug without a specific doctor's note filed with the school's nurse.
Weapons	Bringing or distributing guns, knives, clubs, explosives, or any other device designed to injure other human beings.
Threats of Violence	Student makes verbal or nonverbal threat of violence toward another. Includes spoken, specific threats or gestures indicating that another child or school staff member is in danger.
Physical Assault	The direct injury of another student, school staff member, or visitor of the school.
Provoking Other Student(s)	A student's verbal or nonverbal attempts to encourage or cheer for another student to violate a school rule, or to attempt to get another student angry enough to violate a school rule. This broad category may include students who are watching a fight, instigating fights, or spreading rumors that lead to a fight.
Horseplay	Two or more students involved in physical interactions that seem playful, but may lead to fighting or endanger or obstruct other students, school staff members, or visitors.
Disruption of Learning	
Severe Defiance	A teacher has made multiple attempts to encourage a student to follow a directive, or refrain from disrupting the learning of others, and the student refuses on multiple occasions. This may include a student who is yelling loudly and causing an extreme disruption.
Arguing With a Staff Member	Despite a teacher's repeated attempts to avoid argument, the student continues to disrupt the class by attempting to argue with a teacher.
Verbal Abuse of Peer	One student makes derogatory comments or gestures in writing or verbally about another student. These comments may be "behind the other student's back" or may be "to the other student's face." These comments deliberately injure the emotions or the social standing of others.
Verbal Abuse of Staff Member	One student makes derogatory comments or gestures about a teacher or other school staff member either directly or to other students.
Excessive Tardiness	A student is tardy to class more than three times in a week.
Nonviolent Bullying	Behaviors that deliberately injure the emotional or social functioning of other individuals. These may include spreading rumors, verbal assaults toward an individual, or harassment.

Destruction of Property	
Serious Vandalism	A student either deliberately or carelessly defaces school property, and the damage is difficult to fix by the student. For example, if a student writes on his or her desk, a simple consequence may involve having the student clean that desk or other's desks. Serious vandalism involves permanent damage, damage that requires a professional repair, or damage that the teacher cannot address with a simple consequence and that includes destroying property, (chair, computers, desks, lockers, windows, gym equipment, etc.) or defacing property (painting, writing).
Stealing From a Teacher	A student taking items without permission that are the personal property of the teacher (example, purses, wallets, pens etc.), or are school property that the teacher is using (grade books, teacher's guides etc.)
Stealing From a Student	A student taking items that are the personal property of another student. These items may be school related or not school related. While the school strongly advises all students to leave personal items not necessary for school at home, the school will not tolerate stealing.
Violation of School Rules	
Being in an Unauthorized Area	Any area that has been explicitly marked to forbid students from entering is an unauthorized area. This areas may include teacher's desks, offices, faculty lounges, janitor's closets, stage areas, kitchens, or anywhere outside of school fences. It also includes being in a classroom when not assigned.

Form 8.1: Elementary Student Schoolwide Assessment

Directions: Please circle your answer to the questions.

What grade are you in?

     1   2   3   4   5

Do you feel safe at the school?

     Yes   No

Do you feel scared in ...

The playground?	Yes	No
The hallway?	Yes	No
The school bus?	Yes	No
The lunchroom?	Yes	No
In class?	Yes	No
Other?		

Do you feel scared ...

Before school?	Yes	No
In the morning?	Yes	No
During recess?	Yes	No
In the afternoon?	Yes	No
After school?	Yes	No

What part of the school is the scariest?

_____

_____

Form 8.2: Middle School Student Schoolwide Assessment

Directions: Please circle your answer to the questions.

What grade are you in?

     6   7   8

Do you feel safe at the school?

     Yes   No

Do you feel scared in ...

The playground?	Yes	No
The hallway?	Yes	No
The school bus?	Yes	No
The lunchroom?	Yes	No
In class?	Yes	No
Other?		

Do you feel scared ...

Before school?	Yes	No
In the morning?	Yes	No
During recess?	Yes	No
In the afternoon?	Yes	No
After school?	Yes	No

Where does bullying usually happen?

_____
_____

Form 9.1: Classroom Intervention Form (CIF)

Directions:

1. This form is to be completed by an individual other than the teacher. It may be a member of the problem-solving team or a fellow teacher.
2. The individual should observe the teacher on two separate occasions, preferably during times of the day when behavior problems are more frequent.
3. The observer should mark *yes* or *no* to each question.
4. The teacher should then implement the corresponding intervention when a *no* is answered.

Form 9.1 (Continued)

	Mark *Yes* or *No*	Intervention (If the Response Is *No*, Then Recommend the Corresponding Intervention)
Classroom Rules		
Posted?		Post classroom rules.
Positively stated?		Classroom rules will be positively stated allowing the students to know what they should do.
Simple and observable?		The classroom rules will reflect behaviors that an outsider can see and observe.
Procedures		
Do students have a short activity at the start of each class or period of the day?		The teacher will have an activity ready for students upon entry into the class.
Do students have idle time during the class? When are students idle?		The teacher will create an activity or assignment that students can complete while other students are finishing their work.
Do students remain seated when the bell rings?		When the bell rings, the teacher will have students sit in their seats, and will dismiss them when the class is quiet.
Do students' transition times between activities last less than 2 minutes?		The teacher will practice transition times with the students, and the students will be able to transition from one activity to the next in less than 2 minutes.
Is the teacher able to get hold of important materials and papers to make the lessons work effectively?		The teacher will have all necessary materials available prior to the start of class.
Is the classroom neat and orderly when the students have left at the end of the day or class period?		The teacher will develop and teach students a procedure to neaten the classroom at the end of each day or class period.
Praise		
Does the teacher praise students four times as often as he or she reprimands students?		The teacher will administer four times as many praising statements as reprimands.
Does the teacher praise students for following expectations or demonstrating behaviors?		The teacher will praise students at least one time per 2 minutes for following the expectations of the class.
When giving praise, does the teacher make it clear to the student what he or she did well?		When giving praise, the teacher will inform the students of what they are doing correctly.

Does the teacher praise each student?		The teacher will praise each student during the course of a lesson or class period.
Opportunities to Respond		
Do students have the opportunity to give correct answers two times per minute?		Include two opportunities to respond (OTRs) per minute for students.
Do all students have the chance give correct answers through individual or choral responding?		Include choral responding, responding to partners, individual responding, and writing down correct answers on paper or whiteboards.
Does the teacher acknowledge correct answers?		When a student answers a question correctly, give an acknowledgment of the correct answer.
Do the questions that the teacher asks include at least seven answers the students can answer correctly and quickly?		Write out questions for a lesson. Include seven questions that are facts about the lesson or are review questions.
Effective Reprimands		
When a teacher reprimands is, it done privately?		Issue a reprimand quickly and quietly.
Does the reprimand include a reminder of the expectation?		Tell the student what he or she should do in a reprimand.
Is the student praised or acknowledged as soon as he or she follows the expectation?		After a reprimand, acknowledge the student for following the expectation.
Student Seating		
Are the students seated in such a way to minimize behavior problems?		Arrange a seating pattern that allows the teacher to move quickly between students and, preferably, keeps students an arm's length away from each other.
Does the student seating pattern allow easy access to the desired behaviors?		

Form 9.2: Classroom Observation Form

How many times was a student box checked? _____
Divide that number by 60. _____
Multiply that by 100. _____

How many times was a teacher box checked? _____
Divide that number by 60. _____
Multiply that by 100. _____

Classroom Observation Form (COF)

Classroom Teacher _____ School _____ Grade _____

Date of Observation _____ Time of observation _____ Type of activity _____

1. Every 20 seconds, observe the teacher and one of three students, who are randomly selected from the class.
2. Check teacher boxes if the teacher is involved in instructionally related activity (see "x" for example).
3. Check student boxes if that student is on task. Add the number of checkmarks for all students. Divide by 60 to get a percentage of instructional time.

	Minute 1			Minute 2			Minute 3			Minute 4			Minute 5		
	:20	:40	:60	:20	:40	:60	:20	:40	:60	:20	:40	:60	:20	:40	:60
Teacher															
Student 1															
Student 2															
Student 3															

	Minute 6			Minute 7			Minute 8			Minute 9			Minute 10		
	:20	:40	:60	:20	:40	:60	:20	:40	:60	:20	:40	:60	:20	:40	:60
Teacher															
Student 1															
Student 2															
Student 3															

	Minute 11			Minute 12			Minute 13			Minute 14			Minute 15		
	:20	:40	:60	:20	:40	:60	:20	:40	:60	:20	:40	:60	:20	:40	:60
Teacher															
Student 1															
Student 2															
Student 3															

	Minute 16			Minute 17			Minute 18			Minute 19			Minute 20		
	:20	:40	:60	:20	:40	:60	:20	:40	:60	:20	:40	:60	:20	:40	:60
Teacher															
Student 1															
Student 2															
Student 3															

Form 10.1: Tier II Student Questionnaire Form
(To be completed by the teacher)

Student name: Teacher name:

Date: Grade:

1. What is the behavior that is causing the student to need additional intervention?
   Noncompliance
   Aggression
   Disruption
   Other (please describe) _____
   _____
   _____
   _____

2. When does the behavior occur? _____
   _____
   _____
   _____
   _____
   _____

3. What does this student find to be most enjoyable (e.g., sports, teacher attention, extra recess, peer attention, or edibles; it is appropriate to ask the student)? _____
   _____
   _____
   _____
   _____
   _____

4. What were the student's percentile scores on the most recent standardized test? If standardized test scores are not available, what was the student's performance, as compared to peers, on the most recent math and reading benchmark assessments? _____
   _____
   _____
   _____
   _____
   _____

Form 11.1: Self-Monitoring Form

George's Behavior   Date: _____

Goals:

1. Complete assignments
2. Give my best effort and comply with 75% smiley faces.
3. Be safe and respectful

	Check In	Reading	English	Journal	PE	Lunch	Science	Social Studies	Math	Check Out
Complete Work										
Give Best Effort										
Be Safe and Respectful										

My Goals are   Today I earned:

75% _____

25% _____

10% _____

Mom's Signature _____

Rewards:

*If I reach my daily goal of 75% of smiley faces, I can work on a library computer from 3:00 until the end of school.
* If I receive 10% or less of frowning f aces, I will receive 15 minutes computer time.
*My teachers can reward each smiley face with a Gator Buck, No homework pass, etc...
Extra Bonus Reward: I can earn a reward for my whole class on Friday if I get 75% smiley faces for each day of the week. (Extra outside time, Game time, snacks, etc.)

Form 11.1 (Continued)

How do I get my smiley faces?

1. I must check in and out with Mrs. Jane each morning and afternoon. If Mrs. Jane is not at school, I must report to Mrs. Red, Mrs. Blue, Mrs. White, or Mrs. Black.
2. I will give my folder to all of my teacher's every day.
3. I must learn that if I receive a sad face in one area, I can improve in the next area.
4. For 10% or less of frowning faces, I will receive 15 minutes computer time.
5. I will get my mom's signature each day and return my chart to school each day. I will not be punished at home because of my chart.
6. I will also earn a token from mom for each smiley face I receive at school each day.

Every day is a new day! I can always start over.

Complete Work

- ☐ I will finish all class work as assigned.
- ☐ I will focus on my work until it is finished.
- ☐ While at PE, I will do my exercise and play the game.

Give Best Effort

- ☐ I will comply with adult directions the first time.
- ☐ I will try my best to understand and complete my work.
- ☐ I will stay on task.

Be Safe and Respectful

- ☐ I will speak kindly to my peers and teachers.
- ☐ I will use words to solve problems and frustrations.
- ☐ I will stay in or near my seat.

Form 11.2: Behavioral Contract Form

Student Name: _Benjamin Minova_   Today's Date_____

Directions:
1. At the start of the class period, Benjamin will place this form on the teacher's desk.
2. At the end of the class period, the teacher will give feedback on Benjamin's two goals, and will return the form to Benjamin.
3. At the end of the day, Benjamin will return the form to the CICO coordinator.

Period	Goals	Circle One	Teacher Initials
1	Benjamin came into the classroom, sat down, and got his school supplies out without disrupting other students?	Y N	
	Benjamin followed all directions and rules during the class period?	Y N	
2	Benjamin came into the classroom, sat down, and got his school supplies out without disrupting other students?	Y N	
	Benjamin followed all directions and rules during the class period?	Y N	
3	Benjamin came into the classroom, sat down, and got his school supplies out without disrupting other students?	Y N	
	Benjamin followed all directions and rules during the class period?	Y N	
4	Benjamin came into the classroom, sat down, and got his school supplies out without disrupting other students?	Y N	
	Benjamin followed all directions and rules during the class period?	Y N	
5	Benjamin came into the classroom, sat down, and got his school supplies out without disrupting other students?	Y N	
	Benjamin followed all directions and rules during the class period?	Y N	
6	Benjamin came into the classroom, sat down, and got his school supplies out without disrupting other students?	Y N	
	Benjamin followed all directions and rules during the class period?	Y N	
7	Benjamin came into the classroom, sat down, and got his school supplies out without disrupting other students?	Y N	
	Benjamin followed all directions and rules during the class period?	Y N	

Criteria for success: I will get"Y" circled 9 out of 12 times.
Number circled _____   Criteria met?   Yes   No
Parent signature _____

Form 11.3: Tier II Integrity Checklist (Page 1 of 2)

Student name: Date of integrity check:

A member of the problem-solving team completes this form if he or she is concerned that a Tier II intervention is ineffective.

Corrective Teaching Sequence	✓ if Yes	If the Goal Is Not Checked, the Teacher Should Make the Following Remediation Goal
When Student's Behavior Disrupts the Class, Does the Teacher ...		
Describe the inappropriate behavior?		When the targeted student misbehaves, describe the inappropriate behavior.
Provide a consequence?		When the targeted student misbehaves, provide a consequence.
Describe and demonstrate an appropriate behavior?		When the targeted student misbehaves, describe and demonstrate an appropriate behavior.
Give a reason for an appropriate behavior?		When the targeted student misbehaves, provide a rationale for an appropriate behavior.
Ask for acknowledgment of understanding?		After providing the student with the rationale for the appropriate behavior, ask if the student understands.
Has the student practiced the alternative skill at least two times?		After the student understands the rationale for the appropriate behavior, have the student practice the appropriate behavior two times.
When Giving Directives, Does the Teacher ...		
Use close proximity?		When the teacher is giving a directive to the targeted student, he or she will stand within 5 feet of the student.
Say, "Look at me"?		When giving a directive, the teacher will say to the student, "Look at me."
Praise for eye contact?		When giving a directive, the teacher will praise the student for eye contact.
Give a directive?		When giving a directive, the teacher will be direct.
Use descriptive wording?		When giving a directive, the teacher will describe what the student will do.
Give a 5-second wait?		After giving a directive, the teacher will give the student time to comply with the directive.

Form 11.3: Tier II Integrity Checklist (Page 2 of 2)

Behavioral Contract	✓ if Yes	
Has a specific behavior been identified?		Specific behaviors must be identified.
Were positively stated rules written?		The guidelines must be positively stated and observable.
Has a reward program been included for the student?		The guidelines should include a reward program.

Self-Monitoring	✓ if Yes	
Is the target behavior identified?		Identify target behavior.
Has a self-monitoring system been established and written out?		Create and explicitly spell out a self-monitoring system.
Does the self-monitoring system have a reinforcer built in?		Create a reinforcement schedule.
Has the student been taught the self-monitoring system?		The student will be taught the expectations of the self-monitoring system.
Has the teacher performed reliability checks during the first 3 days of the self-monitoring system?		The teacher will perform counts of the student's behavior during the first 3 days of the self-monitoring system.
If differences exist between the student and the teacher, have the student and teacher problem-solved these differences?		Have the teacher and student meet to problem-solve differences.
Was a procedure built in to fade the system as the student's behavior improved?		Create a fading procedure.

Form 11.5: Daily Behavior Report Card (Younger Students)

My Behavior

Name: _____   Date: _____

Goals: Each day, I will:

	Periods of the day								
Goal 1:									
Goal 2:									
Goal 3:									

At the end of each period of the day, the teacher will give me a

 if I met my goal, a if I come close to meeting my

goal, and a if I don't meet my goal.

My Goals are			Today I earned:	

Parent Signature _____

Rewards:

*If I reach my daily goal, this is what will happen:

Form 11.5: Daily Behavior Report Card (Older Students)

Student name: _____

Today's date: _____

Directions:

1. At the start of the class period, the student will place this form on the teacher's desk.
2. At the end of the class period, the teacher will give feedback on the student's two goals, and will return the form to the student.
3. At the end of the day, the teacher will review the report card to determine if the student earned enough points.
4. The student will take home the form to show to a parent or guardian.

Period	Goals	Circle One	Teacher Initials
1		Y N	
		Y N	
2		Y N	
		Y N	
3		Y N	
		Y N	
4		Y N	
		Y N	
5		Y N	
		Y N	
6		Y N	
		Y N	

Criterion for success: The student will get Y circled _____ out of 12 times.

Number circled: _____   Criterion met?   Yes   No

Parent signature: _____

Form 11.6: Intervention Tracking Form (Page 1 of 2)

Student name	
Behavior of concern	Method of measuring progress

Date	Name of Intervention	Intensity of Intervention	Implementing Intervention	Intervention Integrity Results	Progress Monitoring Data
Ex					
	Self-monitoring	Student self-monitors at the end of every class period.	Ms. Brown	Ms. Beige observed the self-monitoring and found that it was conducted adequately.	Student's office discipline referrals (ODRs) have remained constant. Student's grades have not improved.

Intervention Tracking Form (page 2 of 2)

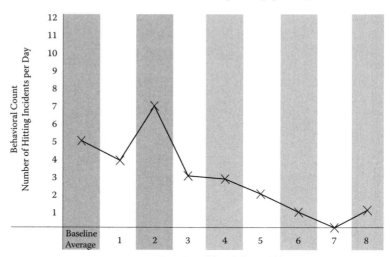

Each note represents a day for Jon

Form 12.1: Target Peer Comparison Form

Directions

Step 1: Determine which 4 behaviors to observe
Step 2: Observe the target student for 10 seconds
Step 3: Record the behaviors for the next 5 seconds under the T column.
Step 4: Observe the student's peer for 10 seconds.
Step 5: Record the peer's behaviors for the next 5 seconds under the P column.
Step 6: Observe the target student again for 10 seconds.
Step 7: Record target student's behaviors for 5 seconds under the T column for 2nd half of the minute.
Step 8: Observe the peer again for 10 seconds.
Step 9: Record the Peer's behaviors for 5 seconds under the p column in the 2nd half of minute 1. The first minute is completed.
Step 10: Return to step 2 until the 20 minutes have elapsed.
Step 11: Add up the number of times a behavior was observed for the target student and for the peer. Record those numbers under the frequency column.

Student Name:
Observer Name:
Date of observation:
Time of observation:

Behavior
1:
2:
3:
4:
5:

Class:
Teacher:
Name of Observer:
Frequency

Target

_____/40 =
_____/40 =
_____/40 =
_____/40 =

Peer

_____/40 =
_____/40 =
_____/40 =
_____/40 =

	Minute 1				Minute 2				Minute 3				Minute 4				Minute 5				Minute 6				Minute 7			
	1st		2nd		1st		2nd		1st		2nd		1st		2nd		1st		2nd		1st		2nd		1st		2nd	
	T	P	T	P	T	P	T	P	T	P	T	P	T	P	T	P	T	P	T	P	T	P	T	P	T	P	T	P
Behavior 1																												
Behavior 2																												
Behavior 3																												
Behavior 4																												
Behavior 5																												

	Minute 8				Minute 9				Minute 10				Minute 11				Minute 12				Minute 13				Minute 14			
					1st		2nd		1st		2nd		1st		2nd		1st		2nd		1st		2nd		1st		2nd	
	T	P	T	P	T	P	T	P	T	P	T	P	T	P	T	P	T	P	T	P	T	P	T	P	T	P	T	P
Behavior 1																												
Behavior 2																												
Behavior 3																												
Behavior 4																												
Behavior 5																												

	Minute 15				Minute 16				Minute 17				Minute 18				Minute 19				Minute 20				Sum			
	T	P	T	P	T	P	T	P	T	P	T	P	T	P	T	P	T	P	T	P	T	P	T	P	T	P	T	P
Behavior 1																												
Behavior 2																												
Behavior 3																												
Behavior 4																												
Behavior 5																												

Form 12.2: Conditional Probability Form

Student Name: _____   Date of Observation: _____

Name of Observer _____

Name of Class: _____   Classroom teacher: _____

		Student Behaviors					FX		Com				Student Behaviors					FX		Com	
		1	2	3	4	5	P	T	Q	E			1	2	3	4	5	P	T	Q	E
1	:00										8	:00									
	:10											:10									
	:20											:20									
	:30											:30									
	:40											:40									
	:50											:50									
2	:00										9	:00									
	:10											:10									
	:20											:20									
	:30											:30									
	:40											:40									
	:50											:50									
3	:00										10	:00									
	:10											:10									
	:20											:20									
	:30											:30									
	:40											:40									
	:50											:50									
4	:00										11	:00									
	:10											:10									
	:20											:20									
	:30											:30									
	:40											:40									
	:50											:50									
5	:00										12	:00									
	:10											:10									
	:20											:20									
	:30											:30									
	:40											:40									
	:50											:50									
6	:00										13	:00									
	:10											:10									
	:20											:20									
	:30											:30									
	:40											:40									
	:50											:50									
7	:00										14	:00									
	:10											:10									
	:20											:20									
	:30											:30									
	:40											:40									
	:50											:50									

Define the student behaviors	Consequences	Compliance	Compliance rate
Student Behavior 1 =	TA = Teacher attention	Q = Teacher directive	Total number of Qs: _____
Student Behavior 2 =	PA = Peer attention	E = Student compliance	
Student Behavior 3 =	ES = Escape/Avoidance		Total number of Es: _____
Student Behavior 4 =	PO = Power		
Student Behavior 5 =	TG = Tangibles		Compliance rate (E÷Q) = _____

Directions:

Step 1: Determine negative or positive student behaviors to observe. Some examples include physical aggression, off-task, out of seat, talking with other peers, throwing items across the classroom, or on-task behavior. If the behavior occurs, mark an X in the box for that 10-second interval.

Step 2: After a student engages in a behavior, mark if the student's peers or teacher give the student attention.

Step 3: If a teacher makes a directive the student should follow, mark a number under the box marked "Q." Mark 1 for the first directive during the observation period, mark 2 for the second directive, and so on. If the student complies with the directive, make an X in the E column for the interval when the child complied.

Form 12.3: Functional Behavior Assessment Form—Teacher Interview (Page 1 of 4)

Student name: Date of birth:

Teacher name: Grade:

School: Interview date:

Describe the behavior of concern (must be observable and measurable): ____
_____
_____
_____

What is an acceptable replacement behavior (must be observable and measurable)? _____
_____
_____

When is the behavior *most frequently* exhibited? (Circle all that apply.)

Time of Day	(a) Before school	(b) Morning	(c) Lunch
		(d) Afternoon	(e) After school
Subject or Class	(a) Reading	(b) Math	(c) Other class
Instructional Style	(a) Independent work	(b) Lecture or class	(c) Discussion
	(d) Small group	(e) Free time	(f) Interruptions
Transitions	(a) Within classroom	(b) Outside of classroom	
Types of Tasks	(a) Easy tasks	(b) Difficult tasks	(c) Hands-on tasks
	(d) Paper-and-pencil tasks		

When is the behavior *least likely* to happen?

Time of Dayl	(a) Before school	(b) Morning	(c) Lunch
		(d) Afternoon	(e) After school
Subject or Classl	(a) Reading	(b) Math	(c) Other class
Instructional Stylel	(a) Independent work	(b) Lecture or class	(c) Discussion
	(d) Small group	(e) Free time	(f) Interruptions
Transitionsl	(a) Within classroom	(b) Outside of classroom	
Types of Tasksl	(a) Easy tasks	(b) Difficult tasks	(c) Hands-on tasks
	(d) Paper-and-pencil tasks		

Where is the behavior *most likely* to occur?

Classroom	Playground	Hallway	Lunchroom	Other (specify)

Where is the behavior *least likely* to occur?

Classroom	Playground	Hallway	Lunchroom	Other (specify)

Form 12.3: Functional Behavior Assessment
Form—Teacher Interview (Page 2 of 4)

What did teachers or staff members do immediately *before* the problematic behavior happens?

Provided direct instruction to the student
Addressed the target student's behaviors
Worked with other student(s)
Led class discussions or lectured
Talked with another adult
Denied the student's request
Issued a directive to the student
Unknown
Other (please describe): _____
_____

What do teachers or staff members do immediately *after* the behavior happens?

Ignore the behavior, or leave the student alone.
Redirect the student.
Send the student out of the classroom.
Give the student a negative consequence or punishment (please describe): _____
_____
Other (please describe): _____
_____

What do other students do immediately prior to the student's problematic behavior? (Circle all that apply.)

Ignore the student
Talk to the student
Make fun of the student
Yell at the student (provoking)
Tell or ask the student to behave appropriately
Negative peer interaction
Other (please describe): _____
_____

What student behaviors immediately followed the student's problematic behavior? (What are the other students doing immediately *after* the behavior happens?) (Circle all that apply.)

Ignoring the student
Talking to the student
Making fun of the student
Yelling at the student (provoking)
Telling or asking the student to behave appropriately
Laughing
Encouraging the student to continue
Moving away from the student
Leaving the student alone
Other (please describe): _____
_____

How did the student perform on the most recent standardized tests (e.g., universal screening or high-stakes testing)?
Name of test:

Reading _____   Math _____

Form 12.3: Functional Behavior Assessment Form—Teacher Interview (Page 3 of 4)

What is the behavior that you want to see instead (i.e., the desired replacement behavior)?

_____

_____

Is there evidence that the student is capable of consistently engaging in this desirable behavior?

                Yes   No

When did this behavior start happening? _____

_____

How long does the behavior last? _____

_____

When is the desirable behavior *most likely* to occur? (Circle all that apply.)

Time of Dayl	(a) Before school	(b) Morning	(c) Lunch
		(d) Afternoon	(e) After school
Subject or Classl	(a) Reading	(b) Math	(c) Other class
Instructional Stylel	(a) Independent work	(b) Lecture or class	(c) Discussion
		(d) Small group	(e) Free time (f) Interruptions
Transitionsl	(a) Within classroom	(b) Outside of classroom	
Types of Tasksl	(a) Easy tasks	(b) Difficult tasks	
	(c) Hands-on tasks	(d) Paper-and-pencil tasks	

When is the desirable behavior *least likely* to occur?

Time of Dayl	(a) Before school	(b) Morning	(c) Lunch
	(d) Afternoon	(e) After school	
Subject or Classl	(a) Reading	(b) Math	(c) Other class
Instructional Stylel	(a) Independent work	(b) Lecture or class	(c) Discussion
	(d) Small group	(e) Free time	(f) Interruptions
Transitionsl	(a) Within classroom	(b) Outside of classroom	
Types of Tasksl	(a) Easy tasks	(b) Difficult tasks	
		(c) Hands-on tasks	(d) Paper-and-pencil tasks

In what location is the desirable behavior *most likely* to occur?

Classroom	Playground	Hallway	Lunchroom	Other (specify)

In what location is the desirable behavior *least likely* to occur?

Classroom	Playground	Hallway	Lunchroom	Other (specify)

Form 12.3: Functional Behavior Assessment Form—Teacher Interview (Page 4 of 4)

What teacher behavior immediately precedes the student's *desirable* behavior? (Circle all that apply.)

Providing direct instruction to the student
Addressing the target student's behaviors
Working with other student(s)
Leading class discussions or lecturing
Talking with another adult
Denying the student's request
Issuing a student directive
Other (please describe): _____
_____

What do teachers or staff do immediately *after* the desirable behavior occurs? (Circle all that apply.)

Ignore the behavior, or leave the student alone.
Redirect the student.
Send the student out of the classroom.
Give the student a consequence.
Provide a positive consequence (e.g., praise).
Other (please describe): _____
_____

What are other students doing immediately *before* the desirable behavior occurs? (Circle all that apply.)

Ignoring the student
Talking to the student
Making fun of the student
Yelling at the student (provoking)
Telling or asking the student to behave appropriately
Other (please describe): _____
_____

What do other students do immediately *after* the desirable behavior happens? (Circle all that apply.)

Ignore the student.
Talk to the student.
Make fun of the student.
Yell at the student (provoking).
Tell or ask the student to behave appropriately.
Laugh.
Encourage the student to continue.
Move away from the student.
Leave the student alone.
Other (please describe): _____
_____

Form 12.4: Antecedent–Behavior–Consequence Narrative Form

Student name: _____

Date and time of observation: _____

Teacher name: _____

Time	Antecedent (What Happened Just *Before* the Behavior?)	Behavior (What Behavior Happened? Be Specific)	Consequence (What Happened Just *After* the Behavior?)

	Events	1	2	3	4	5	6	7	8	9	10	11	12	13	14	15	16	17	18	19	20	21	22	23	24	25	26	27	28	29	30
Antecedent (Trigger)	Teacher issues directive.																														
	Peer says something.																														
	Request is refused.																														
	Students required to work independently.																														
Behavior	Gets out of seat.																														
	Talks to another peer.																														
	Student is off task.																														
	Peer talks to student.																														
	Teacher talks to student.																														
	Student is ignored.																														

Figure 12.5   Antecedent–Behaviour–Consequence (Checklist Version).

Form 13.1: Functional Behavior Summary Chart

Student name: _____

Date form completed: _____

	Antecedent		Behavior		Consequence
What Causes the Problem Behavior?	**What Triggers the Problem Behavior?**		**What Is the Problematic Behavior?**		**What Happens After the Student Engages in the Problematic Behavior?**
What Causes the Replacement Behavior?	**What Happens in the Environment When the Desired Behavior Occurs?**		**What Is the Desired Behavior?**		**What Happens After the Student Engages in the Desirable Behavior?**

Form 13.2: Behavior Plan Worksheet (Page 1 of 2)

Student name: _____

	Antecedent		Behavior		Consequence
How to Avoid the Problematic Behavior?	**What Triggers of the Problematic Behavior Can Be Eliminated?**		**What Is the Problematic Behavior?**		**What Should Occur After the Behavior So That the Student Will Not Continue to Choose to Do the Behavior?**
How Can We Make the Replacement Behavior More Likely?	**How Can We Trigger the Replacement Behavior?**		**What Is the Desired Behavior?**		**How Can the Student Get Their Desires Met by the Replacement Behavior?**
	What Skills Does the Student Need to Learn to Be Successful?				

Form 13.2: Behavior Plan Worksheet (Page 2 of 2)

Communication	Who will be responsible for communicating the behavior plan to the appropriate staff members?
	How will this communication take place (e.g., through writing or oral communication)?
	When will this communication take place?
Social-Skills Training	If any social-skills training is needed for the student, who will be responsible for conducting that training?
	When will the social-skills training occur?
	How long will the skills training need to take place?
Plan Evaluation	How will the behavior-planning team know if the plan is effective (e.g., via review of office discipline referrals [ODRs], absence reports, or systematic classroom observations)?
	Who will be responsible for collecting those evaluation data?
	When will the team review the plan? (The first review should take place within one week of the plan's implementation.)

Signatures: By signing, all participants agree to faithfully implement the portions of this behavior plan.

Parent	
Student	
Classroom teacher	
Problem-solving team members	
School principal	

Appendix B: Intervention Coach Cards

COACH CARD OF OPPORTUNITIES TO RESPOND

- Present a lesson that lasts no more than 5 minutes that describes an important concept or two.
- Ask students questions about the lesson.
- Ask students questions about previous lessons.
- Ensure that students can get 7 out of 10 of the questions correct.
- Aim to offer two opportunities to respond per minute of class time.
- Allow students to respond as follows:
  - Out loud individually
  - Out loud as a whole class
  - Out loud as a small group
  - Sharing an answer with their neighbor
  - Writing down an answer on a sheet of paper
- Praise students briefly for correct answers.
- If a student gets an answer incorrect, ensure that he or she gets a question he or she can answer correctly as soon as possible.

COACH CARD FOR ACTIVE SUPERVISION OF COMMON AREAS

- Those who are supervising a common area arrive on time.
- Those who supervise stay on duty the entire period.
- When students come together in groups, the monitor walks to within 2 feet of that group of students. When moving around in an area, a teacher uses an irregular pattern so that students who wish to misbehave cannot predict when a teacher will look in their direction.
- Escorting students through the common area encourages a monitor to help some students move quicker by walking with them through a transition area. This is especially appropriate for a hallway or thoroughfare where students move from one area to the next.
- Scanning involves teachers constantly moving their heads and eyes to observe the behaviors that are occurring in the common area. Thus, students have the ability to see where the adult is looking, and they know that the adult's attention will soon focus in their direction.
- Teachers interact with students on a regular basis using smiles, touching shoulders, saying hello, or offering some form of interaction. Monitors may consider praising those students who are following the expectations, and providing reminders to rule violators.

COACH CARD FOR PROCEDURE TRAINING

- The goal of the procedure is clear.
- The procedure is broken into multiple parts.
- Each part of the procedure is taught using:
  - Explicit instruction
  - Examples
  - Student practice
  - Corrective feedback
  - Frequent praise
- The students practice the procedure multiple times.
- Once the procedure is mastered, the students practice the procedures again on subsequent days.

COACH CARD FOR BASIC
CLASSROOM MANAGEMENT

- Ensure that the room is laid out in ways that facilitate the goals of the lesson (as space permits). The room layout should:
    - Allow the teacher to move about the classroom with ease
    - Prevent students from being able to hide behind other students
    - Prevent students from being able to reach each other easily
- Use proximity: Move about the classroom on a regular basis so that you are able to stand close to most students.
- Use praise: Make sure praise is specific, genuine, and delivered quietly.
- Redirect inappropriate behaviors: Ensure reprimands are delivered quietly, and tell the students what they should be doing. This should be followed by rapid praise.
- Include many opportunities for students to respond.

COACH CARD FOR THE GOOD BEHAVIOR
GAME (BARRISH, SAUNDERS, & WOLF, 1969)

Select prizes that half of the students in a class can earn. Some examples are a homework pass, an extra point on an upcoming exam, extra recess time, or the chance to line up first for lunch.

- Establish rules.
- These rules should be observable and positively stated.
- The teacher should post the rules.
- Divide the classroom into half with a visible mark.
- Place 10 tally marks on the board.
- When one member of a team breaks a classroom rule, that team loses one tally mark.
- At the end of the class period, the students in the team with the greatest number of points get a prize. If both teams have more than six tally marks, the whole class may earn the prize.

Troubleshooting

Often, one student may take delight in sabotaging his or her team. If this happens, that student should be alone as a member of a third team.

Possible problems: If students in the classroom are aggressive, this intervention may actually exacerbate those problems and create undue levels of tension. If students become overly aggressive when trying to encourage other students to comply, the teacher should stop the Good Behavior Game immediately.

COACH CARD FOR THE CLASSROOM POINT SYSTEM (FABIANO & PELHAM, 2003; FABIANO ET AL., 2007)

This intervention is designed for individuals with attention deficit/hyperactivity disorder. Fabiano and Pelham (2003) created a point system that is an effective means for managing a classroom full of students with limited attention spans. The classroom is set up to allow students frequent opportunities for breaks and a 5-minute recess. If a student has performed well during a segment of the class, that student earns 5 minutes of recess. The other students must remain at their desks working on an assignment.

Point System

- Each student starts with 100 points.
- If a student does not lose points during a segment of class, he or she earns a 5-minute recess.
- The teacher posts the students' points publicly.
- When a student breaks one of the classroom rules, he or she loses 10 points.
- When a student completes an assignment, he or she earns 25 points for completion; he or she can earn an additional 25 points for accuracy.
- The teacher frequently compliments all students who are performing the tasks they need to complete.
- At the end of each week, students have the opportunity to participate in a field trip, field day, or video game party. Those students who earn more than 500 points at the end of the week earn a surprise.

COACH CARD FOR THE EFFECTIVE INSTRUCTION DELIVERY (EID) PROCEDURE

The probability of compliance with adult directives increases with effective delivery of instruction (Matson, Stephens, & Horne, 1978). Effective Instruction Delivery (EID) has proven to increase compliance with severely challenging students (i.e., elementary students in day treatment classrooms). EID is a positive procedure that minimizes the potential of negative side effects during interaction with students. Steps are as follows:

- Establish close proximity with the student (approximately within arm's reach).
- Establish eye contact before you give the instruction to the student.
- Give the student a positive acknowledgment for making eye contact.
- Use a directive rather than a question: "I need you to push your chair in and sit up straight" versus "Will you please sit up straight and push your chair in?"
- Use a quiet-toned voice when delivering the instruction.
- Use a descriptive example: "Answer questions 1 through 5 or sit in your seat or sharpen your pencil."
- Allow a *5-second waiting period* to allow the student time to respond to the instruction.
- Give praise for compliance.

Source: University of Southern Mississippi (2007).

PROCEDURES FOR THE CORRECTIVE
TEACHING SEQUENCE

The Corrective Teaching Sequence (CTS; University of Southern Mississippi, 2007) is best utilized when the student's behavior disrupts the flow of instruction. In correcting students, the teacher provides immediate correction in a manner that is minimally disruptive to instruction. Use the following CTS when correcting a student exhibiting inappropriate behavior.

- Describe the inappropriate behavior.
  - Be specific: Do not force the student to interpret the meaning of your message.
  - Remain calm, nonaccusing, nonmocking, non-threatening, and matter of fact.
- Describe or demonstrate appropriate behaviors.
- Give a rationale for using the alternative behavior.
- Ask student for a verbal response.
- Practice the alternative skill.
- Use praise throughout the process.

COACH CARD FOR THE DAILY
BEHAVIOR REPORT CARD

- Are the goals appropriate? If the child is meeting the goals, is the misbehavior of concern impossible?
- Has a member of the problem-solving team told that teacher that the student has a daily behavior report card?
- Does the student receive a copy of the report card at the start of each day?
- Does the student give the report card to the teacher?
- Does the teacher complete the report card at the assigned times?
- Is the form completely filled out at the end of each day?
- Does the teacher collect the report card and tally the points at the end of each day?
- Does the child earn rewards for meeting criteria for success?

Troubleshooting

If the child is not meeting his or her daily goals, provide a middle step whereby the child can earn partial credit for lower levels of success.

COACH CARD FOR CHECK-IN AND CHECK-OUT

(For a comprehensive checklist for the Behavior Education Program, see Hawken, 2006.)

- Has a coordinator been appointed to meet with students at the start and end of each school day?
- Have several substitutes been named in case the main coordinator is absent or unavailable?
- Is a room available for students to meet?
- Has the coordinator been trained in how to enter data into a spreadsheet?
- Does the student arrive at the check-in and check-out (CICO) coordinator's room at the start of each day?
- Does the student arrive at the CICO coordinator's room at the end of each day?
- Does the student return a completed daily behavior report card?
- Does the child receive the appropriate reward for meeting the criteria for success?
- If contact with a parent is required, does the CICO coordinator make contact with the parent?

Appendix C: Excel Spreadsheet

The following Excel spreadsheet should be used and tracked to sort through Office Discipline Referrals (ODRs). (The names are fictitious. Any resemblance to actual people or events is merely coincidental.)

Date	School	Teacher	Student (Last Name)	Student (First Name)	Infraction	Consequent	Location
9/12/2007	Washington	Ms. Red	Jackson	Elizabeth	Fight	Detention	Playground
9/30/2007	Washington	Ms. Yellow	Boudreaux	Henry	Disrespect	Detention	Classroom
10/1/2007	Washington	Ms. Yellow	Fredricks	Robert	Disrespect	Loss of recess	Lunchroom
10/1/2007	Washington	Ms. Yellow	Phillips	Shanna	Disrespect	Loss of recess	Hallway
10/3/2007	Washington	Mr. Black	Patterson	Dakota	Uniform Violation	Detention	Hallway
10/3/2007	Washington	Ms. Blue	Lincoln	George	Uniform Violation	Detention	Hallway
10/3/2007	Washington	Ms. Yellow	Hebert	Jennifer	Disrespect	Detention	Lunchroom
10/6/2007	Washington	Ms. Green	Bordelon	Michael	Drug Infraction	Detention	Lunchroom
10/6/2007	Washington	Mr. Black	Goldstein	Shawna	Drug Infraction	Explusion	Bathroom
10/6/2007	Washington	Mr. Black	Phillips	Shanna	Disrespect	Loss of recess	Lunchroom
10/9/2007	Washington	Ms. White	Patterson	Dakota	Uniform Violation	Detention	Hallway
10/10/2007	Washington	Mr. Black	Patterson	Dakota	Uniform Violation	Detention	Hallway
10/14/2007	Washington	Mr. Black	Goldstein	Shawna	Drug Infraction	Explusion	Bathroom
10/16/2007	Washington	Ms. Blue	Lincoln	George	Uniform Violation	Detention	Hallway
10/20/2007	Washington	Ms. Green	Phillips	Shanna	Disrespect	Loss of recess	Hallway

If the team wants to sort the list by students, use the following steps:

- Click on Data.
- Click on Sort.

Date	School	Teacher	Student (First Name)	Infraction	Consequent	Location
9/12/2007	Washington	Ms. Red	...th	Fight	Detention	Playground
9/30/2007	Washington	Ms. Yello		Disrespect	Detention	Classroom
10/1/2007	Washington	Ms. Yell		Disrespect	Loss of recess	Lunchroom
10/1/2007	Washington	Ms. Yell		Disrespect	Loss of recess	Hallway
10/3/2007	Washington	Mr. Blac		Uniform Violation	Detention	Hallway
10/3/2007	Washington	Ms. Blue		Uniform Violation	Detention	Hallway
10/3/2007	Washington	Ms. Yell		Disrespect	Detention	Lunchroom
10/6/2007	Washington	Ms. Gree		Disrespect	Detention	Lunchroom
10/6/2007	Washington	Mr. Blac		Drug Infraction	Expulsion	Bathroom
10/6/2007	Washington	Mr. Blac		Disrespect	Loss of recess	Lunchroom
10/9/2007	Washington	Ms. Whi		Uniform Violation	Detention	Hallway
10/10/2007	Washington	Mr. Blac		Uniform Violation	Detention	Hallway
10/14/2007	Washington	Mr. Blac		Drug Infraction	Expulsion	Bathroom
10/16/2007	Washington	Ms. Blue		Uniform Violation	Detention	Hallway
10/20/2007	Washington	Ms. Gree		Disrespect	Loss of recess	Hallway

- Sort by Last Name.
- Select Descending Order.

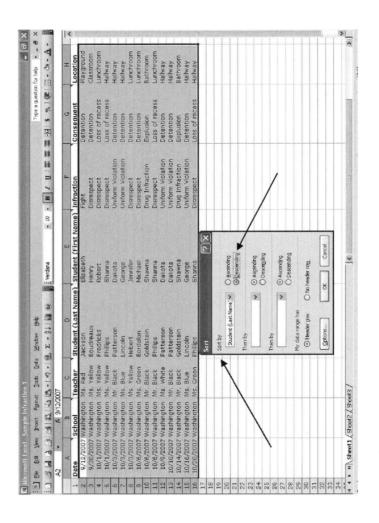

- Data are now sorted.

Microsoft Excel - Sample Infraction 1

File Edit View Insert Format Tools Data Window Help

Type a question for help

Verdana   10   B I U $ %

D19

	A	B	C	D	E	F	G	H
1	Date	School	Teacher	Student (Last Name)	Student (First Name)	Infraction	Consequent	Location
2	10/1/2007	Washington	Ms. Yellow	Phillips	Shanna	Disrespect	Loss of recess	Hallway
3	10/6/2007	Washington	Mr. Black	Phillips	Shanna	Disrespect	Loss of recess	Lunchroom
4	10/20/2007	Washington	Ms. Green	Phillips	Shanna	Disrespect	Loss of recess	Hallway
5	10/3/2007	Washington	Mr. Black	Patterson	Dakota	Uniform Violation	Detention	Hallway
6	10/9/2007	Washington	Ms. White	Patterson	Dakota	Uniform Violation	Detention	Hallway
7	10/10/2007	Washington	Mr. Black	Patterson	Dakota	Uniform Violation	Detention	Hallway
8	10/3/2007	Washington	Ms. Blue	Lincoln	George	Uniform Violation	Detention	Hallway
9	10/16/2007	Washington	Ms. Blue	Lincoln	George	Uniform Violation	Detention	Hallway
10	9/12/2007	Washington	Ms. Red	Jackson	Elizabeth	Fight	Detention	Playground
11	10/3/2007	Washington	Ms. Yellow	Hebert	Jennifer	Disrespect	Detention	Lunchroom
12	10/6/2007	Washington	Mr. Black	Goldstein	Shawna	Drug Infraction	Explusion	Bathroom
13	10/14/2007	Washington	Mr. Black	Goldstein	Shawna	Drug Infraction	Explusion	Bathroom
14	10/1/2007	Washington	Ms. Yellow	Fredricks	Robert	Disrespect	Loss of recess	Lunchroom
15	9/30/2007	Washington	Ms. Yellow	Boudreaux	Henry	Disrespect	Detention	Classroom
16	10/6/2007	Washington	Ms. Green	Bordelon	Michael	Disrespect	Detention	Lunchroom
17								

- Select all columns by clicking the blank cell above the number 1.

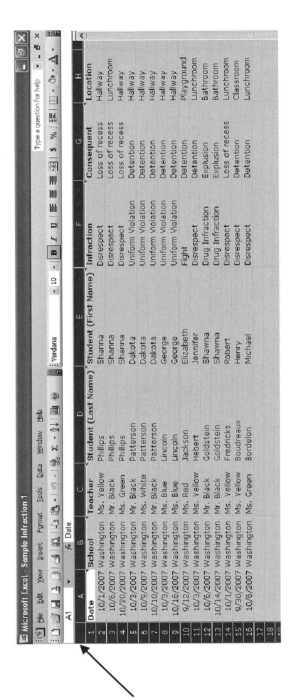

Date	School	Teacher	Student (Last Name)	Student (First Name)	Infraction	Consequent	Location
10/1/2007	Washington	Ms. Yellow	Phillips	Shanna	Disrespect	Loss of recess	Hallway
10/6/2007	Washington	Mr. Black	Phillips	Shanna	Disrespect	Loss of recess	Lunchroom
10/20/2007	Washington	Ms. Green	Phillips	Shanna	Disrespect	Loss of recess	Hallway
10/3/2007	Washington	Mr. Black	Patterson	Dakota	Uniform Violation	Detention	Hallway
10/9/2007	Washington	Ms. White	Patterson	Dakota	Uniform Violation	Detention	Hallway
10/10/2007	Washington	Mr. Black	Patterson	Dakota	Uniform Violation	Detention	Hallway
10/3/2007	Washington	Ms. Blue	Lincoln	George	Uniform Violation	Detention	Hallway
10/16/2007	Washington	Ms. Blue	Lincoln	George	Uniform Violation	Detention	Hallway
9/12/2007	Washington	Ms. Red	Jackson	Elizabeth	Fight	Detention	Playground
10/3/2007	Washington	Ms. Yellow	Hebert	Jennifer	Disrespect	Detention	Lunchroom
10/6/2007	Washington	Mr. Black	Goldstein	Shawna	Drug Infraction	Explusion	Bathroom
10/14/2007	Washington	Mr. Black	Goldstein	Shawna	Drug Infraction	Explusion	Bathroom
10/1/2007	Washington	Ms. Yellow	Fredricks	Robert	Disrespect	Loss of recess	Lunchroom
9/30/2007	Washington	Ms. Yellow	Boudreaux	Henry	Disrespect	Detention	Classroom
10/6/2007	Washington	Ms. Green	Bordelon	Michael	Disrespect	Detention	Lunchroom

- Click Data.
- Click Subtotals.

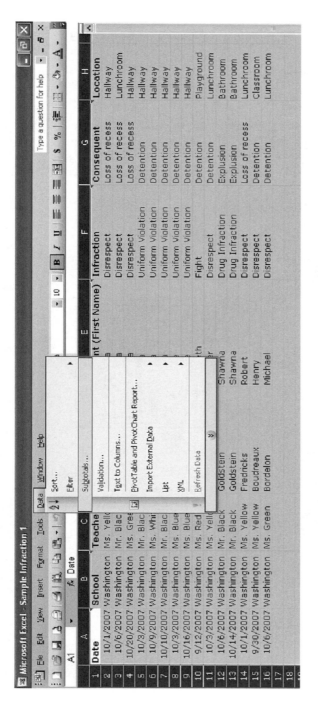

- Under the At Each Change In option, scroll up or down from the dropdown box and select Student (Last Name).
- Under the Use Function option, scroll up or down from the dropdown box and select Count.
- In the Add Subtotal To box, select Student (Last Name).
- Click OK.

Date	School	Teacher	Student (Last Name)	Student (First Name)	Infraction	Consequent	Location
10/1/2007	Washington	Ms. Yellow	Phillips	Shanna	Disrespect	Loss of recess	Hallway
10/6/2007	Washington	Mr. Black	Phillips	Shanna	Disrespect	Loss of recess	Lunchroom
10/20/2007	Washington	Ms. Green	Phillips	Shanna	Disrespect	Loss of recess	Hallway
10/3/2007	Washington	Mr. Black	Patterson	Dakota	Uniform Violation	Detention	Hallway
10/9/2007	Washington	Ms. White	Patterson	Dakota	Uniform Violation	Detention	Hallway
10/10/2007	Washington	Mr. Black	Patterson	Dakota	Uniform Violation	Detention	Hallway
10/3/2007	Washington	Ms. Blue	Lincoln	George	Uniform Violation	Detention	Hallway
10/16/2007	Washington	Ms. Blue	Lincoln	George	Uniform Violation	Detention	Hallway
9/12/2007	Washington	Ms. Red	Jackson	Elizabeth	Fight	Detention	Playground
10/3/2007	Washington	Ms. Yellow	Hebert	Jennifer	Disrespect	Detention	Lunchroom
10/6/2007	Washington	Mr. Black	Goldstein	Shawna	Drug Infraction	Expulsion	Bathroom
10/14/2007	Washington	Mr. Black	Goldstein	Shawna	Drug Infraction	Expulsion	Bathroom
10/1/2007	Washington	Ms. Yellow	Fredricks	Robert	Disrespect	Loss of recess	Lunchroom
9/30/2007	Washington	Ms. Yellow	Boudreaux	Henry	Disrespect	Detention	Classroom
10/6/2007	Washington	Ms. Green	Bordelon	Michael	Disrespect	Detention	Lunchroom

Subtotal

At each change in:
Student (Last Name)

Use function:
Count

Add subtotal to:
☐ Teacher
☑ Student (Last Name)
☐ Student (First Name)

☑ Replace current subtotals
☐ Page break between groups
☑ Summary below data

Remove All   OK   Cancel

- Data are sorted.

Microsoft Excel - Sample Infraction 1

	Date	School	Teacher	Student (Last Name)	Student (First Name)	Infraction	Consequent	Location
2	10/1/2007	Washington	Ms. Yellow	Phillips	Shanna	Disrespect	Loss of recess	Hallway
3	10/6/2007	Washington	Mr. Black	Phillips	Shanna	Disrespect	Loss of recess	Lunchroom
4	10/20/2007	Washington	Ms. Green	Phillips	Shanna	Disrespect	Loss of recess	Hallway
5			**Phillips Count**	3				3
6	10/3/2007	Washington	Mr. Black	Patterson	Dakota	Uniform Violation	Detention	Hallway
7	10/9/2007	Washington	Ms. White	Patterson	Dakota	Uniform Violation	Detention	Hallway
8	10/10/2007	Washington	Mr. Black	Patterson	Dakota	Uniform Violation	Detention	Hallway
9			**Patterson Count**	3				3
10	10/3/2007	Washington	Ms. Blue	Lincoln	George	Uniform Violation	Detention	Hallway
11	10/16/2007	Washington	Ms. Blue	Lincoln	George	Uniform Violation	Detention	Hallway
12			**Lincoln Count**	2				2
13	9/12/2007	Washington	Ms. Red	Jackson	Elizabeth	Fight	Detention	Playground
14			**Jackson Count**	1				1
15	10/3/2007	Washington	Ms. Yellow	Hebert	Jennifer	Disrespect	Detention	Lunchroom
16			**Hebert Count**	1				1
17	10/6/2007	Washington	Mr. Black	Goldstein	Shawna	Drug Infraction	Explusion	Bathroom
18	10/14/2007	Washington	Mr. Black	Goldstein	Shawna	Drug Infraction	Explusion	Bathroom
19			**Goldstein Count**	2				2
20	10/1/2007	Washington	Ms. Yellow	Fredricks	Robert	Disrespect	Loss of recess	Lunchroom
21			**Fredricks Count**	1				1
22	9/30/2007	Washington	Ms. Yellow	Boudreaux	Henry	Disrespect	Detention	Classroom
23			**Boudreaux Count**	1				1
24	10/6/2007	Washington	Ms. Green	Bordelon	Michael	Disrespect	Detention	Lunchroom
25			**Bordelon Count**	1				1
26			**Grand Count**	15				15

Appendix D: Ways to Reward Kids

- Let them get out of something.
  - Earlier dismissal from class at the end of the day (just a few minutes earlier).
  - Get to drop their lowest test grade or skip a test.
  - Class work assignment pass (gets to pick one in-class assignment to skip).
  - Homework pass.
  - Skip a class or leave class for an hour and go to a different setting of their choice (e.g., visit a favorite teacher's classroom to be a helper, help out in the office, go to the library to read, or shoot hoops in the gym).
  - Have a detention removed or shortened.
  - Get to meet with the school psychologist during their least favorite class.
  - Earn time off for a whole group.
- Let them do something fun.
  - Extra recess time.
  - Extended recess time.
  - Free attendance to school events that other students have to pay to attend.
  - Can pick a friend with whom to play a board game and can play the game in a different place on campus while others are in class.
  - Student gets to run down the hallway.
  - Field day.
  - Bring personal pet to school for a day and have designated time to be with the pet (e.g., 30 minutes).
  - Errand person for the day or week.
  - Go to the library and pick out a book when no other students are in the library.
  - Say the morning announcements.
  - Spend time outside doing activity of choice (extra recess period).

- Make a personal call to anyone of their choice during noninstructional time (could be a onetime privilege for a day or once a day for a week).
- Classroom helper for the day or week (or helper to principal, cafeteria manager, etc.).
- Teacher for an hour in their own class or a different class with younger students.
- Computer time.
- Free time.
- Extended gym period.
- After-school basketball.
- Allowed to call parents and tell them that they are doing well today.
- Can do an assignment on the computer instead of a worksheet.
- Extra intervention period with the reading teacher.
- Get to play a class game.
- Let them get something.
- In line first.
- Order lunch and have it delivered to the school.
- Snack.
- Drink.
- Pencil.
- Pen.
- Money.
- Random item from prize box.
- Bonus points in class.
- Stickers.
- Gets to move points forward on a chart.
- Able to bring snacks for the whole class.
- Bubbles.
- iPod.
- Student gets to select a song to play for a party.
- Compliments from the teacher.
- "Good job."
- One-on-one attention with an assignment.
- Football.
- Food coupons.
- Book coupons.
- Bonus points.
- Let them have time with another person.
- Lunch at a special table in the cafeteria.
- Lunch with a favorite adult in a setting other than the cafeteria (e.g., the faculty lounge or a classroom).

- Lunch with friend.
- Assist the librarian.
- Time with the principal.
- Breakfast with the PTA.
- Recognition from the superintendent.
- Play chess with the school counselor.

Appendix E: Topics of In-Services

Effective implementation of behavioral interventions requires a commitment to train faculty and staff members on effective principles of positive behavior support. The list below includes in-service training topics to help teachers be actively involved in the creation of a school's behavior management system.

	In-Service Topic	Who Should Be Involved?
Tier I	The basic roles of a student assistance team	Student assistance team members
	Ways to reward kids	School faculty and staff
	Introduction to positive behavior support	School faculty and staff
	How to teach expectations in the classroom	All teachers and teachers' aides
	How to teach schoolwide expectations	School faculty and staff
	Implementing a schoolwide token economy	Student assistance team members
	Completing schoolwide integrity checklist	Student assistance team members
	Teacher classroom management strategies	School faculty and staff
	Completing the classroom self-monitoring form	School faculty and staff
	Teaching completion of the Classroom Observation Form (COF)	Student assistance team members
	Identifying classrooms in need of support	Student assistance team members
	How to complete classroom intervention form	Student assistance team members
	How to collect office discipline referral data	Student assistance team members
	Identifying areas of the school in need of support	Student assistance team members
	Faculty defines misbehaviors and consequences	School faculty and staff

(Continued)

	In-Service Topic	Who Should Be Involved?
	Completing the classroom intervention form	Student assistance team members
	Administering tickets for positive behavior support	School faculty and staff
Tier II	Identifying students in need of support	Student assistance team members
	How to perform a self-monitoring intervention	All faculty and student assistance team members
	How to implement effective instruction delivery	All faculty and student assistance team members
	Training teachers how to perform the corrective teaching sequence	All faculty and student assistance team members
	Creating a behavior contract	All faculty and student assistance team members
	Building a check-in/check-out system	All faculty and student assistance team members
	Creating daily behavior report cards	All faculty and student assistance team members

Index

No Child Left Behind Act of
    2001 (NCLB 2001). *See*
    NCLB 2001
Nonclassroom settings,
    managing behavior
    problems in, 36–37
Nonverbal directives, 158

O

Observation of classroom
    behavior, 114–116
Office Discipline Referral
    Form, 206–208
Office discipline referrals
    (ODRs), 36, 87
    behavioral psychology
        and, 93–94
    critical information
        for, 88–91
    form for, 91, 206–208
    identifying students
        in need of Tier II
        intervention, 124–125
    meeting regarding, 88–89
    norms for, 95
    problem identification and
        verification, 97–100
    sample Excel spreadsheet
        for, 247–255
On-task behaviors, 61–62
Operant antecedents, 26–27
    activities that support, 34
Operant conditioning, 26
Opportunities to respond
    (OTR), 67–68
    coach card of, 237
Overcorrection, schoolwide
    training and, 40–42

P

Pace of instruction, 68–69
Paraprofessionals, participation
    of on problem solving
    teams, 19
Parents
    participation of on problem
        solving teams, 19

Tier II behavioral
    interventions
    and, 125
Patient teachers, students
    displaying behavior
    problems and, 161
PBS systems
    activities that support, 34
    best practices for, 24–26
    description of, 23
    educational principles
        underlying, 30–31
    program evaluation principles
        underlying, 31–33
    psychological principles
        underlying, 26–30
    students with behavioral
        difficulties and, 121
    token economy systems
        and, 73–75
Peer attention, 157
    behavioral interventions
        and, 78
    group contingencies and,
        118–119
    managing behaviors designed
        to elicit, 163–164
Peer comparison
    observation, 168
Planned transitions, use of for
    students with behavior
    problems, 161
Planning, minimizing
    downtime with,
    61–62
Playground behaviors, defining
    procedures for, 40
Playground monitors,
    participation of on
    problem solving
    teams, 19
Playgrounds, bullying on, 36
Poor judgment, misbehaviors
    caused by, 5
Positive Behavior Ticket
    Template, 205
Positive behavioral support
    (PBS) systems. *See* PBS
    systems